LOOK AHEAD

classroom
COURSE

intermediate

TEACHER'S BOOK

MADELEINE DU VIVIER

ANDY HOPKINS

JOCELYN POTTER

Look Ahead: a partnership between

 BBC English

 The British Council

 University of Cambridge Local Examinations Syndicate (UCLES)

 Longman ELT

 with the cooperation of the Council of Europe

 Longman

Look Ahead Consultants

The authors and publishers would like to thank the following schools and consultants who commented on these classroom materials during their development:

Rob Anderson, Italy   Deanna Donatini, Italy
Ron Banks, France   Escuela Oficial de Idiomas, Vigo, Spain
Ingrid Boczkowski, Germany   Hanna Komorowska, Poland
Anna Cerchietti, Italy   Maggy McNorton, UK
Cultura Inglesa Rio, Brazil

Acknowledgements

Acknowledgements of copyright material used as reference sources for the *Look Ahead* Classroom Course:

Council of Europe: for the use of its revised and expanded Waystage and Threshold level specifications (© Council of Europe 1990).

Simon Greenall and Judy Garton-Sprenger: for their Course Designs created for BBC English for the *Look Ahead* project (© BBC 1993).

Terry O'Neill, Peter Snow and Bob Marsden: for their television scripts (© BBC 1993) for *Look Ahead* programmes 31–45, drawn upon in this book.

We are grateful to the author's agents for an extract from *England Made Me* by the late Graham Greene. Pan edition 1954, originally published by William Heinemann Ltd in 1935.

Designed by First Edition, London

Cover photographs by Longman/Andrew Ward for middle right. Pictor International for top left. Telegraph Colour Library/Bavaria-Bildagentur for top right. Masterfile for bottom. Zefa Picture Library UK Ltd/Stockmarket for middle left.

Illustrated by Ron Dixon

Longman Group Ltd
Longman House, Burnt Mill, Harlow,
Essex CM20 2JE, England
and Associated Companies throughout the world.

First published 1995
Set in Monotype Photina 10.25/11.5pt and Adobe Syntax 9.25/11.5pt
Printed in Spain by Mateu Cromo, S. A. Pinto (Madrid)

ISBN 0582 09840 8

Contents

READING/WRITING	LISTENING/SPEAKING	COMPARING CULTURES
R: Identifying text types and purpose		
R: Quotes describing people's memories R: An article about an unusual lifestyle W: Sentences describing changes W: Gap-fill description of a picture	L: A monologue on how an area has changed L: Short conversations L: A description of a picture S: Giving opinions and reasons S: Role play: meeting new people S: A description of a picture S: Stress in compound nouns	Housing
R: An article about television viewing habits R: A text from a brochure R: A literary extract W: A description of a scene W: Making comparisons	L: Sound sequences L: A conversation about a ride at a film studio S: Agreeing and disagreeing in conversation S: Description of sensations	Postcards
R: An article about borders R: Holiday postcards W: A postcard	L: Brief monologues describing location L: Extracts from conversations connected with air travel L: Conversations at customs S: Describing location S: Discussion: airport security S: Role play: at customs S: Stress and intonation of orders and requests	
R: A report of a crime R: An introductory text about a famous person W: A report of a crime	L: Accounts of crimes L: A monologue by a woman police officer L: A narrative about an incident on patrol L: A story S: Describing a crime S: A short talk	Theft and punishment
R: An article about supermarket sales techniques R: Letters, a memo, an invoice, an order form W: A description of a process W: Letters W: Form completion	L: Extracts from an interview with a car manufacturer S: Describing a process S: Role play: selling a computer S: Discussion: sending a personalised gift S: Sentence stress with *both ... and, neither ... nor, all, none*	
R: An article about small children and fitness R: A literary extract W: Continuing a story creating a mood	L: A medical consultation L: A monologue by a dentist L: Sounds: matching sounds and verbs L: A sound sequence S: Role play: persuading someone to stop smoking S: Role play: calming and advising someone S: Intonation of calming and reassuring someone	At the doctor's Words describing sounds
R: An article about an unusual hotel R: A literary extract	L: Interviews about a ranch hotel L: Dialogue at a hotel reception L: An anecdote about camping S: Asking questions about vocabulary S: Discussion: a holiday at a ranch hotel S: Role play: situations at a hotel S: Telling and retelling stories S: Expressing satisfaction and sarcasm	
R: Case studies of people in different jobs R: An article about a change of career R: Job advertisements W: A brief biography	L: An interview with an art student L: A job interview S: Job interviews S: Using intonation to introduce a new topic	Education

READING/WRITING	LISTENING/SPEAKING	COMPARING CULTURES
R: An article about a model agency W: A short report about people's views on changing their appearance W: Descriptions of people	L: A discussion about changing your appearance L: A monologue about running a model agency L: Sound sequences S: Discussion: changing one's appearance S: Running words together	Clothing for different occasions Ideas of beauty
R: A text about puppets R: A literary extract R: An article about circus animals R: A letter to a newspaper W: A letter to a newspaper giving an opinion	L: An interview with the manager of a theatre L: Monologues giving strong opinions S: Considering possibilities S: Role play: booking tickets for a play S: Discussion: performing animals S: Using stress to show disagreement	Puppets
R: A literary extract R: An article about a biosphere W: Sentences justifying a decision W: A paragraph expressing opinion	L: An interview about generating electricity L: Brief comments about the future L: A radio news item L: A conversation about genetic engineering S: Negotiating a shortlist S: Discussion: freedom and technology in the future S: Using intonation to allow or prevent interruption	
R: Newspaper extracts R: Comments for a survey R: A narrative W: A report about reading habits W: A perspective on events W: A newspaper report	L: A monologue about producing a newspaper L: Short interviews about newspapers S: Discussion: newspapers S: An interview about reading habits S: Interpreting events S: Word stress	Newspapers
R: An article about an unusual exhibit R: An extract from a brochure R: A poem W: Describing an experience	L: Two short talks by museum staff L: A description of a photograph S: A short talk about a museum S: Role play: finding your way around a museum S: Discussion: children S: Describing and responding to a photograph	
R: An article about being a courier R: An advertisement R: An article about the use of home computers R: A report of a survey W: A report of a survey	L: A conversation about a delivery service L: An interview with an emergency service operator L: Phone calls L: A conversation about an accident S: Reporting an experience S: Role play: phone calls S: A report of a conversation S: A survey of home computer use	Telephoning Home computers
R: An article about working holidays R: Persuasive and neutral texts W: Form completion W: A persuasive description	L: A monologue by a travel agent L: A conversation at a travel agent's S: Discussion: advice for foreign students working in your area S: Discussion: holiday destinations S: Role play: checking information about a holiday	Holiday destinations

Introduction

The course

Why is the *Look Ahead* course special?

The Longman *Look Ahead* classroom materials have been produced as a result of a unique collaboration between BBC English, the British Council, the University of Cambridge Local Examinations Syndicate (UCLES) and Longman ELT, with the co-operation of the Council of Europe.

SYLLABUS

The core syllabus for the *Look Ahead* corpus is based on the Council of Europe's revised and extended Waystage and Threshold specifications (Council of Europe Press, 1991), the most comprehensive statement of language learning objectives yet available for the 1990s and the new millennium.

ENGLISH LANGUAGE EXAMINATIONS

New examinations at Waystage level (the Key English Test – KET) and Threshold level (the revised Preliminary English Test – PET) have been devised by UCLES based on these latest specifications.

BROADCAST TELEVISION SERIES

BBC English has used the same Waystage and Threshold specifications to produce a series of sixty television programmes for English language learners. These programmes are accompanied by self-study materials, marketed directly to learners at home by the BBC.

LONGMAN CLASSROOM COURSE

Longman English Language Teaching has produced a four-level classroom course, which takes as its core the Waystage and Threshold specifications. Extracts from the BBC television programmes have been selected according to their appropriacy for classroom use and are available on an optional video cassette which accompanies the Longman classroom materials. These Longman materials form the complete *Look Ahead* course for the classroom.

What levels does the Longman classroom course cover?

The course comprises four levels:

Level 1 Beginner/Elementary
Level 2 Post-elementary/Pre-intermediate
Level 3 Intermediate
Level 4 Upper-intermediate

Look Ahead Level 1 is for students with little or no knowledge of English. *Look Ahead* Level 2 takes students beyond the Council of Europe Waystage level. *Look Ahead Intermediate* and *Upper-intermediate* take students up to and comfortably beyond the Council of Europe Threshold level.

What are the components of the Longman classroom course?

At each level, the course consists of:

– a Students' Book,
– a Workbook,
– a Teacher's Book,
– a set of classroom audio cassettes (Class Cassettes),
– a Workbook audio cassette (Workbook Cassette),
– an optional set of two classroom video cassettes,
– a Video Workbook,
– a Video Teacher's Guide (one guide covers two levels).

Underlying principles of the Longman classroom course

The writing of the *Look Ahead* classroom course has been influenced by the following beliefs about English language learning:

• Learners are intelligent individuals who are already proficient in at least one language.
• Learners want to know what they are learning and why. They also **need** this information in order to become more independent as learners as they progress.

- Learners need to develop at the same time a knowledge of grammar, vocabulary, functional language and communicative skills. Attention to the systems of the language is crucial, but the development of fluency and contextual appropriacy are equally important goals.
- Learning takes place most effectively when learners are actively engaged in the learning process.
- Topics should be interesting, varied and relevant to students' lives.
- Learners need to be provided with every possible opportunity to use new language in contexts which are meaningful to them.
- Cross-cultural understanding is an important aspect of language learning.
- Learners want and need to be able to measure their own progress.
- Learners need resources to help them to continue learning outside the classroom.
- Teachers want materials that take into account all of the above and are presented in a clear, principled manner, but that also allow for flexibility of use.

Key features

What are the key features of *Look Ahead Intermediate* Students' Book?

A MULTI-SYLLABUS APPROACH
Each unit provides presentation, varied practice and contextualised use of grammar, vocabulary, functional language and skills.

FOCUS NOTES
Each double page includes Focus notes in the left-hand margin. These notes highlight the main areas of topic, grammar, functional language, skills, vocabulary development and phonology presented or practised on that double page. This means that learners have a clear understanding at the beginning of each double page of what their learning objectives are.

DISCOVERING LANGUAGE
The Discovering Language boxes in each unit encourage learners to reflect on a particular area of grammar and to deduce rules from clearly contextualised examples. Learners then have the opportunity to test these rules through guided and freer practice activities.

FOCUS ON FUNCTIONS
Activities under the heading Focus on Functions ask students to consider the meaning and appropriate use of particular phrases and language patterns. Students are presented with contextualised examples and are then asked to use the new language in a different context.

SPEECH PATTERNS
Useful patterns of stress and intonation that occur in spoken texts are highlighted and practised.

A WIDE VARIETY OF TASK TYPES
Tasks encourage students' active engagement in the learning process through activities which involve discovery, problem-solving, language use and creative response.

STIMULATING AND RELEVANT TOPICS
Each unit contains a number of related topics. These topics have been chosen for their general interest and for the useful vocabulary and functional language which they generate. Their exploitation encourages personal involvement as learners are asked to relate the topics to their own experiences and interests.

DEVELOPING VOCABULARY
New vocabulary is taught in different ways, but Developing Vocabulary sections help students to explore patterns and relationships within and between words, and to discover useful generalisations.

COMPARING CULTURES
Regular Comparing Cultures sections allow learners to reflect on the similarities and differences between their own and other cultures. The intention is not to promote the value of particular cultural conventions in one part of the world over any other, but to raise awareness of cultural variety.

DOCUMENTARY
The Documentary feature is another strong cultural element of the classroom course. Recordings of real people talking about their lives and work are presented on the Class Cassettes; background information and supporting photographs are provided in the Students' Book. The British and American people who feature in these sections also appear on the *Look Ahead* Classroom Videos, which can be played later for consolidation and enrichment through the additional visual element.

SKILLS

The development of appropriate language skills (reading, writing, speaking and listening) is an important aim of *Look Ahead Intermediate*, and students are presented throughout the book with a wide range of text types and strategies for dealing with them. The third double page in each unit, however, focuses particularly on the development of the skills needed for speaking, functional writing or creative writing. In each unit students are helped, through integrated skills work which is carefully staged and guided, to the production of a spoken or written text. Listening and reading skills development feature throughout the materials.

LANGUAGE REFERENCE

These pages are at the end of each unit and include a two-part summary of the key language presented. The first part lists the forms and explains the uses of grammatical structures that are presented or reviewed in the unit. In the second part, language functions are listed with examples.

PROGRESS CHECKS

There are eight Progress Checks, one at the end of every second unit. These are informal tests of the grammatical, functional and vocabulary development areas presented in the previous unit or units. They can be done in class or as homework assignments. They give students and teachers an opportunity to monitor progress and to decide whether remedial work is appropriate before errors become too firmly established. The keys to these are in the Teacher's Book.

TALKBACK

Talkback pages are an opportunity for students to bring all the language they know to a highly communicative spoken activity. These tasks are intended to be treated lightly and usually with humour; the emphasis is on the development of fluent self-expression.

What are the key features of *Look Ahead Intermediate* Workbook?

LANGUAGE FOCUS

A wide range of activities provides further controlled practice of the main grammatical and functional areas presented in the corresponding unit of the Students' Book. At least one task in each unit involves comprehension of a dramatic episode in the lives of two characters who run a small company. These scenes, recorded on the Workbook Cassette, are audio extracts from scenes on the *Look Ahead* Classroom Videos. The videos can be used for further consolidation of language practised in the Students' Book and Workbook.

EXPLORING VOCABULARY

This section begins with a list of key vocabulary from the corresponding unit of the Students' Book. The wordlist is recorded on the Workbook Cassette so that learners can practise their pronunciation as they revise the vocabulary. It is followed by comprehension tasks, which check understanding of meaning and usage, and awareness of important sound and stress patterns, and development tasks which encourage students to relate vocabulary to other words that they know, sometimes by appropriate dictionary use.

HELP YOURSELF

Six Help Yourself sections provide learner development activities, such as *Grammar contrasts* and *Understanding dictionaries*, which encourage students to reflect on language and the language learning process. Their purpose is to help students to make the most of their own learning potential.

SHORT STORIES

Three short stories, each in three parts, encourage extensive reading for pleasure. The final part of each story is recorded on the Workbook Cassette for extensive listening. Activities focus on general reading and listening skills, such as prediction, inference and personal response, rather than on language analysis.

FLEXIBILITY OF USE

Workbook activities can be used in several different ways, depending on the needs of a particular class:

– as follow-up homework,
– as additional individual study activities, either in class or in a self-access centre,
– as additional class activities with students working together.

A full Answer Key to the Workbook and the Workbook Tapescript are provided at the back of this Teacher's Book.

What are the key features of *Look Ahead Intermediate* Teacher's Book?

This Teacher's Book contains the following information and activities:

INTRODUCTION
The introduction describes the principles which underlie the Longman classroom course and contains general notes on suggested methodology and classroom practice.

DETAILED LESSON NOTES
There are detailed teaching notes for each Students' Book unit to help teachers in their lesson preparation. These are organised under a number of clear headings. Focus notes provide a summary of the main teaching points in each lesson. Like the Focus notes in the Students' Book, they highlight key areas of topic, grammar, functional language, skills, vocabulary development and phonology. These notes are followed by a suggested procedure for each Students' Book exercise. Other ideas for presenting new language are offered under the heading *Alternative presentation*. Background notes give additional cultural information to help teachers from different backgrounds respond to their students' questions. Extra practice sections suggest further, optional activities to supplement those in the Students' Book. Tapescripts and keys to the Students' Book exercises are also provided within the Lesson Notes.

TEACHER DEVELOPMENT TASKS
Towards the back of this book is a unique Teacher Development section for teachers. This consists of photocopiable worksheets with accompanying notes. These worksheets invite teachers to explore – alone or in structured teacher development sessions – areas of language and classroom practice which are particularly relevant to the challenges of teaching intermediate students.

What is recorded on the Class Cassettes?

The set of Class Cassettes contains all the dialogues, listening comprehension materials and speechwork activities in the Students' Book. The tapescripts for each unit appear in the Lesson Notes in this Teacher's Book.

What is recorded on the Workbook Cassette?

The Workbook Cassette contains listening comprehension material: extracts from a drama story about the lives of two people working for an advertising agency, and passages relating to the final episode of each short story. It also contains wordlists which enable students to practise their pronunciation by repeating key vocabulary from each unit, exercises focusing on patterns of sound and word stress, and Help Yourself tasks (where appropriate). The Workbook tapescript is included at the back of this Teacher's Book.

What are the features of the Classroom Videos?

The classroom video material is an optional component of the course. We do not assume that every teacher in every institution will have access to a video player, and the audio Class Cassettes provide all the necessary listening input to the classroom materials.

For those who do have access to a video player, the Classroom Videos are a valuable source of enrichment and extension material. The video material consists of fifteen units, each of which corresponds to a unit in the Students' Book. Each unit is about six minutes in length and includes most or all of the following:

- A short presenter's introduction to the general topic of the unit.
- Scenes from an ongoing story about the personal and professional lives of two people who run a newly-formed company called Marsh Advertising. Extracts from many of these conversations are also recorded on the audio Workbook Cassette and relate to tasks in the Language Focus section of each Workbook unit. It is recommended that the video conversations are used to consolidate new language already presented through the Students' Book.
- Mini interviews intended to highlight examples of functional language in use.
- A short cartoon which exemplifies key language points.
- A real-life interview with someone from Britain or the USA, showing scenes from their everyday lives. Extracts from these interviews are also recorded on the audio Class Cassettes and relate to tasks in the main body of each Students' Book unit. We recommend that this part of the video is used for review and consolidation purposes

after completing the Students' Book unit. This will require access to a video recorder for a maximum of one lesson a week.

A full video tapescript and detailed suggestions on how to exploit the video material are contained in each video cassette box. General suggestions for video exploitation are included in the Methodology and Classroom Practice section below. The Video Workbook, however, provides a complete range of activities which can be done while watching the videos in class or in a self-access centre.

What are the features of the Video Workbook?

The Video Workbook contains fifteen units of activities, each relating to the corresponding unit of the *Look Ahead* Classroom Videos (see above). Each unit can be done in one session with video facilities – in class or in a self-access centre – in about an hour of work. The sections of the Video Workbook relate directly to sections of the videos and the first three pages are written in the sequence of the sections as they occur on the video. The fourth page of each unit is optional and contains activities that encourage learners to reflect on and move out from the video material. Typical activities on this page include role play, discussion and cultural comparison.

Although many of the characters from the video extracts occur in the Students' Book or Workbook, use of the Video Workbook will ensure that the videos are fully exploited.

Methodology and classroom practice

....

Variety and flexibility of approach are crucial if we wish to hold the attention of a class over time. An overview of all the possible teaching techniques is obviously beyond the scope of this short introduction. However, we feel that some explanation of the approaches implicit in *Look Ahead Intermediate*, and some standard procedures for particular activity types, may be helpful.

1 Developing skills

The development of language skills is crucial at intermediate level, and *Look Ahead Intermediate* offers real texts for reading and listening to, as well as stimulating speaking and writing tasks. Grammatical, lexical, functional and phonological knowledge and skills are developed through working with these texts and tasks. In order that contexts and tasks should be realistic, activities that develop individual skills are integrated into a clear sequence that embraces all language skills. A listening or reading text may, for example, be preceded by a discussion activity and lead, via a language focus, to a writing or speaking task. In this way, learners have the opportunity to work in a 'text world' of real language where their understanding and responses are the primary motivating factors, and language work arises in as natural a way as possible.

2 Developing reading and listening

Look Ahead Intermediate contains a wide variety of texts for reading and listening to, including newspaper and magazine articles, letters, signs, literary extracts, radio broadcasts, short stories, interviews, documentaries and informal discussions. Texts have been chosen because they are interesting in their own right, but they offer a range of other features relevant to intermediate learners. Through related activities, students are encouraged to develop awareness of the language and other characteristics of the texts, and of how these are affected by factors such as the purpose of the writer/speaker, the nature and motivation of the intended audience, and the conventions of particular text types.

Longer texts often contain vocabulary and structures which are new to students, but a carefully planned sequence of activities encourages them to understand the main ideas first and to guess the meaning of new language from the context. Most texts have a title or introduction and an illustration; these can help students to speculate about context and content before reading or listening. This prediction stage can be extended if you wish; it is surprising how accurately we can predict not only the general content but also particular vocabulary that is likely to occur and the overall structure of the text.

Texts are accompanied by clear tasks in the Students' Book, and in the Lesson notes in this Teacher's Book, but one possible way of approaching texts for reading and listening is as follows:

- Ask students to think about the title and/or picture, and what these tell them about the text. Ask general questions about the text type, purpose, etc. but do not supply answers, since it is important that students themselves are eventually able to answer the questions correctly by reading or listening.
- If you wish, ask about words that are likely to occur and ask students to justify their guesses.
- Students read or listen, thinking about answers to your general questions and confirming or revising their own predictions. This gives a clear purpose to reading or listening.
- Students can then work alone or together to answer the comprehension questions in the Students' Book. If they work together, an additional benefit will be the need to justify answers to a partner. Before they answer questions on listening passages, give them time to read and think about the questions and then play the cassette a second time.
- After a quick comprehension check, direct students to further activities in the book. You may wish to play key listening passages a third time as students answer the questions. It is also a good idea to play the whole text again at the end so that students have the satisfaction of listening to something they now understand.
- You may then want to analyse the text more closely with your students (see **Presenting new language** and **Expanding vocabulary** below). Note that texts on the third double page of each unit (headed Speaking, Writing and Creative writing) are often presented as 'samples' or 'models' for writing and speaking tasks (see **Developing speaking** and **Developing writing** below).

3 Developing speaking

In *Look Ahead Intermediate* there are three distinct types of speaking activity:

A) Activities that are part of the natural exploration of the topic (such as Getting Started and Comparing Cultures), where the focus is on the sharing of experiences, ideas and knowledge, rather than on the language that students use to express themselves.

B) Activities that focus firmly on particular skills of speaking (giving talks, telling stories, participating in interviews, etc.). Six units end with a double page headed 'Speaking'. Although these pages involve integrated work on all four skills, their main purpose is to prepare students for the development of a substantial spoken output. The particular areas of speaking skills developed are not only important in their own right; they are also areas that commonly feature in the speaking components of public examinations at this level. Fluency and accuracy are both important, as is the appropriate use of vocabulary, functional language, grammar, speech patterns, and features of discourse or style. The main thread of the double page usually involves:

- activities to introduce the topic and learning aims;
- listening to a text which incorporates features that students should aim for in their own speaking;
- reflection on and analysis of the sample – for useful functional language, discourse features, etc.;
- development of vocabulary that students might need to express their own opinions and ideas;
- the main speaking task. This final stage can be set up and managed in the same way as role plays and discussion. (See below.)

C) Activities that provide opportunities for freer practice of target language (grammar and functions). As with all freer practice activities, these are designed to encourage spoken fluency and successful communication rather than complete accuracy, while at the same time showing how well new language has been absorbed and whether remedial work is needed. The two main task types used in *Look Ahead Intermediate* are structured role play and discussion. Also included are lesson-length speaking activities called Talkback (see **Talkback pages** below).

Role play

Role plays are often information-gap activities. Sometimes they involve pairs of students (A and B) looking at different pieces of information, in which case Student B should be directed to the separate section at the back of the book. Students then exchange information in English without looking at each other's books. More often, students are asked to take a role in a conversation and to act it out. In this case, the information gap is created by the students themselves as the conversation develops. A possible procedure for both types of role play activity is as follows:

- Organise students into pairs and ask first A and then B students to identify themselves. Check that students know what to do and are looking at the correct Students' Book page (if appropriate).
- Ask a pair of good students to demonstrate the activity to the class, or demonstrate it yourself with one student.
- Walk around the class and monitor students while they are doing the activity in pairs. It is better not to interrupt unless they are having real difficulty or they ask for help. Note down any common errors relating to language patterns that have just been taught.
- Stop the activity when most students have finished, ask for feedback, and discuss any problems or mistakes that you or individual students have identified.
- Ask students to change roles and repeat the activity, if you wish.

Discussion

Structured tasks encourage students to give their own opinions, to talk about their own lives and to bring their own perspectives as individuals to bear on the topics and texts. Each pair or group discussion is an opportunity for students to develop communication strategies and to say what they mean, even if they do not have quite the right words or complete control over appropriate structures. One approach is as follows:

- Arrange students into pairs or groups, and make sure that they understand the task.
- Start the discussion by asking a question which focuses attention on one aspect of the topic, and then encourage students to continue the discussion in their groups.
- Monitor students while they are talking, intervening if requested but otherwise noting any important problems. Ask additional questions if the discussion is flagging.
- Stop the discussion when a number of groups have stopped talking.
- Ask a student from one group to tell the class about his/her group's feelings or experiences and encourage other students to add to these.
- Ask if students had any language problems during the discussion, and then point out problems that you noticed. Ask the students if they can solve the problems before you provide solutions for them.
- Finally, encourage students to ask you about your own feelings and experiences, particularly if you have a different perspective that they might find interesting.

Talkback pages

The last page in alternate units is called Talkback. Each page provides a major speaking activity that should involve all members of the class. These activities are discussions, games and stimuli for narrative that involve students working co-operatively in order to solve a problem, reach a decision, justify a view or create an effect (of drama, plausibility, etc.). These tasks are highly communicative and are, above all, intended to be fun. Talkback activities are longer than other speaking activities, so full exploitation with teacher feedback can take a whole lesson. They encourage students to draw on all their resources for language appropriate to carrying out the task. Suggestions for management are made in the Students' Book and in the Lesson notes.

CORRECTING SPOKEN ENGLISH

The extent to which correction is appropriate depends, of course, on the aim of each activity. When new language is being presented and practised, accuracy of form is fundamental and students must also be able to produce the correct sound, stress and intonation patterns associated with the language in context. If you are presenting and checking language orally, you will be aware of any problems immediately and can correct mistakes as they occur. During controlled practice of specific language items, students should be able to correct themselves or each other; if they are unable to do this, the language may need re-presenting.

When, on the other hand, your main objective is to encourage an exchange of information and ideas, accuracy will be less important than the fluent and successful communication needed to complete the task. You will, however, probably not wish to ignore errors completely, particularly if they relate to language that has been taught. Some possible ways of dealing with these errors are as follows:

- Encourage students to ask each other or you about mistakes that they think they have made.
- Make notes on common or important errors that you hear while monitoring speaking tasks. After the activity, draw attention to the problems orally or on the board and ask students if they can correct them.
- Record one pair or group of students doing the task. Then play the cassette back to the class. Pause it from time to time to highlight examples of particularly successful communication but

also to demonstrate significant problems. Allow the original speakers the first attempts at correction; then, if necessary, encourage supportive contributions from other students or correct the mistake yourself.

4 Developing writing

There are three main types of writing tasks in *Look Ahead Intermediate*:

A) 'Functional' writing tasks (writing letters, postcards, reports, etc.), which students may well need to carry out in real-life situations, including examinations. Activities help students to construct written texts to conventional guidelines – to produce clear, effective, accurate products.

B) Creative writing tasks, which involve exploring language through a process that includes an imaginative personal response. Although many of these creative writing pages display 'literary' extracts, the purpose is not that students should try to produce 'literary' text but that they should become familiar with the kinds of processes that are crucial to any good writing (e.g. the creation of mood and drama, or the modification of texts for different readers). The emphasis here is on choice (of vocabulary, structure, text type, register) in terms of the effect the writer wants to convey. There is no single correct response to the final writing task; students use their imagination, draw on their entire resource of language and have the opportunity to express in writing what they really want to say.

C) Guided practice of target language items. These written exercises are opportunities for practising the grammatical, functional and vocabulary items that are taught in each unit. They occur mainly in the Workbook and can either be done in class at appropriate points in the unit, or as homework.

MANAGING WRITING TASKS

Teachers are often tempted to view writing tasks as individual activities that take place outside the classroom, partly because of the practical problems caused by some students working faster than others. It is, however, often better for writing to be done, or at least started, in class rather than at home, so that you can monitor the work and provide encouragement. Possible modes for classroom writing are as follows:

- Students write alone.
- Students work in pairs, with one student writing and the other making suggestions, collecting information, using a dictionary to check vocabulary, etc.
- Students work in small groups, with one student writing and the others helping (as above).

One approach to a longer task is as follows:

- Check that students understand the instructions in the Students' Book. (What kind of text is it? How long? What other guidelines are there? Is there a sample/model?)
- Elicit the beginning of a possible text orally, writing it on the board one sentence at a time and asking for improvements.
- Set a time limit for individuals or groups to write their own text.
- When students have finished, ask them to look again at their own work, or to read another piece of work, and to check the overall impact of the text (does it communicate effectively?), the vocabulary (have they chosen the best words?), spelling, etc.
- Collect neat pieces of writing for marking. Ask for heavily edited or untidy scripts to be rewritten and submitted in the next lesson.

MARKING STUDENTS' WRITING

1 Marking 'functional' writing (See a) above.)
Accuracy is important in most types of 'functional' writing. You may find it useful to show errors without correcting them, so that students can have the satisfaction of improving their own work. This requires use of a marking scheme that everyone understands. You can, for example, underline important errors and write a code in the margin to show the type of error, e.g.

O for organisation
G for grammar
V for vocabulary
Sp for spelling
P for punctuation, etc.

Encourage students to improve their texts (to organise them better, to choose more appropriate words, etc.) as well as to correct actual mistakes. Then look at the final text again.

Some teachers feel that it benefits students to be given a formal mark for each piece of writing. This should reflect the desire for students to produce good, effective texts according to clear text conventions (e.g. letter openings and closings). Readers of these texts are concerned solely with the final text, and not the process of producing it. A standard mark sheet might award **two** marks. The first (on a scale of 1–5, say) is an overall impression mark (for communicative effect) based on your feeling about whether the text works (as a letter, as a report, etc.). The second mark is a total of marks for more specific features of the text (organisation, vocabulary, grammar, spelling, punctuation, etc.), with a higher number of possible marks for grammar, say, than punctuation.

Using a standard mark sheet that you give to each student encourages students because it gives information about what is good as well as what is not so good about a piece of work. It also allows you and/or your students to keep a record of their written work.

2 Marking 'creative' writing (See b) above.)
It is, we feel, more important that creative and highly personal writing should be displayed (read aloud, put on the wall, etc.) and therefore given positive value than that it should be graded. If you feel you have to give a grade, we suggest an impression mark based on three main criteria:

- active individual participation in the process leading up to writing;
- degree of co-operation with writing partners;
- the effect of the final text, based on the degree of creative experimentation that the text displays.

3 Marking written exercises (See c) above.)
These should be marked for the accuracy of the language items which are being tested.

5 Expanding vocabulary

There are two distinct vocabulary expansion threads in *Look Ahead Intermediate*.

The first concentrates on understanding and using vocabulary related to the topics in each unit. Exercises in the Students' Book encourage interpretation of these words in the context of listening and reading texts. (See **Developing reading and listening** above.) A quick, lively drill (repetition in chorus and then individually) is helpful to establish sound and stress patterns before the words are used more freely. Exploring Vocabulary sections of the Workbook provide a wide range of activities based on a list of important new words, which is also recorded on cassette. Consider allowing students to do vocabulary practice activities in groups, and ensure that they have access to a good dictionary so that it becomes an automatic and valued

resource. Encourage students to write down additional new words in a way that is both meaningful and accessible to them so that they can refer to and build on their lists later. Quick quizzes, simple crosswords, word boxes and word games will remind students of vocabulary from previous units as the course progresses. Finally, encourage students to experiment freely and without inhibition in activities where the main aims are fluency and successful communication rather than total accuracy. This will help them use new language with confidence.

The second thread, Developing Vocabulary, concentrates on aspects of vocabulary form, meaning and use – such as affixation, sense relations and compounds – that go beyond the topic areas. These exercises can be done in small groups, or you can present them as open class activities. Access to a good dictionary is crucial, as tasks often ask students to generate new words and expressions using a particular pattern.

6 Presenting new language

New language in *Look Ahead Intermediate* is always presented in the context of a reading or listening text. These texts are normally **not** specially constructed vehicles for particular language items, but are genuine texts in their own right in which key language occurs naturally. They should therefore be treated as real texts first and only afterwards as contexts for language work. Procedures for dealing with reading and listening texts have been discussed above (see **Developing reading and listening**). After focusing on the purpose and content of a text, one possible approach is as follows:

- Ask questions that draw attention to the use of the new language (*Is this a formal or informal conversation? What do we say when we ask a friend to do something?*) and then to the form (*Which verb form follows 'Would you mind ...?'*).
- Ask students to identify other examples of the new language.
- Move on to the Discovering Language or Focus on Functions activities (see below), or straight into controlled practice activities.

DISCOVERING LANGUAGE BOXES
These boxes draw students' attention to contextualised examples of new language structures. They are designed to assist an inductive (guided discovery) approach to

grammar teaching, encouraging students to reflect on language patterns and to formulate possible rules. Students can work through the activities in pairs or small groups and then feed back to the whole class. Alternatively, you can ask students to read the relevant examples and to formulate aloud possible rules in English. Write the best rule or rules on the board, eliciting improvements where possible. In the early stages of the course you may need to provide clear rules at the end of the discussion, but students can also be referred to the Language Reference section at the end of each unit for more help with form and usage. Discovering Language exercises are always followed by guided and freer practice activities in the Students' Book, and further practice is given in the Workbook. You may like to do these practice exercises in class or set some of them for homework. The Lesson Notes in this book often suggest further practice activities.

FOCUS ON FUNCTIONS
By focusing on functional language in context, these sections draw attention to the use of particular forms of expression for effective and appropriate communication. Guided and freer practice activities allow practice in using this functional language through the unit, and the Talkback pages provide a further opportunity for using it freely and by choice. Focus on Functions exercises are usually best done as small group work.

ALTERNATIVE PRESENTATIONS
Not all teachers will wish to use the particular inductive approaches in the Students' Book all of the time; some may prefer to present new language in their own way and then to use the reading or listening texts in the book for consolidation. For this reason, suggestions for alternatives are given in the Lesson Notes in this book under the heading Alternative Presentation. Another possibility for alternative presentation is to use the Language Reference pages (see below).

THE LANGUAGE REFERENCE PAGES
These are placed towards the end of each unit and include notes and examples for new aspects of grammar (form and use) as well as examples of new functional language. Possible uses for these pages are:

- as a reference resource for students working in an inductive mode with the Discovering Language boxes and Focus on Functions exercises;

- as a learning tool for students to read **before** working with the text material in which the new structures occur;
- as a revision aid for students and as a reminder while they do related Workbook exercises outside class.

7 Handling guided practice

Practice activities in the book follow the presentation of new language. Task types vary, but the aim at this stage is normally accuracy – the correct manipulation of language patterns. You may wish to supplement these activities in class with further tasks from the Workbook, or to add more of your own. It may be beneficial for students to work together so that they can learn from each other, since the practice activities are designed as teaching and not testing tools. You may wish to inject an element of competition into, say, a gap-filling exercise, so that students with correct answers score points for their team. Here is one simple approach to a guided practice activity:

- Remind students of the new language (if the presentation of that language took place in a previous lesson), for example, by asking a pair of students to act out a conversation that includes it.
- Ask students to read the instructions. Check that they have understood by giving them a minute or two to think about the first question and then eliciting the answer, accepting corrections from other students if necessary.
- Tell students to work through the activity in pairs and then turn to a different partner to compare and if necessary amend their answers.
- Ask individuals for answers in an appropriate form for that activity. If the task was the completion of a chart, for example, you may want to draw the chart on the board (or an OHT) and ask individual students to come to the front and complete different boxes.
- Identify any problems that some students still have. Highlight them and draw attention to relevant sections of the Language Reference page at the end of the unit. Make a note to do a further check when the language is recycled later in the unit. Alternatively, ask students to do a related Workbook exercise.

8 The importance of pronunciation, stress and intonation

Students should be intelligible when they speak English both to native speakers of English and to non-native speakers with whom there is no other language in common. Inappropriate speech patterns can lead to misunderstanding. For this reason, pronunciation is an important thread in the *Look Ahead* multi-syllabus.

In the Intermediate Students' Book the emphasis is on stress and intonation above word level. Attention is given, for example, to patterns associated with certain functions (like orders and requests), and patterns that have real discourse value (introducing new topics or interrupting). A useful standard procedure for dealing with the sections headed Speech Patterns is as follows:

* Organise students in pairs and play the relevant extracts from the cassette while they look at the questions in their books.
* Ask students to discuss the meaning of particular features of pronunciation, and what the effect of different patterns would be.
* Take feedback in open class.
* Play the cassette again, stopping for individual and choral repetition of key sentences.
* Move into a freer speaking activity (such as a role play) in which the new pattern is likely to occur.

The different sounds of English, which students should be able to recognise and produce, are presented methodically through *Look Ahead 1* and *2*. In *Look Ahead Intermediate* the pronunciation of new words is given attention in the Workbook, where an alphabetical list for each unit is provided in written form and recorded on the accompanying cassette. The Workbook activities invite students to repeat the words on the cassette – best done individually out of class – and also encourage students to recognise, and group together, words that share similar sound and stress patterns.

It is always useful to do some revision of the pronunciation of new words in the classroom after students have done the Workbook exercises. You can, for example, choose words from the list at random and ask individuals to contextualise them in sentences to show that they understand the meaning, and to allow you to check the pronunciation of the words in context. Another idea is to write a stress pattern on the board (e.g. O o o – <u>ex</u>cellent) and give pairs of students one minute to list five words with that pattern.

9 Supplementing the coursebook

This course, with its different components, is complete and needs no specific supplementation. Indeed, in some situations teachers may feel that they are unable to cover all the tasks presented in a particular lesson, so the Lesson Notes in this book contain suggestions for omitting exercises or setting them for homework. However, each teacher has an individual style of teaching just as each class has its own needs, and the progression of tasks through the Students' Book does not in any way rule out additional activities which you might want to introduce. Some are suggested in the Lesson Notes. Others might include:

* games and puzzles for all kinds of purposes;
* further practice in reading skills using locally available English language texts (such as articles from English language newspapers) that relate to a unit topic, and using graded readers;
* project work suggested by topics in the book and involving teamwork inside and outside the classroom. An example would be the preparation of an English language guidebook for a local museum, including floor layouts, photographs, explanatory text, and so on;
* formal debates on subjects of interest, with students preparing short talks in support of and against a proposition.

Specific ideas for these and many other activity types can be borrowed from teachers' resource books, or from friends and colleagues.

10 Integrating the videos

While use of the *Look Ahead* Classroom Videos is optional and the course is complete without them, they were developed at the same time as the books and audio cassettes and are linked to them in fundamental ways (through topic, situation, character and language focus). The visual element provides additional layers of richness to Documentary sections in the Students' Book and drama sequences in the Workbook; some parts of the videos (such as the short animations) will be completely new to students. Teachers are advised to use the video material for consolidation **after** completing each Students' Book unit, and the Video Workbook provides activities that exploit and move out from this material. Detailed suggestions for using the videos are given in the Video Teacher's Guide that accompanies the Video Workbooks.

Lesson Notes

Welcome to Look Ahead Intermediate

. . . .

The aims of these two pages are to familiarise the students with some of the topics and people presented in the book and to stimulate their interest in the subjects they are going to study.

EXERCISE 1

Direct the class to the pictures and the questions in the exercise. The students discuss the questions in pairs and then as a class. Do not confirm their answers yet, as they can check them in Exercise 5.

KEY

A works for a newspaper
B emergency services operator
C hotel owner
D police officer
E works for a model agency
F an ambulance
G handcuffs
H printing press
I cards from a model agency
J a room key (hotel)
K the front cover of an information leaflet on crime; its purpose is to inform; it might be read by householders
L a sign showing that the area is for horses only; its purpose is to warn/inform; car drivers
M the front cover of a magazine; its purpose is to persuade readers to open the magazine; it would be read by women (usually)
N a sign on an office door; its purpose is to inform people who the occupant of the office is; it might be read by people working in/visiting the office
O part of a street map; its purpose is to illustrate location/directions; it might be used by a taxi driver/visitor to the city/emergency services operator

EXERCISE 2

Write A–E on the board and ask *Which object (F–J) goes with person A?* Elicit the students' answer and write H next to A on the board. Then ask *Which text (K–D) goes with person A?* Elicit the answer and write N on the board. The students then work in pairs and do the same for the other four people. Check their answers as a class.

KEY
A–H–N, B–F–O, C–J–L, D–G–K, E–I–M

EXERCISES 3 AND 4

Divide the class into pairs of A and B students. Direct the As to the pictures on pages 6 and 7 and the Bs to the contents chart on pages 2 to 5. Ask the Bs to read out some of the unit titles. Then the As describe the pictures and the Bs decide which unit titles they refer to. Each pair of students compares their answers with another pair. Check answers as a class.

KEY

A / H / N = News and views
B / F / O = In touch
C / J / L =   Away from home
D / G / K = Rights and wrongs
E / I / M =   Skin deep

📼 EXERCISE 5

Tell the students that they are going to listen to the five people in the pictures to check their answers. Play the extracts. The students compare answers with their partners and then check as a class.

KEY

1 = D   2 = A   3 = C   4 = E   5 = B

TAPESCRIPT

One. CATHY ELLISON
I've been with the Austin Police Department for thirteen-and-a-half years. Currently I'm assigned to crimes against property, the theft division.

Two. IVAN FALLON
Working for *The Sunday Times* is dramatically exciting. You are absolutely at the centre of what are the most exciting events that particular week.

Three. JOHN EGAN
Horseback riding is a very important feature of Rancho Encantado and it's certainly one of the reasons that people come from around the country to, to stay at the ranch.

Four. CHRIS OWEN
I think that there's a great satisfaction in finding someone, grooming them, putting them on the road to success, and watching them grow . . . I mean, the change you see in some of the models over a two or three year period is quite astonishing.

Five. MICHELLE REDFERN
The main aim of my job is to help the public and get

them the ambulance there as soon as we can – in the shortest time possible.

Finally, ask the students to look at the contents chart again, to find out the topics of the other ten units. Students discuss in pairs or groups which topics they think they will find most interesting.

1 *Patterns of life*

Changes

Focus	
TOPIC	SKILLS
• Changes in surroundings	• Reading: people's memories
GRAMMAR	• Listening: a monologue
• *Used to* + infinitive	• Writing: about changes
	• Speaking: giving opinions and reasons

GETTING STARTED EXERCISE 1

Background note
In the 1980s there was a new development of houses and offices in East London in the Docklands area, formerly a poor area, along the River Thames. It includes the Canary Wharf tower, which is the tallest building in Europe. In the 1990s, the area was hit by the recession and development stopped. There is an electric railway (The Docklands Light Railway) which connects the area to the City of London.

The overall theme of this unit is to discuss how life/the area where you live can change. To introduce the topic, direct the class to Pictures B and C in the Students' Book and ask *What do you call this place?* Elicit *the docks*. Discuss if the students have dockland areas in their countries and if their purpose has changed. Then direct them to the exercise and, in pairs, they discuss the two questions. Get quick class feedback for both questions, but do not confirm their answers to question 2 yet.

KEY
1 A = 1990s   B = 1970s   C = about 1910

🖭 LISTENING EXERCISE 2

Tell the students that they are going to listen to a conversation to check their answers to question 2 from Exercise 1. Play the cassette. Ask them to compare their answers in pairs and then check as a class.

KEY
It used to be a busy area with lots of work at the docks; now it has become a commercial area.

TAPESCRIPT
Docklands is an area in the east of London, along the River Thames, where boats used to come in and dock. In the last century and the first half of this century, the area was very busy; there were lots of ships coming in, and lots of work for the people who lived there. But things changed in the 1950s and 60s: the docks closed and industries moved out. Then, in the 1980s there was another great change: new buildings went up in Docklands, and new companies moved in.

READING EXERCISE 3

Write WORK, PLEASURE, HOME, THE RIVER on the board and ask the students to read the first text. Elicit which topic the text is about. Write A under THE RIVER. The students do the same with the other texts in pairs. Check as a class and write their answers on the board under the correct headings.

KEY
A the river   B pleasure   C home   D work

EXERCISE 4

This exercise helps students to practise intensive reading. To demonstrate the task, direct the class to the first statement and get them to find the information in the text which shows if it is true or false. Then students do the same with the other two statements. Encourage them to compare answers in pairs. When checking as a class, make sure they read out the relevant part of the text.

KEY
1 False: the housing was cramped (Text C), children didn't have toys (Text B), the father often had no work (Text D), money was always a problem (Text D).
2 True: people were very friendly with their neighbours, they went to the park with other families on Saturday evenings (Text B).
3 True: it provided work for the men (Text D), it was exciting for people to watch the ships (Texts A and B).

EXERCISE 5

This exercise focuses on the names of different types of boats and jobs. If you wish, write BOATS and JOBS on the board and ask the students to read the questions in the book. They answer the questions in pairs. Check their answers as a class and write them on the board under the two headings.

KEY

1 Boats: tugs, police launches, sailing barges, river buses, pleasure boats. River buses and pleasure boats carried members of the public as passengers.
2 Jobs: (a) a conjuror   (b) a stevedore   (c) a foreman

DISCOVERING LANGUAGE EXERCISE 6

Note: Students may be confused by the fact that the *s* is pronounced /s/ in *I **used to** /juːstə/ play football* (as opposed to /z/ in *I **used** /juːzdə/ a bowl*). They may also try to pronounce the final *d* on *used*.

Alternative presentation

You may wish to present *used to* before doing the exercise. Draw/find some pictures of the past and present (sing/watch TV, coaches/fast cars, old houses/blocks of flats).

Draw/put the first picture on the board and ask *What did people use to do in the evenings a hundred years ago?* Elicit *They used to sing.* To check the concept, ask *Do people usually sing in the evenings now?* (No) *Did they use to in the past?* (Yes) *Was it a habit then?* (Yes) *Is it a habit now?* (No) *Why not?* (Because things have changed.) Then drill *They used to sing in the evenings* chorally and individually. Show the picture of a TV and elicit *People didn't use to watch TV in the evenings.* Use the same concept questions and drill the sentence, concentrating on the pronunciation of *didn't use to.* Make sure the students do not pronounce a *d* on the end of *use to.* Repeat the procedure with your other pictures.

To elicit the question form, point to your first picture and say *What's the question?* Elicit *What did people use to do?* Drill the question chorally and individually. Then get the students to ask and answer in pairs. If you wish, write the questions and sentences on the board with the students' help and highlight the form and pronunciation of *used to.*

Direct the class to the questions in the Students' Book which help the students to focus on the form and meaning of the language. Encourage them to work in groups to discuss their answers and then check as a class.

KEY

1 c. It refers to the past.
2 No, it is not probable. *Used to* refers to a past habit.
3 Infinitive without *to.*
4 We never used to have, we used to go out, That used to be, Dad often used to come home, Mum used to cry, Dad didn't use to pay. The two negative forms are: *never used to, didn't use to.*
5 Did you use to enjoy life in Docklands?

Extra practice

Find more pictures of the past: your local library could be a good source. If possible, group them into subjects: clothes, transport, food and drink, people, housing, leisure activities, social customs. Divide the students into groups (one per topic) and give each group a large piece of paper with the topic written on the top. Using the pictures and their own ideas, they write sentences about the past, e.g. *Children used to play in the streets. People didn't use to eat convenience foods,* etc. Give them about ten minutes. Then rotate the pieces of paper and the next group adds more ideas. Do the same until all the groups have had a chance to add something – keep the pace going and prompt as necessary. Return the paper to the original group for them to read the others' suggestions and to correct any errors of information or language. You can read out some of the more interesting sentences and display them on the noticeboard if you wish.

EXERCISE 7

Write the topics on the board: *home, school, free-time, family holidays.* Elicit other ideas for *anything else* (e.g. food, sports, drinks). To demonstrate the task, indicate students to ask you questions about the prompts. If they have problems with the question form, drill a question for each of the topics on the board, e.g. *What did you use to study at school? Did you use to wear a uniform? What did you use to do in your free time? Where did you use to go on holiday?* The students then interview each other in pairs. Make sure they make notes under the headings *used to* and *didn't use to.* Monitor and make a note of any errors you hear. Get class feedback: if you have a large class, get them to tell each other in groups. Finally, use the board to correct any errors you heard.

Extra practice

Write a *Find someone who . . .* based on your students. If you don't have access to a photocopier, write this chart on the board and ask the students to copy it into their notebooks, e.g.

FIND SOMEONE WHO USED TO	NAME
– do ballet	. . . .
– live in the countryside	. . . .
– have a rabbit as a pet	. . . .
– quarrel with their brothers/sisters	. . . .
– go on holiday to the same place every year	. . . .
– wear shorts at school	. . . .
– eat lots of sweets	. . . .
– play hide and seek	. . . .

🔊 Documentary

LISTENING EXERCISE 8

The aim of this exercise is to pre-teach vocabulary that the students will need for the listening task in Exercise 9. Ask them to work in groups to do the first part of the exercise. If they find the vocabulary difficult, read out definitions to check understanding, e.g.

T: *a line of houses*
SS: *row*
T: *a job that needs special training*
SS: *a skilled job*

In the same groups, they then complete the phrases in the second part of the exercise. Encourage them to check their answers in pairs and then as a class. If necessary, drill their answers and write them on the board: mark the stress and highlight the linking and weak forms in:

a row of houses, the spirit of our time, a modern housing estate, sink at sea, thrive in forests.

KEY

1 row /rəʊ/   2 skilled/pro'fessional   3 'purchase
4 de'serted   5 'spirit   6 pro'fessional/skilled   7 thrive
8 sink   9 e'state

📼 EXERCISE 9

Ask the students to copy the headings from the exercise into their notebooks. Play the cassette once and the students check their answers in pairs. If necessary, play the cassette again and check their answers as a class. Remind the students of the texts they read in Exercise 3 about Docklands. Ask *What new information have you learnt about Docklands?* and they discuss in groups. If necessary, play the cassette again, segmenting it to elicit the new information.

KEY

1 JOBS: Professional people live there, not people who work on the docks.
  WEEKENDS: Docklands is deserted at weekends because the professional workers only live there during the week and then go to weekend homes in the country.
  COMMUNITY LIFE: There is no social/community life any more because people are not there at weekends.
2 There were whole estates and rows of houses lived in by people who worked on the docks. Some docks had their own social clubs with dances on Saturday nights and parties for children.

TAPESCRIPT

TERRY WARD

The kinds of people and the, the jobs that they used to do in, in the last century in the docks were all relevant to Docklands itself and the industries which were joined to it. Today, of course, the people are completely different and there are a lot of professional people now, skilled accountants, doctors, lawyers. They're the kind of people who would have a town house and then would want to get away to the country, somewhere in the countryside. A lot of the flats and houses that have been purchased in the docks, well at the weekends they're empty. You don't see them. They're only used during the week when the people are working. Therefore they don't really constitute a community, because at the weekend, when the social life used to be at its most active, now it tends to sink and go quiet. And an awful lot of the new docks estates and areas are deserted at weekends. And you've got nothing any more. In fact it's like a ghost town.

When Docklands was really thriving many years ago and they, they used to have whole estates and rows and streets of houses which were all dockers or related industries, all the people lived there, they had a very close-knit community spirit. And they certainly used to make all their own entertainment, an awful lot of it; and they used to organise trips – you know, days down to the seaside and things like that. Certain docks used to have their own social clubs, for instance, where they'd have dances on Saturday nights and things, and various parties for the children.

WRITING EXERCISE 10

Direct the class to the prompt in the exercise and elicit a complete sentence from the students (see Key). Write it on the board. Ask the students to work in groups to write at least six sentences. Monitor and help. To check their answers, each group reads out their sentences and the other groups say if they are grammatically and factually correct.

SUGGESTED KEY

People in Docklands used to live and work on the docks, but now professional people live there. The river used to be very busy, but now there are very few ships. There used to be lots of work on the docks, but the docks closed. People used to live in houses, but now they live in modern blocks of flats or houses. They used to go to the park on Saturday evenings, but now the people who live there go to their country houses at the weekend. There used to be a strong community life, but there isn't any more because people are rarely there at weekends.

SPEAKING EXERCISE 11

Give an example of one area in your country that has changed and discuss if the students think it is better or worse, and why. If they need some guidance, brainstorm other areas that have changed on the board and then get them to discuss the exercise in groups. Monitor and note down any errors you hear with forms of *used to* and use the board to correct them at the end of the students' discussion.

Extra practice

If your students are interested in the topic of 'change', ask them to write about how a specific area in their country has changed. They can present their writing to the class in the form of a wall poster, if possible with pictures.

Short of time?

Exercise 10 can be done for homework. Exercise 11 can be omitted.

Moving on

Focus	
TOPIC	**SKILLS**
• Changes in lifestyles	• Reading: an article
GRAMMAR	• Listening: conversations
• Present simple	• Speaking: role play
• Adverbs of frequency	**VOCABULARY DEVELOPMENT**
• Present progressive for current events	• Compound nouns (noun + noun)
• Present progressive for fixed future plans	**STRESS PATTERNS**
FUNCTIONS	• Stress in compound nouns
• Greetings	
• Asking/talking about health	
• Introductions	
• Responding to introductions	

GETTING STARTED EXERCISE 1

To introduce the topic, write *change* on the board and ask *Is it positive or negative?* Discuss the students' ideas. Then direct them to the questions in the book and give them a few minutes to make brief notes about themselves. Then they work in pairs and discuss the questions with their partner. If you wish, get quick feedback.

READING EXERCISE 2

Direct the class to the picture in the Students' Book and ask students to describe what they can see. Then write the headline (*A flatful of rubbish*) on the board and discuss as a class what it might refer to. Next, ask *Can you think of a connection*

between the picture and the headline? and discuss as a class. Finally, they read the article to see if their guesses were correct. Check as a class.

EXERCISE 3

Background notes

A **mortgage** is a loan to buy a flat or house over 20 to 25 years. In Britain, it is common to get a mortgage from a **building society** or from a bank. **British Telecom** (the company Andrew Weston-Webb used to work for) is the largest telecommunications company in Britain. It used to be a nationalised company and was privatised by the Conservative Government in the 1980s.

This is a real article from **The Observer** (a serious British Sunday newspaper) about a man who had a relatively normal lifestyle with his wife and daughter. After a number of crises in his life, he went to Australia under a false name. Later, he confessed to the authorities and returned to Britain. He now lives alone in a flat provided by the local council.

Note: *skip* is British English. In American English, they use *a dumpster*.

Write the four vocabulary items in the exercise on the board. Refer the students back to the article and ask them to find the words. In pairs, they discuss what the words mean and check in their dictionaries. Check as a class and highlight what part of speech they are and the stress. Drill as necessary.

KEY

skips: (noun) builders' large metal containers for taking rubbish away

'left-over: (adj) (e.g. food) unwanted/not sold

'mortgage /'mɔːgɪdʒ/: (noun) money borrowed from a bank or building society to buy a house/flat

'pension /'penʃn/: (noun) an amount of money paid regularly (by the government or a company) to someone who has retired

EXERCISE 4

First the students read the questions and then they find the answers in the article. Check that the students understand *suburbs*. Ask them to compare answers in pairs and then check as a class.

KEY

1 They come from other people, builders' skips.
2 Because he is concerned about the environment and wasting things unnecessarily.
3 He sells them to other people at street markets.
4 He used to be an executive with British Telecom and used to live in a large house in the suburbs.

5 Yes. He says 'I feel much happier living here. Life's an adventure this way.'

6 Open answers.

DEVELOPING VOCABULARY EXERCISE 5

The aim of this exercise is to make students aware of the formation of compound nouns. Write the examples as headings on the board and tell the students to copy them into their notebooks. Discuss the first question and establish why they are called 'compound nouns' (two words together which make a new noun). Then demonstrate the task in question 2 with *identity*. Elicit the answer and write *identity cards* under *phone cards* on the board. Ask the students to do the same with the other words in pairs. Check their answers and write them on the board. Then follow the same procedure with the third question.

KEY

1 A compound noun is made up of two words which together make a new noun. In these examples, the compound nouns are all made up of two nouns.

2 *identity* cards   *day*-time   *vegetable* markets
  fish hooks/markets   *curtain* hooks
  kitchen shelves/chair/hooks   *bed*-time

3 *book*case/ club/end
  *arm*band/hole/ rest
  *lamp*post/stand
  coat hanger/ stand
  phone book/ box/ kiosk/
  *street*car (American English for *tram*)/life
  *night*cap/dress/fall/life/light/ porter/ shift/shirt/ watchman

🔊 SPEECH PATTERNS EXERCISE 6

Refer the students back to the compounds on the board from Exercise 5. Play the first compound and mark the stress on the board as a class. Then play the complete cassette again. Students check their answers in pairs and then discuss the pattern as a class. Play the cassette again, stopping to drill each compound chorally and individually.

KEY AND TAPESCRIPT

In compound nouns, the main stress is generally on the first noun.

• bookshelves   • armchair   • lampshades   • night-time

• coat hooks   • phone cards   • street markets

Extra practice

Draw an outline of a room on the board (see below).

Dictate the description to the students and they draw a picture of the room. Then they describe the room to you. Complete the drawing, then write their description on the board as a class and encourage correction of any errors, especially the stress patterns of the compound nouns.

Description

The bed is opposite the door and there is a bookcase next to the bed on its right. Under the window, there is a dining table with a fruit bowl on it. Opposite the window on the wall, there are some bookshelves with an armchair under them. In the middle of the room is a round table with two phone books and a phone card on it. There are three coat hooks on the back of the door. Hanging from one of them is a nightdress. On the left of the door, there is a coat stand.

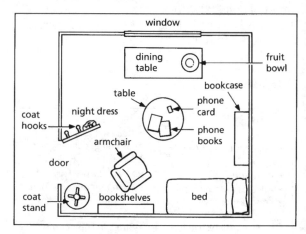

DISCOVERING LANGUAGE EXERCISE 7

The aim of Exercises 7 and 8 is to check that the students understand the difference in use between the present simple, present progressive used to express temporary activities in the present, and present progressive used to express the future. This should be revision for the students so direct them immediately to the exercise and ask them to discuss the questions in pairs. Monitor to see how good their knowledge is. Check their answers as a class.

KEY

1 a – C   b – A   c – B

2 a – present progressive (*is going down*)
  b – present simple (*hardly ever buys/goes out/looks through/sells them/I tell them/pass on/people love it*)
  c – present progressive (*is sitting*)

EXERCISE 8

Refer the students back to the first paragraph of the article and get them to find the missing adverb of frequency (*hardly ever*). Write the sentence on the board and ask *Does he often buy new things?* (No) *How do you know?* (Because of *hardly ever*). Establish that *hardly ever* has the same meaning as *rarely/occasionally* and that it means that he almost never buys new things. Highlight the position of the adverb in the sentence (before the main verb). If you wish, remind students of the position of adverbs of frequency with the verb *to be* (they come after the verb) and the position of expressions such as *once a week, every month* (at the end of the phrase).

KEY

1 hardly ever
2 always, sometimes, frequently, often, rarely, occasionally

Extra practice

If your students need revision of adverbs and expressions of frequency, write these on the board and draw the time scale below:
always, most evenings, once a year, sometimes, frequently, often, rarely, occasionally, hardly ever, almost never, all the time, never

ALWAYS – – – – – – – – – – – – – – – – – NEVER

The students plot the adverbs and expressions on the scale.

SPEAKING EXERCISE 9

Write these headings on the board: *clothes, homes, possessions, routine.* Ask the question *Are your clothes the same as Andrew's?* and discuss some of the differences as a class. The students then work in pairs and discuss the differences between their lifestyles and Andrew's, using the headings. Monitor and note down any errors you hear with the language from Exercises 7 and 8. Discuss as a class and use the board to correct any errors you heard. Then ask the pairs to write down questions that they would like to ask Andrew, *e.g. Do you ever feel hungry?* Elicit their questions as a class and write them on the board. Leave them there for the next exercise.

EXERCISE 10

Divide the students into pairs and direct them to the information about their roles in the exercise. Establish that the As (*Andrew*) are at the street market and the Bs (*the students*) have read about him but have not met him before. To demonstrate the task, role play the beginning of the

conversation with an A student. The students then role play their conversations in pairs. If you wish, they can change roles. Monitor and note down any errors you hear. Correct them at the end of the activity on the board.

FOCUS ON FUNCTIONS EXERCISE 11

Note: See *Look Ahead 1* Teacher's Book, Unit 3, page 29 for information on conventions for greeting people in Britain.

First, as a class, discuss how the Bs greeted Andrew in the role play, e.g. shook hands. Then the students discuss question 1 in pairs or as a class. Next, write the two headings in question 2 on the board and elicit possible phrases. As you elicit them, ask the students to decide if they are formal or informal and group them on the board accordingly. Leave them on the board for the next exercise. Finally, discuss question 3 as a class.

SUGGESTED KEY

1 Open answers.

2 Formal greetings:	Good morning/afternoon/ evening/night.
Informal greetings:	Hello. Hi. How are things? How are you?
Formal introductions:	I'd like to introduce you to . . . Can/May I introduce you to . . .? How do you do? I'm pleased to meet you.
Informal introductions:	Hello, my name's . . . This is . . . , Nice to meet you.

LISTENING EXERCISE 12

Direct the class to the two questions and play the two conversations. Encourage the students to discuss their answers in pairs and then check as a class. Refer the students back to the expressions on the board from Exercise 11. To demonstrate the task, play the cassette again, stopping after *Hi* and together tick it off the list or add it to the list. Then play both conversations. Students check what they have ticked and added to their lists. Then use the board to check as a class. Drill for polite intonation as necessary.

KEY

1 The first one is informal. The second one is formal.
2 open answers

TAPESCRIPT

One.

JULIE: Hi, Madeleine! Good to see you again. How are you?

MADELEINE: Hello, Julie . Fine, thanks. And you?

JULIE: Oh, fine. How's Charlie?

MADELEINE:	Oh, he's well. Anyway, Julie, this is Dan. He's working with us today.
JULIE:	Hi, Dan.
DAN:	Hi. Nice to meet you.

Two.

WOMAN:	Julie, let me introduce you to Signor Bettinelli. Signor Bettinelli is the mayor.
MAYOR:	Good evening. How do you do?
JULIE:	How do you do?
DIRECTOR:	And Signora Bettinelli, this is Julie Simms.
JULIE:	How do you do?
SIGNORA BETTINELLI:	Pleased to meet you.

SPEAKING EXERCISE 13

First divide the students into groups of four and allocate roles (A, B, C, D). Tell them to read the situation and roles in the book. It is more realistic if students do this exercise standing up. Make sure they change roles so that they role play the conversation four times. Monitor and make notes of any mistakes you hear and use the board to correct them at the end of the activity. Monitor carefully for polite intonation patterns. In the feedback, you may also wish to discuss if it is appropriate to shake hands (you might do so in Britain in this situation).

Short of time?
Exercise 1 can be omitted.

SPEAKING: Describing pictures

> **Focus**
>
> TOPIC
> • Housing
>
> FUNCTIONS
> • Describing location/people/buildings
>
> SKILLS
> • Listening: a description
> • Speaking: a description
> • Writing: gap-filling

GETTING STARTED EXERCISE 1

If you think the vocabulary in the questionnaire will be new for your students, describe the school or other familiar buildings as a class to teach it. You may need to drill the vocabulary for correct pronunciation. Then ask the students in groups to describe the three types of houses in the book. If you wish to guide their description, write the headings *type of house?/age?/materials?/roof?/ condition?/special features?* on the board. Monitor for correct pronunciation. Get feedback as a class and then decide which home the questionnaire is describing. Next, ask the students to fill in the questionnaire about their homes; they can just write the answers in their notebooks. Monitor and help with vocabulary, especially for *special features*. Before they interview each other, you may need to check their question forms. To do this, direct them to the first two questions and say *What do you ask?* (What kind of house do you live in?) If necessary, drill chorally and individually. Then do the same with the other questions and elicit *How old is it? What's it made of? What's the roof made of? Is the outside in good condition? Are there any special features on the outside of the building?* Next, put the students into pairs to interview each other. If you wish, they can make notes to report back to the class.

KEY

1 the picture in the centre

COMPARING CULTURES EXERCISE 2

Copy the types of housing in question 1 onto the board. Ask *Which type of building can you see in the picture on the left?* (block of flats). Make sure students use a full sentence to identify the buildings. Do the same with the other two pictures. If necessary, ask questions to check the students understand the other vocabulary, e.g.
T: *What's a caravan?*
ss: *It's usually a holiday home. You can pull it behind your car.*
They then work in pairs and do the same with the other types of building. Monitor and help with any unknown vocabulary. Elicit their answers and tick each type of building as they mention it. Drill chorally and individually for correct pronunciation. Then write *Most people / Some people /A few people* on the board and get the students to discuss in groups where people live in their countries. Monitor and make a note of any pronunciation errors you hear for correction on the board at the end of the activity.

KEY

1 The picture on the left shows a block of flats.
  The picture in the centre shows a cave.
  The picture on the right shows houses on stilts.
2 Open answers.

Extra practice

1 If possible, take your students on a short walk around your town, naming the different types of buildings they see. e.g. *terraced houses, blocks of flats, detached houses, a cottage.*
2 The students work in pairs and design their ideal home. They can use the questionnaire in Exercise 1 to decide on the type of house. They also decide on the number of rooms, layout, etc.

and draw a plan. Then they work with another pair to describe their homes to each other. If you have a small class, they can mingle and compare homes, and then with their original partner, decide which home they would like to live in.

🔲 LISTENING EXERCISE 3

Direct the students to the pictures again and the questions in the Students' Book. Play the cassette and get them to compare answers in pairs. Check as a class.

KEY

1 the picture in the middle   2 b, then a   3 b,c,a
He describes them in this order because his main interest is in the cave dwellings. The cave that he describes first is the most important feature of the picture.

🔲 EXERCISE 4

Organise the students into groups of three and ask them to read the three questions and between them to choose one each to answer. Quickly check which student in each group is answering 1, 2 and 3. Play the cassette once. Now explain that in their groups, they are going to pool and use their notes to describe the picture as the speaker did. Monitor and make a note of any errors of information. Finally, get one group to describe the picture to check their answers to the questions.

KEY

1 a) painted white, inhabited, cool and pleasant
  b) quite poor, wearing casual summer clothes
  c) flat plain, plateau, not much vegetation
2 a) the house   b) the painted facade
  c) the brown rock   d) the picture   e) this same hill
  f) the house   g) the sloping rock
  h) this particular rock   i) the two high points
  j) the next building
3 It's probably . . .   I can't really tell.   I suppose . . .
  It's quite possible . . .   perhaps . . .   . . . appears to
  be . . .   They're probably . . .   I don't imagine . . .
  . . . presumably . . .   I'm not quite sure . . .
  . . . looks like . . .   This must be . . .   I should think . . .

TAPESCRIPT

This is an amazing picture. In the foreground there's a house built into the side of a bare hill. The house is actually cut out of the rock, and the front is painted white. There's a single window with a, a pink curtain across it and a wooden door. At least, it's probably made of wood; I can't really tell.

This rock house is clearly inhabited because in front of the house I can see washing hanging on a washing line in what looks like the front yard. Then, above the painted facade of the house, they've built a chimney . . . so there's a white chimney pot on top of the brown rock. They've also put up a television aerial, which is right in the centre of the picture, so I suppose there's electricity inside. It's quite possible that at the back of this same hill there's another door – or the facade of another house, perhaps.

At the side of the house, to the left and below the sloping rock, there's a flat area and the family seems to be using it as a patio. Anyway, they've got chairs there, and one person appears to be serving food. They're wearing casual summer clothes and they're probably quite poor because I don't imagine that the house is very luxurious. Further to the left and below the patio area is another chimney, which presumably belongs to a different, lower cave dwelling.

Em, in the background, a long way from this particular rock, there's another range of hills. Then, between the two points, there's a relatively flat plain – or a plateau, I'm not quite sure – and then there's a small town. It looks like a town because there are a lot of white houses and each one is quite close to the next building.

This must be a hot country because the sky is blue and there isn't much vegetation. I should think the cave dwellings are actually really cool and pleasant to live in.

WRITING EXERCISE 5

The students work in the same groups to do this exercise. Get them to read the whole text first and then to identify which of the pictures it is describing (the one on the left). Then they complete the gaps. Monitor and help. Write 1–10 on the board. Elicit their answers and write the correct ones on the board.

SUGGESTED KEY

1 casual   2 probably   3 At the side of/in front of
4 perhaps   5 close   6 on top of   7 Below
8 Between   9 painted   10 sloping

SPEAKING EXERCISE 6

The aim of this exercise is to give oral practice of the vocabulary and prepositional phrases of location in this unit. Direct the students to the picture and exercise in the Students' Book. They discuss the picture in groups of four. Then ask them to regroup with members of other groups to exchange their ideas. If you wish, discuss as a class.

EXERCISE 7

Ask the students to close their eyes and tell them they are standing outside their home. Ask them to visualise it, what it looks like, what season it is, and what the people inside are doing. Then divide them into pairs and tell the As to describe what they have visualised and the Bs to draw it. Explain that the Bs should ask questions if they are not sure about what to draw and they may need to make notes about the people's lifestyles. When they have finished, they swap roles and the As draw B's building. Monitor and note down any errors you hear.

EXERCISE 8

The students then tell the class about their partner's home. If you have a large class, they can give feedback in groups of four. Finally, use the board to correct any errors you heard in Exercises 7 and 8. If you wish, they can write the description for homework.

Short of time?
Exercise 5 can be done for homework.

Please refer to the Introduction to the Teacher's Book for ways of using the reference section.

Progress check: Unit 1

Grammar and functions

EXERCISE 1

1 used to study   2 does she do   3 did Tim use to work?   4 do he and Sheila live   5 Do they go
6 do they do   7 Did Tim use to go   8 did Sheila use to go   9 Does she go   10 Did they use to go

EXERCISE 2

1 Sheila didn't use to go to concerts. She used to go to discos and clubs.
2 Sheila and Tim don't live in a flat. They live on a houseboat.
3 They don't work in an office. They work in a school.
4 They didn't use to go on walking holidays. Sheila used to go on holidays abroad. Tim used to go on cycling holidays.
5 Tim doesn't go to concerts. He goes to parties.

EXERCISE 3

1 Sheila used to study Arabic and Persian.
2 Not possible.
3 Tim used to cycle with friends at weekends.
4 He used to go to concerts once or twice a week.
5 Not possible.

EXERCISE 4

1 They are visiting his parents next weekend.
2 They often give parties on the boat.
3 Sheila is teaching at the moment.
4 Tim is not working this morning.
5 They hardly ever go out on weekdays.

EXERCISE 5

1 hello/hi   2 Fine thanks   3 And you?   4 this is
5 Pleased/Nice to meet you   6 Good morning
7 Let me introduce you to   8 How do you do
9 How do you do

Vocabulary

EXERCISE 6

1 houseboat   2 lifestyle   3 street market
4 film show   5 community spirit   6 river bus
7 insurance company

2 *Pleasures*

An evening at home

Focus	
TOPIC • Television viewing	**FUNCTIONS** • Stating preferences
GRAMMAR • Adjective + preposition + noun/-*ing* • *Love, like, enjoy, hate, prefer* + -*ing*	**SKILLS** • Reading: an article

GETTING STARTED EXERCISE 1

To introduce the topic, ask students to name common hobbies and leisure activities they do, and count how many mention 'watching television'. Then divide them into pairs to discuss the question. Monitor and help with any new vocabulary for the types of programmes. Discuss as a class and write the types of programmes on the board. Drill for correct pronunciation as necessary.

Extra practice
Build up a list of programmes on the board, e.g. *the news, weather forecast, documentary, soap opera, drama series, situation comedy, films,* etc. Give out copies of newspapers with TV guides (of the same day if possible). Students work in groups and find examples of the different types of programmes.

READING EXERCISE 2

Direct the students to the cartoons and headline of the article and ask *What do you think the article is about?* Elicit their ideas and then ask them to read the two questions and the introductory paragraph. Encourage them to compare their ideas in pairs and then discuss as a class.

KEY

1 The Carter family, who watch TV all the time, had to live without one for a month. The Fox family, who have never had a TV, borrowed the Carter's TV for a month.
2 open answers

EXERCISE 3

Background note
MTV is a satellite TV station which plays rock and pop music all the time.

Ask the students to copy the chart into their notebooks. They read the article and complete the chart. Encourage them to compare their answers in pairs and then check as a class.

KEY

	BEFORE THE EXPERIMENT	DURING THE EXPERIMENT
George	ate in front of the TV	ate/talked with the family
Sandra	watched MTV all evening	played games with the family had more time to do her homework and started piano lessons
Angela	ate/talked together as a family	watched a few programmes but had to plan her life around the TV rarely saw children conflicts over homework
Peter	played family games and read	enjoyed watching TV programmes helped with his schoolwork

EXERCISE 4

If you have a large class, copy the exercise onto the board. To demonstrate the task, ask the students to find another word for *television* in the headline of the article. Elicit their answer (Box). The students do the same for the other words. Elicit their answers and write them on the board.

KEY

1 box (headline)   2 to rush away (George)
3 to miss (George)   4 crazy (Sandra)   5 nag (Angela)
6 depressing (Angela)

DISCOVERING LANGUAGE EXERCISE 5

Note: The expression *-ing (verb) form* is used in *Look Ahead Intermediate* instead of 'gerund' or 'present participle'.

Write *interested, bored, tired* on the board and ask the students to find the words in the article. Then ask *Which preposition follows 'interested'?* Write *in* next to *interested* on the board. Do the same for *bored* and *tired*. Follow the same procedure with question 2 and write the forms next to the adjective and prepositions on the board. Finally, the students discuss question 3 in pairs. Elicit their answers and highlight the forms on the board.

KEY

1&2 interested + in + noun/(an *-ing* verb form)
      bored + with + an *-ing* verb form/(noun)
      tired + of + an *-ing* verb form/(noun)
3   *-ing* verb form

EXERCISE 6

To introduce the exercise, ask *What can you do at home in the evening?* and ask the students to write down their ideas. If you wish, discuss their ideas as a class and write any new vocabulary on the board. To demonstrate the task, ask a student *Are you interested in painting? Are you bored with watching TV?*, using the forms in the previous exercise and make notes on the board. The students then use their list to interview each other. Make sure they make notes about their partner. Monitor and correct any errors you hear with the prepositions/-ing forms.

Use your notes on the board to write a couple of sentences about the student you 'interviewed'. The students then use their notes to write about their partner. Next, they swap their descriptions with their partner, who checks for any factual or language errors. If you wish to display their writing, they can write the name of their partner in large letters at the top of a piece of paper and then write their description underneath.

Extra practice
To revise the language in Exercises 5 and 6, write these prompts on the board: *I'm interested in/I'm bored with/I'm tired of/I love/I hate*, and ask the students to write five sentences about themselves, using the prompts. Each sentence should be on a

separate piece of paper. Take them all in. Read them out and ask the students to guess who wrote each sentence.

FOCUS ON FUNCTIONS EXERCISE 7

Copy the examples onto the board and ask three pairs of students to read out the dialogues, each with a different response. Then the students discuss the questions in the exercise. Check as a class and use the board to highlight the students' answers (see Key).

KEY

1 a) 2, 3   b) 1
2 1 prefer + . . .-*ing* form
   2 'd rather not + infinitive without *to*
   3 'd rather + infinitive without *to*
3 would
4 I'd rather not eat at home.
5 No.
6 The expressions are much more polite than just saying *No*.

EXERCISE 8

Divide the students into pairs and ask them to read the instructions. Then ask a pair to read the example exchange in the Students' Book. Explain that they can accept the invitation only after they have refused four times. You may need to remind the class of ways of accepting invitations. Elicit *I'd love to/that's a good idea/that'd be great*, etc. Make sure the students change roles. Monitor and note down any errors you hear with the language for refusing and accepting invitations. Use the board to correct the errors at the end of the activity.

Extra practice

If students need more practice in inviting and accepting/refusing invitations, ask them to draw a diary page in their notebooks and fill it in with activities for three days. They then mingle and invite each other to any of the events they have planned. The aim of the activity is to persuade as many people as possible to come with them on each day. The students are only allowed to agree to one invitation per evening. If they find that they have accepted an invitation and then get a better one, they must go back to the original student and make an excuse which means that they can't go after all!

A day out

> **Focus**
>
> TOPIC
> • A visit to a film studio
>
> GRAMMAR
> • *So do I.*
> • *Neither/Nor do I.*
>
> FUNCTIONS
> • Agreeing and disagreeing
>
> SKILLS
> • Reading: texts from a brochure
> • Listening: sound sequences, a conversation
> • Speaking: agreeing and disagreeing in conversation

GETTING STARTED EXERCISE 1

Background notes

Universal Studios is one of the largest film companies in the USA. The original film studio was in Hollywood, Los Angeles but now there is also one in Florida. It is possible to visit the studios as a tourist and see where and how films are made. **Ghostbusters** was a popular film made in 1984 about an imaginary firm in New York which tries to get rid of ghosts. A sequel was made some years later. **King Kong** was a film made in 1933 (remade in 1976) about a giant gorilla which terrorised the people of New York, taking a young woman prisoner and climbing the Empire state building, holding her under his arm. **Earthquake** (1974) was a popular 'disaster movie' about a huge earthquake which destroys Los Angeles.

Find out if the students have ever been to a film studio and what it was like. Then direct the class to the brochure at the top of the page and the questions. You may need to pre-teach *set* e.g. *Are films always made in houses, outside?* (No) *Do they have houses in the studio?* (Yes) *What do we call these?* (Sets).The students read the brochure. Encourage them to compare their answers in pairs and then check as a class.

KEY

1 in Florida, USA   2 films   3 Hollywood
4 Visitors can: go on rides (a), see where films are made (c), and meet actors (d).

SPEAKING EXERCISE 2

Note: The word *attraction* is used to describe the special rides at Universal Studios, as the effects are such that they are more than just rides.

Refer the students back to the pictures and discuss which attractions they think are shown. Check they understand attractions – you could find out if they have visited an adventure park or theme park (like *Disneyland*) and if they enjoyed the attractions.

KEY

A is from *Ghostbusters*, B is from *Kongfrontation*,
C is from *Earthquake ... The Big One*.

READING EXERCISE 3

Copy this grid onto the board (without the text):

	ATTRACTION	WHERE ARE THE VISITORS?	WHAT 'DANGER' ARE THEY IN?
1	*Kongfrontation*	trapped in a tram above the East River	King Kong is angry and he is smashing things
2	*Earthquake ... The Big One*	trapped in an underground train	they could be buried alive, crushed, burnt or drowned

The students copy it into their notebooks. Direct
the class to the three descriptions of the
attractions. Ask them to read the first one and
elicit which attraction it is describing, where the
visitors are and what imaginary danger they are
in. Complete the grid on the board. The students
then work in pairs and do the same with the
second description. Check as a class.

KEY

1   1 *Kongfrontation*   2 *Earthquake*   3 *Ghostbusters*
2   See above.

EXERCISE 4

Copy the adjectives in List A onto the board and
ask the students to find them in the texts from
the brochure and in Exercise 3. Then direct them
to the adjectives in List B. Ask a student to read
out the sentence which contains *fantastic* from
the text. Elicit which adjective in List B has a
similar meaning and write *great* next to *fantastic*
on the board. The students then do the same
with the other adjectives. Encourage them to
compare answers in pairs. Then check as a class
and write the students' answers on the board.
Mark the stress and drill for pronunciation as
necessary.

KEY

fan'tastic – great   'terrifying – very 'frightening
'crazy – wild   in'credible – unbe'lievable
huge /hjuːdʒ/ – e'normous   'famous /'feɪməs/ – well-
'known ('well-known when before a noun)
'evil /iːvəl/ – bad and 'dangerous

EXERCISE 5

Direct the students to the exercise and the five

explanations. To demonstrate the task, ask the
students to read the first description again to find
the verb for 'breaking violently'. Elicit their
answer and write *smashing* on the board. The
students then work together in pairs and do the
exercise. Check their answers as a class and write
the verbs on the board. Drill for correct
pronunciation as necessary.

KEY

1   'smashing /'smæʃɪŋ/ (Text 1)
2   'crushing /'krʌʃɪŋ/ (Text 1)
3   trapped /'træpt/ (Text 1)
4   sur'vive /sə'vaɪv/ (Text 1)
5   co'llapses /kə'læpsɪz/ (Text 2)
6   'buried /'berɪd/ (Text 2)

📇 Documentary

LISTENING EXERCISE 6

Students work in pairs to imagine the sounds
that might be heard at each attraction, and make
notes. Encourage them to ask you/check with a
dictionary for any sounds they can't say in
English.

SUGGESTED KEY

Kongfrontation: the sound of King Kong roaring,
smashing buildings and cars, people
screaming
Ghostbusters: the sound of guns firing, people
shouting
Earthquake: the sound of water rushing, buildings
collapsing, fire, trains

📼 EXERCISE 7

Refer the class back to the pictures and texts in
Exercises 1, 2 and 3. Ask the class *Which
attraction is it?* and play the first sound on
cassette. Elicit the attraction and what the people
are doing (screaming and shouting). Then play
the other sequences and the students note down
which attraction and what is happening.
Encourage them to discuss their ideas in pairs
and then check as a class.

KEY

(Tapescript is sound effects only)
1   *Kongfrontation:* King Kong is roaring, people are
screaming, helicopters are flying,
people are running
2   *Ghostbusters:*   people are shouting, guns are firing
3   *Earthquake:*   the ground is rumbling, people
are screaming, buildings are
collapsing, water is rushing

EXERCISE 8

Direct the students to the questions in the Students' Book. They discuss them in groups of three or as a class. Encourage them to use the adjectives from Exercise 4. Monitor for correct pronunciation.

KEY

open answers

▦ EXERCISE 9

If your students find listening difficult, you may wish to play the conversation twice. The first time, direct them to question 1. Play the conversation and encourage them to compare their answers with their partner before you check as a class. Then play the conversation again, pausing the cassette to give the students time to write the expressions down. The students check their answers in pairs and then as a class. Write their answers to question 2 on the board. Leave the expressions there for the next exercise.

KEY

a) Neither do I.   b) Oh, I did.   c) So am I.
d) Nor am I.

TAPESCRIPT

WOMAN: Wow. That was fan*tastic*! Did you like it?

MAN: Oh, yes. It was *great*, wasn't it?

WOMAN: That part where the train was coming towards us. I was terrified!

MAN: So was I. And then that burning oil tanker. All those flames. They were *real*. I mean, it was a *real fire*. I don't know how they do it.

WOMAN: Neither do I. It was amazing. And that last part ...whew!!

MAN: What? The water, you mean? I didn't like the water.

WOMAN: Oh, I did. It was really frightening.

MAN: Yes, but you know I don't like water. I've always been afraid of it.

WOMAN: But that's the point.

MAN: What do you mean?

WOMAN: Well ... that's why people go on these rides ... because they're frightening.

MAN: Huh? Well, I suppose that's right. But that was a bit too frightening for me. Anyway, do you want something to drink? I'm really thirsty.

WOMAN: So am I. There's a restaurant over there.

MAN: Oh, no! Food? After that ride? I'm not interested in food at the moment.

WOMAN: Nor am I ... let's find a shop and get some drinks.

DISCOVERING LANGUAGE EXERCISE 10

In groups, the students discuss the questions in the exercise. Compare their answers as a class and write them on the board. Leave them on the board for the next exercise.

KEY

1 a) So was I.   So am I.
   b) Neither do I.   Nor am I.
2 Oh, I did.
3 The verb comes before the subject when the speaker agrees, e.g. *So can I.* It comes after the subject when the speaker disagrees, e.g. *Oh, I did.*
4 The same verb form is used in the comment and in the response, e.g. *I was terrified!   So was I.*

SPEAKING EXERCISE 11

Tell the students that you are going to ask them some questions and they must write down the answers in their notebooks. Ask *Where were you born?* and make sure the students write down *I was born in ...* Then ask *How old are you? Are you married? What do you enjoy doing? What don't you enjoy doing? What did you do yesterday evening?* You may wish to add other questions which are not included in the exercise, e.g. *Can you dance? Do you have to get up early in the morning? Have you been to Italy?* As you are asking the questions, monitor to check that the students are writing down full sentences. To demonstrate the next part of the activity, ask a student to read out their first sentence (e.g. *I was born in ...*) and agree or disagree with it (*So was I/I wasn't*). Students then do the same in pairs. Make sure they change roles. Monitor and correct any errors you hear.

Extra practice

Divide the class into teams of four to six. Each team writes ten statements about themselves using a range of tenses and modal verbs (present simple/progressive, past simple, present perfect simple, *can, have to, should*). Then the first team reads out a statement and the team which agrees/disagrees the fastest gets a point.

Short of time?

Exercise 6 can be omitted.

CREATIVE WRITING: Describing scenes

Focus

TOPIC
• Landscapes

SKILLS
• Speaking: description of sensations
• Reading: a literary extract
• Writing: a description of a scene, making comparisons

VOCABULARY DEVELOPMENT
• Adjectives associated with colour words
• Verbs referring to light

SPEAKING EXERCISE 1

Refer the students to the picture in the Students' Book. Read out the introduction to the exercise as the students look at the picture. Ask them to work in pairs and to make a list in their notebooks of the nouns they can see in the picture. Elicit their answers and write the nouns on the board. Then ask the students to think of adjectives that can describe the nouns – do the first one together. Monitor and help them. Elicit their answers and write appropriate adjectives next to the nouns. Then tell them that they are the person in the picture. Tell them to close their eyes. Ask *How do you feel? What can you hear? What can you smell? What can you taste?* Pause between each question to give them time to think. Then they open their eyes and tell their partner how they felt and what they heard, smelt and tasted.

READING: A LITERARY EXTRACT EXERCISES 2 AND 3

Background notes

Capri is an Italian island near Naples. It is very popular with tourists. **Sainsbury's** is a large chain of British supermarkets, selling mostly food, drink and household goods.

Ask the students to read the introduction to the exercise and establish that the author is standing on the same hill that they have just imagined. Check that they understand *dusk*: the picture should help them. Direct them to the four questions in Exercise 2 and the text. Encourage them to compare their answers with their partner and then check as a class. Follow the same procedure for Exercise 3.

KEY FOR EXERCISE 2

1 It's early evening and the sun is going down.
2 200–300 feet above the sea.

3 Not very windy – there's a gentle breeze.
4 There are lemon trees, pine trees and honeysuckle.

KEY FOR EXERCISE 3

1 No. He has never been to this spot before. He describes himself as a tourist.
2 Yes. He describes the scene in the first person (I).
3 No. The sliver of moon, the pale blue evening sky and dusk suggest that the sun has already set.
4 It is a British supermarket. He refers to 'the household products section of Sainsbury's'.
5 Perhaps, because he relates the smell of the plants to a supermarket, which is an unexpected reference in the context.

EXERCISE 4

Copy the exercise onto the board and ask the class to find a word that means 'vertical'. Elicit 'sheer' and write it on the board. The students do the same for the other words. Encourage them to compare answers in pairs and then check as a class. Write the words on the board and drill for correct pronunciation as necessary.

KEY

1 sheer /ˈʃɪə/   2   aquamarine /ˌækwəməˈriːn/
3 jagged /ˈdʒægɪd/   4 faintest /ˈfeɪntɪst/
5 sliver /ˈslɪvə/   6 honeysuckle /ˈhʌnɪsʌkəl/

EXERCISE 5

Write the headings from the exercise (*see/hear/smell/feel*) on the board. As a class, discuss the words and phrases which describe what the writer can see and make brief notes on the board if you wish. The students then work in pairs and make notes under the other headings. Check their ideas as a class.

SUGGESTED KEY

a) *see:* breathtaking, never seen anything half as beautiful, spilling down the hillside, twinkling lights, sheer drop, sliver of moon, brilliantly white, hung in a pale blue evening sky
b) *hear:* sea . . . washing against the jagged rocks, the sound of breaking waves
c) *smell:* the scent of lemon, honeysuckle and pine
d) *feel:* I had the feeling that no one had been there for years, a warm breeze pulled gently at my hair

DEVELOPING VOCABULARY EXERCISE 6

Discuss question 1 as a class. Then the students discuss question 2 in pairs. Check as a class and establish that it is not often possible for the nouns to collocate with other colours, e.g. *sea black* or *mud red*.

KEY

1 deep blue – dark blue   pale blue – light blue
   brilliant blue – bright blue
2 a) rose pink – pale to dark pink
      sea green – dark green
      jet black – deep black
      mud brown – dark brown
      blood red – deep red
   b) open answers
   c) emerald green, grass green, sapphire blue, snow
      white, canary yellow, lemon yellow, chocolate
      brown, ruby red, . . .

Extra practice

To practise the different colour collocations, bring
in pictures/objects e.g. jewellery. The students
describe the colours in the pictures/objects and
things in the classroom, e.g. *Her nail varnish is
blood red.*

EXERCISE 7

Refer the students to the exercise and copy the
headings below onto the board. To demonstrate
the task write *sun* under *noun* on the board and
ask *What verb goes with 'sun'?* Elicit *shines* and
write it on the board next to *sun.* The students
work in pairs and match the nouns and verbs in
the same way. Elicit their answers and write them
on the board.

KEY

NOUNS	VERBS
the sun	shines
diamonds	sparkle
lightning	flashes
stars	twinkle
candles	flicker

EXERCISE 8

Direct the class to the picture in Exercise 9 and
discuss what the girls can see, hear, smell and
how they feel. Then ask a student to read the
example sentence to you and write it on the
board. Highlight the constructions *so + adjective
+ that* and *it was like + -ing.* Divide the students
into groups of four and ask the students to write
three sentences for each construction. Monitor
and help. Then elicit their sentences and write
them on the board. Leave them on the board for
the next exercise.

WRITING EXERCISE 9

Direct the students to the text and ask them to
read it. In pairs, they make notes about the
sensations illustrated in the picture. Using these,

and the notes on the board, they continue the
description of the scene.

EXERCISE 10

The aim of this exercise is to involve the students
in the process of editing their writing and to focus
on language and style. Ask the students to read
the questions, discuss each one if necessary, and
then to check their writing in pairs. If your
students know each other well, they can swap
their texts with another pair and edit each
others' writing.

EXERCISE 11

Ask the students to think of a scene that they can
remember vividly. Then ask them the questions
from Exercise 1 but allow them to write down
their impressions after each question. They can
use these notes to lead them into the writing
which can take place in the class or for
homework. Encourage them to use the questions
in Exercise 10 to edit their work.

Short of time?
Exercise 11 can be done for homework.

Talkback

. . . .

Working it out

1 The aim of this page is to give the students some
   speaking practice around the topic of job
   satisfaction. It gives students the opportunity to
   practice language of liking and disliking, stating
   preferences and agreement/disagreement.
   First, find out from your students if they have
   jobs and if they don't, what jobs they would like
   to do. Then encourage them to discuss in small
   groups what they like and dislike about the job
   they have or why they would like to have a
   particular job. Direct the students to the pictures
   and ask them to make a list of the things that
   may be important in a job: company car,
   helping people, working outside, opportunities
   to travel, opportunity to run your own business
   and be your own boss, money, long holidays,
   comfortable office and a good position.
2 Discuss as a class what the students have on
   their lists and then ask them to add other
   things: e.g. responsibility, promotion chances,
   variety, meeting people, flexitime, interesting
   work.

3 The students then work on their own and prioritise the features from the most important to the least important.

4 The students compare their lists with their partners and discuss why the things are more or less important. They should express agreement/ disagreement, and then justify their reasons.

5 In pairs, they try to think of jobs that would match each list.

6 Finally, each pair reports back to the class about the jobs they would like and why. If you wish, students can write a paragraph about their own job preferences for homework.

3 *Borders*

Lines on a map

Focus	SKILLS
TOPIC	• Listening: brief monologues
• National borders	• Speaking: describing location
GRAMMAR	• Reading: an article
• *Have to, must, needn't*	
FUNCTIONS	
• Talking about obligation, absence of obligation, prohibition	

GETTING STARTED EXERCISE 1

Write A, B, C, in a column on the board and direct the students to the three pictures in the Students' Book. Ask *What is the natural feature you can see in Picture A?* Elicit their answers and write them on the board next to A. The students then work in pairs and do the same for pictures B and C. Check their answers as a class and write them on the board. Next, refer the students to the three pairs of countries. They quickly discuss in pairs which picture represents which border. Then check as a class.

KEY

1 Picture B: a river (the Rio Grande)
2 Picture C: mountains (the Andes)
3 Picture A: a desert (the *Rub al Khali* – the Empty Quarter)

🖭 LISTENING EXERCISE 2

Refer the students to the questions in the Students' Book. Explain that they are going to listen to three people talking about the position of their countries. Play the cassette once. Encourage

students to compare answers in pairs. If necessary, play the cassette a second time. Check answers as a class.

KEY

1 1 Spain   2 Sweden   3 Brazil
2 a) to the south   b) in the north
    The preposition *to* suggests a feature is outside the country or area; the preposition *in* suggests inside.
3 east, west, north-west, north-east

TAPESCRIPT

One.
There are mountains in the north which form the border with France. To the south and east of the country is the Mediterranean Sea, and in the west there's a land border with Portugal. To the north-west of the country is the Atlantic Ocean.
Two.
The south of the country is fairly flat with a lot of forest, but there are mountains in the north-west on the border with Norway. The border in the north-east is with Finland, but most of the south and east of the country is surrounded by the Baltic Sea.
Three.
It's a huge country with the Atlantic Ocean to the east. The borders with Peru, Bolivia and Colombia are in the forest areas in the west. A river forms most of the border with Paraguay in the south.

SPEAKING EXERCISE 3

Ask the class *What's the position of (+ your country)?* and discuss its position and borders. Then, to demonstrate the task, think of a country and tell the students that they have to guess which country you are thinking of. Describe the position of the country, e.g. *It's a small country without any sea borders. Mountains form the border with Germany to the north, . . .* Students guess which country it is. Divide the class into pairs. A thinks of a country and describes it. B guesses where it is. Make sure they change roles. Monitor and note down any errors you hear. Use the board to correct them.

Alternatively, the students have to ask questions to guess the country. You think of a country and the students ask questions, e.g. *Is it in the north? How many countries does it share its borders with? What size is it?* Once they have guessed your country, they work in pairs and do the same.

Extra practice

Divide the classroom into compass points like this:

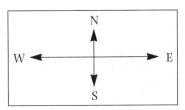

The students stand in the middle of the room. Explain that the classroom is the world and establish where north/south/east/west are. Tell them to go to the country they like most. They move and then turn to the students standing near them and say which country they have chosen and why they like it. You can do the same with: the country they don't like, the country they would most like to visit, the country which is the most dangerous, etc.

READING EXERCISE 4

Background notes

Liechtenstein is a very small country between Austria and Switzerland with a population of approximately 28,000. **Wiener schnitzel** is a famous Austrian dish which is made of a thin slice of veal covered with breadcrumbs and fried quickly in oil.

Direct the students to the title of the article. Discuss the two possible meanings and what they think the article will be about.

KEY

The two meanings of *cross* in the title are:
1 to go/pass over a border   2 angry

EXERCISE 5

Establish that the students know where and how small Liechtenstein is and what *Wiener schnitzel* is. Ask the students to read the first paragraph and then discuss what they think is going to happen next. If you wish, write some of their ideas on the board.

EXERCISE 6

Write *What happened to the writer? Why did he become so worried?* on the board and ask the students to read the text. Encourage them to discuss their answers with their partner and then discuss as a class. If you wrote their ideas on the board in Exercise 5, confirm which ideas were accurate.

KEY

He got lost and crossed the border from Liechtenstein into Austria by mistake. He was worried because he did not have his Australian passport or an Austrian visa with him. As he came from the former Soviet Union, he thought he would be in a lot of trouble because of crossing the border illegally.

EXERCISE 7

Ask the class *What do you think happened next?* and organise the students to work in pairs to discuss the ending. Then regroup them into fours to exchange ideas. Discuss their ideas as a class and then tell students to look at page 31 to find out what happened. Once they have read the ending, discuss as a class.

EXERCISE 8

Direct the students to the questions about the article. They discuss them in threes and make brief notes. Discuss their ideas as a class.

KEY

1 He used to live in the former Soviet Union.
2 He's got an Australian passport.
3 He left it in his hotel room in Liechtenstein.
4 He became really worried, he froze with fear.
5 Because it used to be illegal to move within or outside the country without permission from the State.
6 Because he is worried that the immigration officials will start asking questions if he appears too confident.
7 Because he thinks he will be treated like a criminal as he doesn't have any documents with him.

EXERCISE 9

Write 1–6 on the board and direct the class to the gap-fill exercise in the Students' Book. Ask the students to read the complete paragraph first to get the general meaning. Then do the first gap together. Encourage the students to work in pairs. Monitor and help. Then elicit their answers and write them next to the numbers on the board.

KEY

1 border post   2 frontier guards   3 immigration office   4 passports   5 visas   6 stamp

Next, ask the students to write in their notebooks any new words from the text that they are not sure about. Elicit the words and write them on the board. Divide the students into fours and ask them to explain the words that they know to each other. Then ask them to check the meaning of the unknown words in their dictionaries. Monitor and help. As a class, check the meaning of the words that are new to most of the students.

DISCOVERING LANGUAGE EXERCISE 10

Ask the students to read the example sentences in the exercise and to discuss questions 1–4. Monitor and help. Check as a class and use the board to highlight the forms.

KEY

1 infinitive without *to*
2 have to – don't have to   must – mustn't
   The negative of *need* can be *needn't* or *don't need to.*
3 H – I *have to* get to the station.
   I – You *needn't/don't need to* pay for children.
4 H – I *had to* get to the station.
   I – You *didn't have to* pay for children.

FOCUS ON FUNCTIONS EXERCISE 11

Note: Students are often confused by how to express the concepts of obligation/absence of obligation. They may be confused by the difference between *don't have to* and *mustn't.*

Copy the headings in the exercise onto the board and ask the students to write them in their notebooks. Ask questions to check that they understand the three concepts, e.g. *Do you have a choice? Why do you do it?* (Because it's a rule/law), *Is it necessary?* Then ask the students to find sentences in Exercise 10 which express these ideas. Do the first one together to demonstrate the task. Encourage them to work in pairs and monitor to help. Elicit their answers as a class and write the expressions under the headings on the board.

KEY

Obligation: Sentences A, C and H
Absence of obligation: Sentences B, D, E, F and I
Prohibition: Sentence G

EXERCISE 12

Write 1–5 on the board and direct the class to the signs in the exercise. Elicit the rule for the first sign and write it on the board next to 1. Make sure the students use the language from Exercise 10. The students then write sentences for the other signs in pairs. Check their answers as a class and write their sentences on the board.

KEY

1 British passport holders *do not have to/needn't/don't need to* have a visa for the USA.
2 You *mustn't* take Latvian currency out of the country.
3 You *can* pay with American Express cheques.
4 You *must / have to* walk on the right.
5 First class passengers *don't have to/needn't/don't need to* wait.

Extra practice

Divide the class into groups of four. Each group thinks of a place, e.g. classroom, airport, library, restaurant, etc. They write five rules for their place using the different forms in Exercise 10. They then read out their rules one by one. The other groups must guess the place. If they do so after the first rule, they get five points, after the second rule, four points, etc. If no one guesses the place, the team gets ten points.

Short of time?

Exercises 9 and 12 can be done for homework.

Coming and going

Focus	
TOPICS	SKILLS
• Air travel	• Listening: extracts from
• Customs	conversations,
	conversations at customs
GRAMMAR	• Speaking: discussion, role
• Reported requests and	play
orders	SPEECH PATTERNS
	• Stress and intonation of
	orders and requests

GETTING STARTED EXERCISE 1

Direct the class to the cartoon and the questions. Students discuss the questions in pairs and then as a class.

KEY

1 The cartoonist is commenting on the high level of security at airports today. He/she probably thinks that it is too high.
2 & 3 open answers

LISTENING EXERCISE 2

The names of these jobs should be revision for the students. Write *a – g* on the board. Encourage the students to do the exercise in pairs and then check as a class and write the jobs next to the letters. Mark the stress and drill for correct pronunciation. Leave the vocabulary on the board for the next exercise.

KEY FOR EXERCISES 2 AND 3

a se'curity guard (2)   b 'customs officer (4)
c 'passport officer (6)   d 'flight attendant (1)
e 'check-in clerk (5)   f 'porter (7)   g 'pilot (3)

🔲 EXERCISE 3

Explain that the students are going to listen to seven extracts from conversations and they must decide which people from Exercise 2 are speaking. Tell them that they will hear only one extract per person. Play the first extract, stop the cassette and elicit the answer. Write *1* next to *flight attendant*. Then play the other six extracts. Encourage the students to compare answers with their partner and then check as a class.

TAPESCRIPT

1 Could you put your seat belt on now, sir?
2 Empty your pockets.
3 Ladies and gentlemen, we've just hit a patch of bad weather, so would you please return to your seats and fasten your seat belts.
4 Open the blue case, please.
5 Please don't go into the departure lounge until eleven o'clock.
6 Can I see your passport, please?
7 Could you give me something smaller, sir? I'm afraid I haven't got any change.

Note: The voice usually rises at the end of a polite request, and falls at the end of an order. However, the authority of a person making a request can sometimes mean it functions as an order, whatever the intonation.

🔲 EXERCISE 4

Ask the students to copy the grid below into their notebooks.

Play the first extract again and elicit if it is an order or a polite request. Write *1* under POLITE REQUEST. Play the orders/requests. The students can quickly compare answers and then check as a class.

KEY

ORDER	POLITE REQUEST
2 3	1
4 5	6 7

DISCOVERING LANGUAGE EXERCISE 5

Alternative presentation
Students close their books. To introduce the two dialogues, draw three people on the board like this:

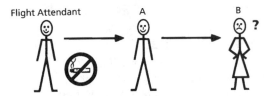

Ask *What is the flight attendant saying?* and elicit *Please don't smoke here.* Then draw a question mark next to B and mime that she didn't hear. Say *What did B ask?* and elicit *What did he say?* Practise the two lines chorally. Then point to the

flight attendant and ask *What did he say?* and elicit *He told us not to smoke here.* Drill the exchange chorally and individually. Then draw this picture on the board:

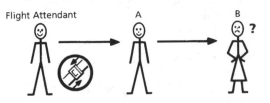

Elicit the second dialogue in the same way. The students can practise the dialogues in threes – encourage them to change roles. Then write the two dialogues on the board with the students' help.

Direct the class to the two dialogues in the Students' Book and the questions. The students discuss the questions in pairs. Check as a class. Use the board to highlight the form, like this:

VERB	OBJECT	INFINITIVE
He *told*	us	not to smoke here.
She *asked*	us	to fasten our seat belts.

KEY

1 Dialogue 1 – d) giving an order
   Dialogue 2 – c) making a request
2 giving an order: to tell   making a request: to ask
3 object pronoun
4 infinitive without *to*
5 *to order* Other possibilities are *insist* and *demand*, but these take a different construction (+ *that . . .*).

EXERCISE 6

Divide the students into threes and allocate them A, B, C roles. Ask one group to read out the example exchange to demonstrate the task. Next, direct the groups to the six requests/orders and establish that A must read all six requests/orders. Make sure each group changes roles twice. Monitor and note down any errors. If you wish, some groups can role play their conversations for the whole class before you use the board to correct any errors you heard.

SUGGESTED KEY

1 He told you to put your seat belt on.
2 She told/ordered you to fill in the form.
3 He asked you to bring him a glass of water.
4 He told/ordered you not to put the bags under the seats.
5 She asked you to open the case.
6 She told/ordered you to stand over there.

Extra practice

For more controlled practice, divide the class into threes. Each student writes down five commands or requests, e.g. *Stand up, Could you be quiet? Can you help me?*, etc. A reads out their first command/request to B and C reports it, e.g.

A: *Stand up.*

C (to B): *He told you to stand up.*

🔲 Documentary

🔲 LISTENING EXERCISE 7

Direct the students to the pictures and discuss the questions in pairs or as a class.

KEY

1 a customs officer with two travellers/passengers
2 at customs
3 in the USA
4 Where have you been? Why? Have you got anything to declare? Did you buy anything there? How long have you been away? Was it your first visit?
5 to declare things that you have bought in another country

EXERCISE 8

Write 1–6 on the board and refer the students to the form. Ask *Which phrase means 'I have a US passport'?* and elicit *I am a US citizen*. Write this next to 1 on the board. Direct the class to the other definitions in the exercise. Encourage the students to work in pairs to find the phrases in the form. Check their answers as a class and write them on the board.

KEY

1 I am a US citizen.   2 I reside permanently in the US.
3 currency   4 goods I purchased
5 goods we acquired abroad   6 on reverse side

🔲 EXERCISE 9

Direct the class to the spaces on the declaration form. Play the conversation, stop the cassette after *I'm in the oil business* and elicit the answer next to question 8 on the form (*business and pleasure*). Next, play the complete conversation. Encourage the students to compare answers with their partners and then check as a class on the board. Make sure that students realise that some of the answers come from the exercise instructions. Tell them that they won't be able to complete all the gaps on the form.

KEY

TAPESCRIPT

OFFICIAL: Good afternoon, folks. May I see your passports and declaration?

FATHER: Certainly.

OFFICIAL: OK. Let's see, can you tell me where you've been, sir?

FATHER: We've been to England and France.

OFFICIAL: Why? What was the purpose of your trip?

FATHER: Uh … partly business and partly pleasure.

OFFICIAL: What is, what is your business, sir?

FATHER: I'm in the oil business.

OFFICIAL: OK. Um, I see you're bringing back $500; can you tell me what you're bringing, Carrie?

CARRIE: Just clothes.

OFFICIAL: Oh. Did daddy buy you some stuff?

CARRIE: Yes.

OFFICIAL: Good. Tell me, have you, were you on a farm or on a ranch of any kind?

FATHER: No.

OFFICIAL: OK. Are you bringing back any food items?

FATHER: No, sir.

OFFICIAL: What about any plants, anything like that, animals?

FATHER: No.

OFFICIAL: OK.

🔲 EXERCISE 10

Direct the class to the questions in the Students' Book. Play the complete conversation. Encourage the students to compare answers with their partners. If necessary, play the conversation again and then check as a class.

KEY

1 a hat, gloves, small handbag, a child's drawing book, perfume
2 the child's drawing book
3 London Gatwick Airport
4 £25.00
5 Because she bought the perfume in Britain where it is duty-free of tax but it is not duty-free in the USA.

TAPESCRIPT

OFFICIAL: Are these all gifts?

TRAVELLER: They are just gifts.

OFFICIAL: OK. Can you tell me what you have here?

TRAVELLER: Certainly. That's a hat and gloves.

OFFICIAL: OK. What about this one?

TRAVELLER: A small handbag.

OFFICIAL: OK. And this one here?

TRAVELLER: A child's drawing book.

OFFICIAL: OK. I'm going to look at it, OK?

TRAVELLER: Mmm.

OFFICIAL: This is all your own personal clothing?

TRAVELLER: Yes, it is.

OFFICIAL: And what is this here?

TRAVELLER: That's some duty-free perfume that I bought back at London Gatwick. I don't have to declare that though, do I?

OFFICIAL: Is it for personal use or is it a gift?

TRAVELLER: It's a gift.

OFFICIAL: Um, I'm afraid so, yes. Did you not include it in your, in your exemption here?

TRAVELLER: No, I didn't.

OFFICIAL: How much did you pay for it?

TRAVELLER: £25.

OFFICIAL: Yes, I'm afraid that you'll have to include it in

your declaration, because it's only duty-free from the country you're buying it in, not from the country that you're bringing it into. If you haven't added it to your declaration, you'll have to add it on to it, OK? Why don't you do that right now?

TRAVELLER: OK.

🔲 SPEECH PATTERNS EXERCISE 11

Write the sentence on the board twice numbered 1 and 2. Ask *Which is an order and which is a request?* Play the two sentences and elicit the answer. Then ask *Does the voice go up or down at the end?* and play the sentences again. Elicit the students' answers and mark the intonation on the two sentences with the help of the students. Write *order* and *request* next to the appropriate intonation pattern. Then play the two sentences for the students to practise the patterns. Write *Could you wait there?* on the board and get the students to practise saying the sentence in pairs with different intonation.

KEY AND TAPESCRIPT

1 Could you open your bag, please? Request

2 Could you open your bag, please? Order

SPEAKING EXERCISE 12

This exercise is an information-gap role play. Divide the students into pairs. A reads the instructions on page 27 and B reads the instructions on page 128. If necessary, brainstorm some of the questions that the customs officer asked in Exercises 9 and 10 and write them on the board. Check that the As know who they are (customs officers) and do the same with the Bs (travellers). Also check that the As know how many parcels they are going to ask the Bs to open (2). The pairs then role play their conversations. Monitor and make a note of any errors. When the customs officers have looked at two of the parcels, the students can change roles and role play conversations about the other two parcels. Use the board to correct any errors you have noted down.

KEY

The parcels are: a poster, a video cassette, a bottle of perfume, a shirt.

WRITING: Sending postcards

Focus	
TOPIC • Holiday postcards SKILLS • Reading: postcards • Writing: a postcard	VOCABULARY DEVELOPMENT • Adjectives describing places, feelings and experiences • Adjectives ending in -ed/-ing

COMPARING CULTURES EXERCISE 1

Direct the class to the postcards in the Students' Book. The students discuss the questions in threes. Then discuss as a class.

READING EXERCISE 2

Refer the students to the two postcards and questions in the Students' Book. Encourage them to compare answers with their partners. Check as a class.

KEY

1 B (because the word England is included in the address)
2 a) Jenny and Sarah are friends.
  b) Ken and Julie are boyfriend/girlfriend or husband/wife.
3 a) both postcards – *Take care* (*Love* if Jenny and Sarah are good friends)
  b) neither postcard – *Yours faithfully/ Yours sincerely* (too formal)
  c) Sarah's postcard only – *Regards*
  d) Julie's postcard only – *Love* (unless Jenny and Sarah are good friends)

EXERCISE 3

The aim of this exercise is to show the students how the information on the postcard is organised. Refer the students to the exercise and check that they understand the features listed in question 1. Then ask *Which postcard includes descriptions of general feelings about the holiday?* and elicit *Both*. The students then read the two postcards and identify the features. Encourage them to compare answers and then check as a class. You may wish to discuss question 3 as a class if your students find it difficult.

KEY

1 Both postcards include a, b, d, e, g, h.
2 kisses
3 the omission of *Dear* and of subject pronouns, the verb *to be* and *there is/are*
  Postcard B: Arrived last night after an awful flight – long delays at the airport. The hotel's very noisy and the food's really disgusting. Having a rotten time –

miss you a lot. At least the weather's not too bad. Going down to the coast later today to try to find a quiet beach. Can't wait to see you again. All my love, Julie XXXX

DEVELOPING VOCABULARY EXERCISE 4

Refer the students back to Postcard A and, as a class, elicit the adjectives that go in the gaps. Then write 1–4 on the board and direct the students to the list of adjectives. They should be revision for the students but, if necessary, reassure them that it is not important for them to know all of the adjectives to do the exercise. Indicate the first gap and ask *What other adjectives in the list can you use instead of 'fantastic'?* Elicit *amazing, dreadful,* etc. The students then work in fours and categorise the adjectives according to the context. They do not have to keep the same meaning. Monitor and help with any new vocabulary. Check their answers as a class and write the adjectives next to the numbers on the board. Then point to the first adjective and ask *Is it usually positive or negative?* Elicit *positive* and write *P* next to *amazing* on the board. The students then work in their groups and do the same with the other adjectives. Check as a class and mark the adjectives with a *P* or *N* as appropriate. Some of the adjectives could depend on the situation.

KEY

1 1 fantastic 2 huge 3 sandy 4 great
2 1 amazing, dreadful, awful, miserable, wonderful, OK, nice, good, marvellous, exciting, lovely, appalling, superb, fine, tolerable + *time*. It is possible, but colloquial to use *OK* before a noun.
  2 small, long, tiny, immense, enormous
  3 stony, empty, sheltered, rocky, crowded
  4 amazing, dreadful, awful, beautiful, miserable, wonderful, OK, nice, good, not bad, marvellous, lovely, appalling, superb, fine, tolerable
3 Positive feelings: amazing, beautiful, wonderful, OK, nice, good, not bad, marvellous, exciting, lovely, superb, fine
  Negative feelings: dreadful, awful, stony, miserable, appalling, tolerable
  Depends on the context (often neutral): small, empty, long, tiny, sheltered, immense, rocky, enormous, crowded
  Other words: 1 great, terrible, super 2 gigantic, little 3 lonely, golden 4 sunny, disgusting, windy

EXERCISE 5

Write the two sentences on the board and ask the students *How did the person feel?* Elicit *terrified* and *disgusted.* Then ask *What was the experience like?*

and elicit *terrifying* and *disgusting*. To check understanding, ask *Which adjectives do we use to talk about feelings?* (*terrified/disgusted* – ones that end in *-ed*) and *Which adjectives do we use to talk about experiences?* (*terrifying* and *disgusting* – ones that end in *-ing*). Then draw this grid on the board:

EXPERIENCES	FEELINGS

Direct the class to the exercise and ask the students to discuss question 2 in pairs. Elicit their answers and write them in the correct column. Then write a – e on the board. Students work in pairs to do question 3. Check as a class and write the answers on the board.

KEY

1 terrified, disgusted
2 Experiences: exciting, appalling, frightening
  Feelings: bored, interested, disappointed, amazed, relaxed, surprised, depressed
3 a) depressing   b) excited   c) surprised
  d) frightening   e) interesting

WRITING EXERCISE 6

Direct the class to the postcards in the Students' Book and ask the students to write 1– 4 in their notebooks. They work in pairs and discuss the questions to plan their writing. Monitor and make sure they make notes. If the students want to know, the postcards are (left to right): Athens, the Seychelles, Hong Kong, Iceland.

EXERCISE 7

Before the students start writing their postcard, read the outline in the exercise as a class to make sure they know how to organise their writing. Monitor and help as they write in pairs. Encourage them to check for mistakes. They can then read their postcards out to the whole class.

Extra practice

If the students enjoy writing postcards, bring some blank ones into class. They can work in pairs and choose another pair of students to write to in the class. If you have a large class, you may need to tell them who to write to. Then, using the picture on the card and their imaginations, they follow the organisation outline in Exercise 7 and write the postcard. Then they 'post' it to the 'recepients', who read it.

Short of time?

Exercise 7 can be done individually for homework.

Progress check: Units 2–3

Grammar and functions

EXERCISE 1

1 Neither/nor did I.   2 Neither/nor have I.
3 So was I.   4 So am I.   5 Neither/nor can I.

EXERCISE 2

1 She asked me to help her with the housework.
2 She asked me to clean the kitchen.
3 She told me to turn the television off (immediately).
4 She told me not to talk to her like that.
5 She asked me to do the washing-up and not to leave the saucepans for her.

EXERCISE 3

1 A – D; B – C.
2 A: We had to arrive early.
  B: We didn't have to arrive early.
  C: We didn't need to/have to arrive early.
  D: We had to arrive early.

EXERCISE 4

1 I'd rather go to Ireland.   2 I enjoy fishing.
3 Yes, he'd (he would) probably like to come./Yes, he probably would like to come.
4 I'd prefer to drive there.   5 Ken hates flying.

Vocabulary

EXERCISE 5

1 A: terrified/B: terrifying   2 A: tiring/B: tired
3 A: annoying/B: annoyed   4 A: relaxed/B: relaxing
5 A: confusing/B: confused

4 *Rights and wrongs*

Bag snatchers

Focus	
TOPIC	**SKILLS**
• Crime	• Reading: a report
	• Listening: accounts of crimes
GRAMMAR	• Writing: a report
• Past progressive	• Speaking: describing a crime
• Past simple	
• Conjunctions: *while/when*	**VOCABULARY DEVELOPMENT**
	• Words related to crime

GETTING STARTED EXERCISE 1

Ask the students to look at the title and the pictures in Exercise 1. Ask them if they can work out what *bag snatchers* are, and what the verb *snatch* means. Establish that the four pictures are all scenes from the same story but are not in the correct order. The students work in pairs and discuss an appropriate order. Check their answers. Then ask a student to read out the example description in the Students' Book for the first picture. In pairs, they describe the other pictures. Get feedback as a class. If the students are having problems with the formation of the present progressive, write one of the descriptions on the board with the students' help and check how the present progressive is formed.

KEY

Order of pictures: D – B – C – A

In the second picture, the woman is looking at her watch and one of the boys is approaching her. The woman's husband is opening the car door while her two children are looking in the shop window.

In the third picture, the boy is just snatching the woman's bag from under her arm. The woman is not sure what is happening.

In the fourth picture, the boy is running off with the handbag and the woman's husband is shouting at him. Her two children are looking at the thief.

READING EXERCISE 2

Refer the students to the report and questions in the Students' Book. Check that the students understand *witness*, e.g. ask *What do you call the person who saw the crime?* (a witness). Once they have answered the questions, encourage them to compare answers in pairs. Check answers as a class.

KEY

1 The witness was sitting in a café on Queen Street.
2 The boys were standing in a doorway opposite the café.
3 The woman was in the street, a few metres away from them.
4 She looked at her watch.
5 He snatched her bag and ran off down the street.
6 He started to walk away from the shop.

DISCOVERING LANGUAGE EXERCISE 3

Alternative presentation

Draw these pictures of the scene on the board:

Point to the first picture. Ask the class *What was the time?* (One o'clock), *What was the woman doing?* (She was waiting in the street). To check the concept of the past progressive, ask *Was this a sudden action or one in progress?* (One in progress). Then ask *What were the boys doing?* (Standing in a doorway). Use the same question as before to check understanding. Then point to the second picture and ask *What did the woman do?* (She looked at her watch) and *What did the boy do?* (He snatched her bag). Ask the question from above to check that the students understand that these were sudden actions. To check the difference between the two tenses, draw this timeline on the board:

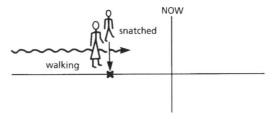

Ask the questions again to check concept. Practise the exchanges in open and closed pairs.

Refer the students back to the report (in Exercise 2). They discuss the questions in pairs. Then discuss as a class.

KEY

1 Present progressive (*I was sitting*) describes a situation in progress. Past simple (*I noticed*) describes a sudden action.
2 Past progressive: *they were watching/she was waiting/she was standing/the thief was running.*
   Past simple: *she looked/one of the boys snatched/she turned and shouted/he ran off/the other boy started to walk*
   The writer is describing an episode in the past. The past progressive provides the background to the past simple actions.
3 *While* is commonly used to introduce a progressive verb form.

When is commonly used to introduce a simple verb form.

Extra practice

Write these two sentences on the board:

A: *When the police came, I saw one of the thieves again.*

B: *While the police were coming, I saw one of the thieves again.*

The students work in pairs and discuss the difference in meaning. To check their answers, you can draw the timelines below on the board and elicit which sentence they refer to. The students can also draw the timelines in their pairs.

KEY

In Sentence B, the police were still coming and had not arrived. In Sentence A, the police had arrived.

EXERCISE 4

The aim of this exercise is to focus on the formation of the past progressive. The students work in pairs and write the complete dialogue in their notebooks. Then elicit their answers and write the dialogue on the board with the students' help.

KEY

OFFICER: What were you doing when your wife lost her bag?

MAN: I was opening the car door.

OFFICER: Were you watching your wife?

MAN: No, I was facing the car.

EXERCISE 5

Refer the students back to the pictures in Exercise 1. Ask a student to read out the example sentence. They then work in pairs and make sentences beginning with *while*. Check their answers as a class.

SUGGESTED KEY

While the boys were standing in the doorway, the woman looked at her watch.

While she was looking at her watch, one of the boys snatched her bag.

While one boy was running away, the other one started to walk away from the shop.

While the man was opening the car door, the thief approached the woman.

If you wish, you can use the pictures to remind the students that you use the progressive form to describe actions that were happening at the same time. Ask *What was the man doing in the third picture?* (He was unlocking his car.) *And what was*

the thief doing?* (He was snatching the woman's bag.) *Were the actions both continuing at the same time?* (Yes). The students then work in pairs and make sentences using two progressive forms, e.g. *While the man was unlocking his car, the thief was snatching the woman's bag.*

Extra practice

To practise the past progressive, copy this diary schedule on the board:

YESTERDAY	
15.00	playing with dog
16.00	
16.30	

etc.

The students copy it into their notebooks and make notes next to each time with what they were doing, e.g. *15.00 playing with dog.* They then mingle and find other people who were doing the same thing at the same time, e.g.

A: *What were you doing at three o'clock?*

B: *I was playing with the dog.*

A: *So was I/I wasn't. I was working in my office.*

📼 LISTENING EXERCISE 6

Direct the class to the four pictures and establish that they show different crimes in progress. Play the first description, stop the cassette and elicit which picture the speaker is talking about. Then play the other three descriptions. Check answers as a class.

KEY

Crime 1 = Picture D   Crime 2 = Picture C
Crime 3 = Picture A   Crime 4 = Picture B

📼 EXERCISE 7

Copy these headings onto the board and ask the students to copy them into their notebooks:

A PERSON	A CRIME	SOMETHING A CRIMINAL DOES

Refer the students to the vocabulary in question 1 and play the cassette again. Stop after *shoplifting* and decide as a class which heading to write it under. Then do the same with the other words, stopping after each one to give the students time to write. Encourage the students to compare answers in pairs. Then elicit their answers and write them on the board. Leave them there for question 2.

Now direct the class to the chart in question 2. If necessary, ask the class to copy it into their notebooks and copy the headings onto the board. As a class, decide which words go in the first row (*burglary, steal*). Write them under the correct heading and tick them off the list from question 1. The students work in pairs to complete the chart. To check answers, complete the chart on the board with the students' help. Mark the stress and drill for correct pronunciation where necessary.

KEY

1 a) *a person*: burglar, pickpocket, thief, arsonist
   b) *a crime*: shoplifting, burglary, theft, vandalism, murder
   c) *something a criminal does*: steal, burgle, rob, mug, murder

2

PERSON	NAME OF CRIME	ACTION VERB
'burglar	'burglary	'burgle
'pickpocket	-	pick 'pockets
'vandal	'vandalism	'vandalise
'arsonist	'arson	set 'fire to
'mugger	'mugging	mug
'robber	'robbery	rob
thief	theft	steal
'shoplifter	'shoplifting	steal
'murderer	'murder	'murder

TAPESCRIPT

One.

PENNY

I was working in the newsagent's – as I do every Saturday. It's always busy on Saturdays and I was the only person serving. I looked up from the till at one point and noticed a very well-dressed woman behaving rather strangely. She was looking at some pens and had a couple of them in her left hand. Her right hand was moving under her coat, as if she was putting something in an inside pocket. It was my first experience of shoplifting, and the problem was I wasn't sure she *was* stealing. The woman looked up and saw me. Then she brought one of the pens over to the till to pay for it. I simply didn't have the courage to ask if there was another one inside her coat, so I just let her leave.

Two.

JONATHAN

I found a burglar in my house one night. It was all a bit strange. It was the middle of the night and I was in bed upstairs. I woke up and thought I heard a noise in the kitchen. We get a lot of burglaries around here, so I thought, 'Oh, no!' I crept downstairs and noticed that light was shining under the kitchen door. I opened the door suddenly and a man ran across the room and out of the back door. On the kitchen table was my video

recorder, a pile of CDs, and a half-eaten banana. It's a horrible thought. While I was asleep, that man was calmly stealing my video and eating my food!

Three.

MARY

Nobody has ever burgled my house, but someone robbed me once. They stole my purse while I was watching a football match. I didn't realise until I was on the bus afterwards. Pickpockets are so good at stealing these days, aren't they? You don't feel anything. The worst thing is that when it's happened to you once, everyone looks like a possible thief.

Four.

GEOFF

I was in Los Angeles on the night of the riots. It was really frightening. There was a lot of theft and vandalism. People were smashing shop windows and stealing everything – televisions, computers . . . even washing machines and fridges. And they were just damaging things for fun. They were going into some shops with guns and demanding money from the owners. Arsonists were starting fires . . . gangs of youths were mugging anybody who happened to pass by. I stayed in my hotel room while all this was happening – I was too terrified to go out. The next day I heard there were quite a number of murders too. The whole experience was just awful.

SPEAKING EXERCISE 8

Allow the students to choose a picture from Exercise 6 or to describe a personal experience. If they choose a picture, establish that they tell the story as the person who experienced the crime. Give them a few minutes to make notes about what happened. Divide them into pairs to tell each other about their experience. Explain that they may need to ask questions to find out more information. Monitor and note down any errors you hear and use the board to correct them at the end of the activity.

WRITING EXERCISE 9

The students use their notes from Exercise 8 to help with writing the report, and the report in Exercise 2 as a model. They can exchange reports with their partners and correct any errors in each other's writing. If you wish, for feedback, they can read out their reports in groups of four.

COMPARING CULTURES EXERCISE 10

Background notes

1 **Public embarrassment** means a punishment which physically shows other people that someone has committed a crime, e.g. putting an obvious sticker on a car that is illegally parked.

2 In Britain, it is possible to have a **suspended sentence**, e.g. a six-month sentence, suspended for two years. This means that if the person commits another crime within two years of the first one, they are automatically sent to prison for six months.

First, elicit from the students the names of non-violent theft and write them on the board. Then direct them to the six kinds of punishment in the Students' Book and check that they understand them. The students then work in threes and discuss the most common punishments for the crimes on the board. Monitor and help them with the names of other kinds of punishments as necessary. If you wish, discuss as a class.

Short of time?
Exercise 9 can be done for homework.

Women in the front line

Focus	
TOPIC • Women police officers	FUNCTIONS • Agreeing and disagreeing with opinions
GRAMMAR • Reflexive pronouns	SKILLS • Listening: a monologue, a narrative

GETTING STARTED EXERCISE 1

Direct the class to the picture and title. In pairs, students discuss what is happening, and the meaning of the title. Then discuss as a class.

KEY

In the larger picture several police officers, including a woman, are dressed in 'riot gear', i.e. the clothes and protection used at riots.
In the smaller picture a woman police officer is arresting someone. *The front line* is the place where the fighting/action takes place.

FOCUS ON FUNCTIONS EXERCISE 2

If you wish to revise the expressions for agreeing and disagreeing, write the two headings on the board and brainstorm the expressions the students know.

To introduce the topic, discuss if the students have women police officers in their country/ countries and if they do the same work as their male colleagues. Ask them to read the four comments in the Students' Book. The students discuss in pairs which opinions they agree or disagree with. Monitor and make a note of any mistakes they make with language for agreeing and disagreeing. To extend the activity, divide the students into groups which either agree or disagree with women officers being on the front line. They make a list of their reasons for their opinion. Then regroup them into pairs of opposite opinions. Students try to persuade each other that their opinion is correct. The student to 'win' is the one who keeps arguing for the longest!

DISCOVERING LANGUAGE EXERCISE 3

Ask a student to read out the three example sentences. Students then work in pairs and answer the questions. Check as a class. Then copy this list of subject pronouns (not the reflexive pronouns yet) onto the board:

I	⟶ ?	*myself*
You	⟶ ?	*yourself*
He	⟶ ?	*himself*
She	⟶ ?	*herself*
It	⟶ ?	*itself*
We	⟶ ?	*ourselves*
You	⟶ ?	*yourselves*
They	⟶ ?	*themselves*

Elicit the reflexive pronouns and write them next to the subject pronouns.

KEY

1 a) themselves   b) herself   c) himself
2 *-self* is for singular forms and *-selves* is for plural forms.
3 *I, you, we*: possessive adjectives (*my + self, your + self/selves, our + selves*).
  He, she, it, they: object pronouns (*him + self, her + self, it + self, them + selves*)

EXERCISE 4

Direct the class to the first picture and elicit a sentence with a reflexive pronoun. The students then work in pairs and do the same for the other pictures.

KEY

A He's introducing himself.
B It's looking at itself in the mirror.
C She's defending herself.
D They're weighing themselves.

🖻 Documentary

📼 LISTENING EXERCISE 5

Refer the students to the questions in the exercise and check that they understand the vocabulary. Play the cassette once and encourage the students to compare answers with their partners. If necessary, play the cassette again. Check their answers to questions 3 – 6. The answers to questions 1 and 2 are checked in the next exercise.

KEY

3 c)   4 a)   5 c)   6 a)

TAPESCRIPT

CATHY ELLISON

I've been with the Austin Police Department for thirteen-and-a-half years. Currently I'm assigned to crimes against property, the theft division. Theft entails several areas: we investigate white collar crime, we investigate property crimes, we investigate anything to do with embezzlements or any kind of stolen property – we investigate all those types of crimes.

When you graduate from the academy everyone is assigned to patrol; so you have to do at least two years in patrol, and that's what I did. One of the things you do is you learn how to get from one place to the other quickly; you learn what your major streets are; and so you just drive around, trying to find out who lives where and who knows what's going on. Every district has an area where one person knows what's going on, all over.

And I think that people tend to trust people of the same race. And I found that, even when I was taking police calls with another officer who was not a black officer, if the person that we were talking to were black, they would just – for some reason – turn to me and not the other officer.

I get afraid a lot of the times, but one of the things that you're taught in the cadet class is if people don't see that you're frightened, and if you just do your job, and I've talked my way out of a lot of things.

EXERCISE 6

First the students read the text to check their answers to questions 1 and 2 from Exercise 5. Check as a class. Then write the five expressions in italics in the text on the board. The students work in pairs to guess the meanings of the words. Discuss as a class and write the best definitions next to the expressions on the board.

KEY FOR EXERCISE 5

1 b)   2 c)

SUGGESTED KEY FOR EXERCISE 6

currently – at the moment
crimes against property – theft, vandalism, arson, etc.
white collar crime – crimes committed in
    offices/business e.g. fraud
embezzlements – stealing money which you are
    responsible for, usually from a business/company
investigate – to find out more information about
    something

▭ EXERCISE 7

Explain that the students are going to hear Cathy Ellison tell a real story that happened to her. They listen with their books closed. Encourage them to make notes as they listen. They can compare their notes in pairs. If necessary, play the story again. Then the students complete the summary in the Students' Book. Remind them to think about which past tense they use. To check their answers, write 1–13 on the board. Ask a student to read out the first sentence. If the class agrees that the verb form is correct, write it on the board next to 1. Do the same with the rest of the summary. The summary can be completed for homework.

KEY

1 was working   2 received   3 was   4 was hiding
5 drove   6 were talking   7 shouted   8 crept
9 were walking   10 blew   11 pulled   12 shot
13 was

TAPESCRIPT

CATHY ELLISON

Several years ago when I was working patrol in north-west Austin, I received a call of a female who was distraught. She said that someone was in her home. I was the first officer there – I didn't know where my backup was. And she ran to the door and she goes: 'They're in here, they're in here right now.' So, as we were walking through her home, it was dark – her lights weren't on, and she was behind me, you know, just stuck to me like I don't know … it was just really funny but she was saying that the person was in the bedroom – that's where she saw them. And as we were walking through her apartment, her apartment, the wind came through and blew a curtain right in to me and I thought there was a person that pushed that curtain, and I had my gun drawn and almost shot that curtain.

SPEAKING: A short talk

Focus	
TOPIC • Legendary heroes	VOCABULARY DEVELOPMENT • Rephrasing more concisely
SKILLS • Reading: an introductory text • Listening: a story • Speaking: a short talk	

GETTING STARTED EXERCISE 1

Direct the class to the picture in the Students' Book and ask the students to discuss the questions in pairs or as a class. The photograph is a still from the film *The Outlaw Josey Wales*, with Clint

Eastwood, but ensure that your students are discussing the general context, not the film/actors in the picture.

KEY

1 The cowboys and Indians lived in the USA.
2 The Indians were the native inhabitants and lived in tribes. There were many different Indian languages. They lived in wigwams (tents) and hunted with bows and arrows. They were eventually forced to live in special areas called reservations.
3 In American films, the cowboys are usually depicted as the heroes. (Some films today, however, try to give a more balanced view.)
4 open answers

READING EXERCISE 2

Refer the students to the title of the article and use the board to brainstorm what they know about *Robin Hood* – accept any contribution. Then ask the students to read the text to find out the answers to the questions in the exercise. Check as a class and tick the ideas on the board that the text mentions.

KEY

1 Robin Hood lived in a forest in the fourteenth century.
2 He robbed and murdered people in authority. Those he stole from included the Sheriff of Nottingham, rich landowners and members of the church.
3 The poor.

EXERCISE 3

Refer the students back to the text to answer the questions. Encourage them to compare answers in pairs and then discuss as a class.

KEY

1 fiction, apparently, (according to the) legend, historical 'detectives' have tried to find evidence, there *was* an outlaw, Robin Hood was a symbol, new stories about him have appeared through the centuries, a legendary figure

2 POSITIVE	NEGATIVE	IT DEPENDS
hero justice	criminal	rebel authority outlaw

3 Someone who fights against injustice on behalf of a group of people who cannot defend themselves.

EXERCISE 4

The aim of this exercise is for students to use the words for different types of people in Exercise 3. Encourage them to discuss their answers in pairs and then compare as a class.

SUGGESTED KEY

1 hero, rebel, fighting for justice
2 hero, fighting against authority and injustice
3 criminal, outlaw

DEVELOPING VOCABULARY EXERCISE 5

Write and complete, with the students' help, the first example from the exercise on the board (*. . . people who own land*). Then ask *How can you explain 'the poor'?* and elicit *The poor are people who do not have any/enough money*. The students then write their own definitions for numbers 3 – 8. Get feedback from the class and, if you wish, write the definitions on the board.

KEY

3 home owners   4 factory owners   5 car owners
6 the rich   7 the famous   8 the young

🔲 LISTENING EXERCISE 6

Background note

In former times, **a knight** was a man of noble rank who was trained to fight, especially on horseback. Nowadays, **a knight** is a man who has been given the title *Sir* by the king or queen. **Note:** The narrator of the story uses the present simple for dramatic effect.

First, check that the students understand *knight*. (The *Longman Dictionary of English Language and Culture* has a picture.) Then direct the class to the seven events in the story and establish that they are not in chronological order. Play the cassette, stopping after *accidentally killed someone*. Elicit that (c) is the first event. Then play the complete story. Encourage the students to compare answers with their partners and, if necessary, play the story again. Then check as a class.

KEY

1 c   2 e   3 b   4 g   5 d   6 f   7 a

🔲 EXERCISE 7

Explain that you are going to play the story again and the students must write down the important words and phrases. Play the cassette, pausing to allow the students time to write. Then they work in pairs and compare the information they have – make sure they add any extra information to their notes. Next, copy this grid onto the board:

TIME	CAUSE AND EFFECT

Direct the class to the words in question 3. If your students do not understand the meaning of *cause and effect* write this sentence on the board and ask them to complete it: *I went to the bank yesterday because . . .* (I needed some money). Highlight *because* and elicit/explain that this is giving a reason (cause); going to the bank is the effect. Then write this sentence on the board: *Yesterday morning, I went to the bank.* Highlight *yesterday morning* as a time marker. Play the cassette again, stopping after *one day* and write it under *time* with the students' help. Then play the complete story, stopping as necessary to give the students time to write. Elicit their answers and write them in the appropriate columns on the board. If there is disagreement, play the relevant part again for the class to decide.

KEY

a) time: one day, when, the next day, until, in the meantime, a few weeks later
b) Cause and effect: so, as a result, because

TAPESCRIPT

I'll tell you a story about Robin Hood. One day Robin and his men are walking through the forest on their way back to the their camp when they meet a poor knight. Robin likes having guests so he invites the knight to eat with them. When they finish eating, Robin asks the knight to pay for his meal, because he and his men don't have much money. But the knight explains that he has nothing and in fact he owes a large sum of money to a rich landowner. The reason for this is that the knight's son was in a shooting competition and accidentally killed someone. As a result, the knight has to pay the landowner four hundred pounds or he will lose his land. He asks Robin to lend him the money and Robin agrees. The next day the knight goes to the rich landowner and pays the four hundred pounds. Now he has to repay Robin Hood's loan.

But Robin feels sorry for the knight and has other ideas. He and his men wait on the road until some rich travellers arrive on their way to London. Robin demands money from them but they say that they have little money themselves. 'If that's true,' says Robin, 'then I am sorry for you and I will give you some money for your travels.' He searches their baggage and finds eight hundred pounds. The travellers run away and Robin Hood keeps the money. In the meantime, the poor knight has worked hard to find the money to pay Robin Hood back and a few weeks later, he appears in the forest and gives it to Robin. But Robin says he does not need the money because he already has it, and he gives the knight the other four hundred pounds from the rich travellers. The knight is delighted and rides home to tell his wife the good news.

SPEAKING EXERCISE 8

Divide the students into pairs. Explain that they are going to retell the story from the cassette, using their notes and the phrases from Exercise 7. Indicate a pair to read out the example sentences: A reads out the first sentence and then B continues with the second. Establish that they must take it in turns to say a sentence but there is no need to write. Monitor and make a note of any errors you hear. If you wish, elicit the story from the pairs and write each sentence on the board exactly as the students say it. Encourage correction and improvement (including the use of the linking phrases). The students may wish to write it in their notebooks.

EXERCISE 9

Divide the class into fours. Explain that the students must think of other legendary figures. If necessary, give them some examples, e.g. King Arthur, William Tell, Rasputin. They each then think of one person and use the questions in the exercise to make notes about them. Monitor and help.

EXERCISE 10

The aim of this exercise is for the students to share all their information. They work in groups of four and take it in turns to tell each other about their character – the others add any extra information they know. Make sure they add this to their notes.

EXERCISE 11

The groups of four divide into pairs and each pair chooses one of the characters they have discussed. The students can reorganise their notes but do not need to write the talk down.

EXERCISE 12

The aim of this exercise is to give the students confidence in giving short talks. You will need to make sure they speak clearly. If you wish, make notes of any serious errors on slips of paper. When they have all finished their talks, hand them the slips with the errors on for them to correct in pairs. If you have a large class, they can tell their stories in groups of six.

Talkback

What's your story?

The aim of this activity is to provide an opportunity for free speaking, where the students will need to use past tenses, but should draw on their whole language resource. The story-telling in Unit 4 will help them in this.

1 Direct students to the pictures and explain that they are going to listen to a story on cassette. They must decide which picture the speaker is talking about. Play the cassette and get feedback as a class.

KEY AND TAPESCRIPT

Picture C

I couldn't believe it. It was terrible. It happened two days ago. I was walking along the street . . . I was doing some shopping, and there was a woman in front of me – she was probably about fifty. Anyway, something fell from her bag – just a piece of paper – and I picked it up. She was walking quite fast so I ran after her. When I caught up with her I put my hand on her shoulder to attract her attention. She turned round suddenly and I felt this spray go into my face and . . . well . . . I was terrified. I couldn't see anything. Then someone punched me and I fell onto the ground . . . I didn't know what was going on. Anyway, when it was all over and she realised what was happening, she apologised. The spray was a security thing that some people carry in the States. It's a kind of foam with a coloured dye in it and it leaves its mark for about seven days. The idea is that you can identify someone who has tried to rob you. So . . . I've got to walk around like this for a whole week. People think I'm either crazy or a thief. I don't think it's very funny!

2 Next, divide the students into pairs. They choose one of the other pictures. First they brainstorm ideas for their story orally and then they make notes.

3 Finally, they tell their story to the class. You can organise it so that those who chose the same picture tell their stories one after the other. They can discuss how the stories are different. As they tell their stories, you can make a note of any serious errors for correction on the board after the activity. If you wish, you can also ask students to write up their story for homework.

5 *For sale*

The science of shopping

<table>
<tr><td>Focus</td><td>SKILLS</td></tr>
<tr><td>TOPICS
• Shopping
• Supermarkets
• Processes
GRAMMAR
• Present simple passive</td><td>• Reading: an article
• Writing: a description of a process
• Speaking: describing a process</td></tr>
</table>

GETTING STARTED EXERCISE 1

To introduce the topic, discuss with the students how often they/their families go to supermarkets. Check the students understand *to display something* and then ask them to discuss the exercise in pairs. Discuss the questions as a class to see if pairs have the same answers. Do not confirm their answers as the article in Exercise 2 discusses the principles of supermarket layout.

READING EXERCISE 2

Note: The *s* in *aisle* is silent, /aɪl/.

Ask the students to read the newspaper article and ask if it answers any questions raised in Exercise 1. Elicit feedback and then discuss the two questions in Exercise 2 as a class.

KEY TO EXERCISE 1

1 The entrance is usually on the left of the building because customers look to their left and move clockwise.

2 It displays fresh fruit and vegetables to give the impression that only healthy food is sold.

3 The basic foods are kept in different places in the supermarket so that customers will have to pass other products to find them, and may buy some of these other goods.

4 Customers move more slowly.

5 At the end of aisles or at eye level.

6 The supermarkets try to keep them full as customers do not like to buy from half-empty shelves because they think there is something wrong with the products that are left on the shelf.

EXERCISE 3

Direct the class to the diagram of the supermarket and the words in the Students' Book and write A – H on the board. Ask *What do we call A?* and elicit *the checkout*. Write *checkout* next to A on the board. The students then do the same in pairs. Elicit their answers as a class and write them on the board. Drill for correct pronunciation.

KEY

1 F   2 D   3 E   4 B   5 C   6 H   7 G   8 A

DISCOVERING LANGUAGE EXERCISE 4

Alternative presentation

Ask the class *What is your town/country famous for?* Elicit *X* (e.g. cheese, chocolate, etc.) and repeat one of the students' answers using the passive, e.g. T: *So cheese is produced in . . .* Then ask another student *What is produced in X?* and elicit *Cheese is produced in . . .* To check the concept of the passive, ask *Do you produce it yourselves?* (No, someone else does), *Is it important that we know who produces it?* (No). Drill the sentence chorally and individually and then ask *What other things is your town/country famous for?* and elicit more examples. Make sure that the examples include both countable nouns (e.g. shoes, cars, clothes) and uncountable nouns (e.g. chocolate, rice, leather). Follow the same procedures to check concept, and drill as necessary. Make sure the students understand the verb forms with countable and uncountable nouns. In pairs, they can make sentences about other products from their region.

Refer the students to the three sentences from the text in the Students' Book. The students then work in pairs and find other examples of sentences using the passive form in the text. Check as a class. Then the students discuss questions 2 and 3 in pairs. Discuss their answers as a class.

KEY

1 the layout is designed, healthy food is sold, they are kept, customers are taken, shoppers are encouraged, supermarkets are paid, sweets are often placed, more is bought
2 *to be* + a past participle
3 Because the position of the sweets is more important than who put them there.

WRITING EXERCISE 5

Check that the students understand 'green beans' (fresh, long, thin ones rather than dried round ones) and where they are grown (Kenya). Refer them to the flow chart. Ask a student to read out the example sentence and get the rest of the class to finish it (e.g. *. . . and taken to the packing house*). Make sure the students copy the sentences into their notebooks. They then work in pairs to write the description. To check their answers, ask volunteer pairs to read out each stage. If you

wish, write the stages on the board for the students to check their answers.

SUGGESTED KEY

. . . and taken to the packing house. They are weighed and packed and then are put into cold storage. On Day 2, they are driven to Nairobi airport and are flown to London. On Day 3, they are inspected by customs in London and are then transported to the central supermarket store. On Day 4, they are distributed to supermarkets (where they are displayed).

SPEAKING EXERCISE 6

To demonstrate the task, tell the students the main foods you eat and write them in a list on the board. Then the students do the same for themselves. Next, refer them back to your list on the board and discuss as a class where the foods are grown/made. The students then work in pairs, compare their food items and discuss where they are grown/made and how they are processed. Monitor and note down any errors you hear with the simple present passive. Discuss as a class and use the board to correct any errors you heard.

Extra practice

Each student makes a list of ten passive sentences, e.g. *Bananas are grown in the West Indies, Coffee is drunk in cafés, Films are watched in cinemas, Cars are made in factories*, etc. They work in groups of three. The first one reads out their sentence with a subject pronoun instead of the noun, e.g. *They are grown in the West Indies*. The other students must guess what the subject is. They can each have one guess. The student who guesses correctly gets one point; if no one guesses correctly, the student who read out the sentence gets three points.

Making a sale

Focus		SKILLS
TOPICS		• Listening: interview extracts
• Cars		• Speaking: role play
• Production of cars		
• Advertising		SPEECH PATTERNS
GRAMMAR		• Sentence stress with *both ... and, neither ... nor, all, none*
• *Both, neither, (...nor), all, none*		

📖 Documentary

📼 LISTENING EXERCISE 1

Background note

The **Morgan Motor Company** is a small family company which makes expensive and exclusive sports cars. The company has deliberately not changed the way it makes the cars for the last 70 years. They value the fact that many of the parts are handmade by their own craftsmen in the small factory in Malvern. There is a seven-year waiting list for each car.

Direct the students to the pictures and discuss what kind of car is advertised. Then they discuss question 2 in pairs. Check as a class and make sure they use the adjectives, e.g. *I think the cars are not mass produced/are handmade*, etc.

SUGGESTED KEY

1 a Morgan car
2 British, handmade, expensive, luxurious, traditional, attractive, comfortable, reliable

📼 EXERCISES 2 AND 3

Explain that the students are going to listen to an interview with Charles Morgan, Production Manager of the Morgan Motor Company. Direct them to the questions and check they understand the vocabulary. Play the cassette, encourage them to check answers in pairs and then check as a class. Repeat the same procedures for Exercise 3.

KEY FOR EXERCISE 2

1 Charles is his grandson   2 about 100
3 The frame of the car is made of wood (ash) and it is then covered with metal (aluminium or steel). This is how coaches used to be made many years ago.

TAPESCRIPT FOR EXERCISE 2

PRESENTER

Listen to the first part of an interview with Charles Morgan, the Production Manager of the Morgan Motor Company. The company was started by Harry Morgan, his grandfather, and it makes the famous Morgan sports cars. There are only about a hundred workers at the factory; it is small and very traditional.

CHARLES MORGAN

The Morgan is built using a technique which we call coach building. Coach building was very popular in the 1920s and in fact all the best cars in the world were always coach built. And what that means is that, rather like in the olden days with coaches being built out of a wood frame and metal panels, we still build the car that way. We start with the ash tree, and we make a frame, and we then cover it in either steel or aluminium.

KEY FOR EXERCISE 3

1 the customer's name
2 b and d
3 fifty per cent
4 It's unique in its appearance, its character, the way it's built and the fact that each person who works on the car gives something of themselves.

TAPESCRIPT FOR EXERCISE 3

CHARLES MORGAN

The car, once it's finished as a chassis, has a ticket put on it with the customer's name on it; and even at this stage when the car is only two or three days old, the customer can see his particular car going through our factory. The Morgan is built out of a combination of parts which we obtain from external suppliers and parts that we manufacture ourselves. We manufacture many of the major components ourselves because we want to give the car its particular character. The metal parts are made out of a flat sheet of metal in every case. We make, for example, the fuel tank of the car; we make the radiator of the car.

We have agents in approximately fifteen different countries. The proportion of cars that are exported compared to the proportion that are, are sold in the UK is, is half and half; so approximately 50% are, are exported. The Morgan sports car has a unique look, but it also has, I think, a unique character, and that character comes from the materials that are used in the making of the car, and it comes from the, the way it's built, and the people who build it – because undoubtedly of the hundred people who build this car they all put a little bit of themselves into the car.

EXERCISE 4

The students can discuss the exercise as a class or in pairs.

EXERCISE 5

Write the heading IN COMMON on the board and refer the class to the advertisements and the brochure for Morgan cars. Ask *What have they got in common?* and elicit a quality, e.g. *expensive*. You may need to remind the students of the adjectives in Exercise 1. They work in pairs and make a list of similarities. Discuss their ideas and write the adjectives on the right-hand side of the board. Leave them there for the next exercise.

DISCOVERING LANGUAGE EXERCISE 6

Direct students' attention to the exercise. Point out those which are the same as the students' ideas in Exercise 5. Then direct the class to the two language questions and ask the students to discuss them in pairs. Check their answers as a class and highlight the forms on the board (see

Key). Leave the statements on the board for the next exercise. If you wish, the students can write complete sentences using their adjectives from Exercise 5 and the same structures. Elicit their sentences and write them on the board. If necessary, highlight the use of the singular and plural forms.

KEY

Both the car *and* the necklace (= 2 objects) *are* handmade.
Neither the necklace *nor* the perfume (= 2 objects) *is* British.
Both of them (= 2 objects) *are* handmade.
Neither of them (= 2 objects) *is* British.
All of them (more than 2 objects) *are* expensive.
None of them (more than 2 objects) *is* cheap.

🖭 SPEECH PATTERNS EXERCISE 7

Refer the students back to the statements from Exercise 6 in their notebooks. Play the first sentence and mark the stress together on the board. Then play all the statements, pausing if necessary to allow the students to mark the stress. Encourage them to compare answers with their partner. Then elicit their answers as a class and mark the stress on the board. Play the statements again, pausing to allow the students to repeat.

KEY AND TAPESCRIPT

A Both the <u>car</u> and the <u>neck</u>lace are hand<u>made</u>.
B <u>Both</u> of them are hand<u>made</u>.
C Neither the <u>neck</u>lace nor the <u>per</u>fume is <u>Brit</u>ish.
D <u>Neither</u> of them is <u>Brit</u>ish.
E <u>All</u> of them are ex<u>pen</u>sive.
F <u>None</u> of them is <u>cheap</u>.
A and C have a different stress pattern.

EXERCISE 8

To demonstrate the task, write the names of three products on the board. Make one example sentence using the language from Exercise 6 and elicit others from the class. Then, divide the class into threes and ask each group to write down the names of three products which are advertised a lot in their countries. They then compare them using the language from Exercise 6. Monitor and make a note of any errors you hear. To check their answers, either ask the students to say their sentences to the whole class or reorganise the students into different groups of three to give feedback to each other. Finally, use the board to correct any errors you heard.

Extra practice

Write these prompts on the board:

can sing   likes dogs   travels to school by bus
went shopping at the weekend   likes watching
sport on TV   has got two brothers
has met a famous person   is going out tonight
The students work in pairs and interview each other. They then report back to the class or write sentences about themselves, using *both of us, one of us, neither of us* ... Next, they mingle and interview other students in the class using the same prompts. They return to their original partner and write more sentences using *some of us, none of us, all of us.*

SPEAKING EXERCISE 9

Copy the chart from the exercise onto the board and direct the class to the different kinds of computer software in question 1. In threes, students discuss which software would be suitable for which people and complete the first column of their chart. Encourage them to compare answers with another group and then discuss as a class. Next, refer them back to the adjectives in Exercise 1. They work in the same groups and discuss which adjectives can describe qualities of the computer which might appeal to each group of people. Again, discuss as a class.

SUGGESTED KEY

	SOFTWARE	QUALITIES OF THE COMPUTER
teenagers	word-processing games home study music-making	modern, mass produced, fun, attractive, green
parents buying for children	games home study music-making	practical, modern, cheap, mass produced, fun, attractive, reliable
people in business	word-processing design accounts & book-keeping desktop publishing	international, practical, modern, comfortable, reliable, environmentally-friendly

EXERCISE 10

Divide the students into pairs and ask them to read the information about the two roles in the Students' Book. Allocate A and B roles. Before they role play the situation, give them a couple of minutes to think about what they are going to say. Monitor and make a note of any errors you hear. Make sure that they change roles and use the board to correct any errors at the end of the activity.

Short of time?

If you wish, you can omit Exercise 4 from this lesson.

WRITING: Letters

> **Focus**
>
> TOPIC
> • Sales
>
> FUNCTIONS
> • Letter-writing conventions
>
> SKILLS
> • Reading: letters, a memo, an invoice, an order form
> • Writing: formal letters, form completion
> • Speaking: discussion

GETTING STARTED EXERCISE 1

Direct the class to the picture in the Students' Book and discuss the questions in pairs or as a class.

SUGGESTED KEY

1 She produces T-shirts with slogans/pictures on them.
2 by mail order
3 They are personalised and are specially printed.
4–6 open answers

READING EXERCISE 2

Copy these headings onto the board and ask the students to copy them into their notebooks:

FROM	KIND OF LETTER
a customer	order for a T-shirt

Students work in pairs and make a list of the letters that they think Sandra receives under the two headings. Think of the first one together to demonstrate the task. Discuss their ideas as a class and write them on the board.

EXERCISE 3

Refer the students to the letters in the Students' Book and tick those on the board which correspond with the ones in the book. Make sure they know what each piece of writing is called (*order form, invoice,* etc.). Then direct them to the questions. Encourage them to compare answers with their partner and then check as a class.

KEY

1 A and E, C and F
2 Sandra knows the writers of B (addresses her by first name; note form) and F (informal; addresses her by first name)

3 A – from a customer, to order a T-shirt
   B – from Sandra's secretary, to give her a message
   C – from a wholesalers, to request payment
   D – from a customer, to make a complaint
   E – from a customer, to give a message for a T-shirt ordered
   F – from an acquaintance, to apologise for a delay and to accompany C.
4 she was expecting C/F (. . . you asked for)

EXERCISE 4

Write 1 – 6 on the board and tell the students that they are Sandra and they must decide the order in which they are going to deal with the correspondence. They discuss in pairs or as a class.

SUGGESTED KEY

She will probably deal with B first (urgent). She will probably deal with A/E next (to satisfy a new customer), then she will probably deal with the complaint (D), and finally C/F, as these are not urgent.

FOCUS ON FUNCTIONS EXERCISE 5

Background note

For information on letter-writing conventions, see *Look Ahead 1* Teacher's Book, Unit 2, page 28 and *Look Ahead 2* Teacher's Book, Unit 14, page 118.

The aim of this exercise is for the students to revise what they know about British letter-writing conventions. Encourage them to work in threes to discuss the questions. Then discuss as a class.

KEY

1 below it
2 a) 4th   b) 2nd   c) 1st   d) 3rd
3 a) 9th January   b) 22nd October   c) 1st April
   d) 23rd February
4 Dear (name) + Yours sincerely
   Dear Sir/Madam + Yours faithfully
5 Can you phone him . . . ? (B) Please send . . . (D/E)
   could you please include . . . (E)

READING EXERCISE 6

Direct the class to Letter E and the list of the eight parts of the letter. Encourage the students to compare answers in pairs and then discuss as a class and establish how the conventions are different in their countries.

KEY

a) 4   b) 8   c) 6   d) 1   e) 7   f) 5   g) 3   h) 2

SPEAKING EXERCISE 7

The students discuss the exercise in pairs. Monitor and help. There is no need for class feedback as this exercise prepares the students for the writing tasks in the next two exercises.

WRITING EXERCISE 8

Encourage the students to complete both writing tasks in pairs. First, they copy the order form and, using their ideas from Exercise 7, write the message. They then use Letter E as a model for their own writing. If you wish, they can swap letters to see what they have ordered and to check for any errors.

EXERCISE 9

If necessary, brainstorm some expressions for apologising and write them on the board. Then compare them with the expressions in the Students' Book. The students write Sandra's reply to Letter D. Again, if you wish, the students can edit each other's writing.

Short of time?
Exercise 4 can be omitted if necessary and Exercise 9 can be done for homework.

Progress check: Units 4–5

Grammar and functions

EXERCISE 1
1 When did he live?   2 What did he do?
3 No, he didn't.   4 tried   5 wrote   6 Yes, he did.

EXERCISE 2
1 were walking   2 arrested   3 was riding   4 ordered
5 was preparing   6 took out   7 shot
8 was still applauding   9 asked   10 said   11 was

EXERCISE 3
1 are eaten   2 is   3 eat   4 are grown   5 is used
6 is made

EXERCISE 4
1 a) yourself   b) myself
2 a) yourselves   b) ourselves
3 a) themselves   b) herself/himself

EXERCISE 5
1 All of these people are young.
2 Both of the men are wearing jackets.
3 Neither of them has long hair.
4 All of them are drinking.
5 One man is not carrying a bag; both the other people are.
6 None of them is smoking.

Vocabulary

EXERCISE 6
1 stole, theft   2 set, arsonist   3 robbed, mugged

6 Body and mind

Staying well

Focus	
TOPIC • Health and fitness **GRAMMAR** • First conditional • Second conditional	**SKILLS** • Reading: a magazine article • Speaking: a role play **VOCABULARY DEVELOPMENT** • Prefix *over-* • Suffix *-able*

GETTING STARTED EXERCISE 1

To introduce the topic, ask the class *What things do we do which are bad for our health?* Use the board to collate students' ideas, e.g. *don't sleep enough, have bad eating habits, smoke, don't take enough exercise*, etc. Direct the class to the headlines in the Students' Book and compare these with their ideas. Then ask a student to read out the example piece of advice in the exercise. The students work in pairs and make a list of pieces of advice in the same way. To check their advice, ask one pair to read out their list; the other students then read out any pieces of advice that were not mentioned by the first pair.

SUGGESTED KEY
You shouldn't smoke. You shouldn't eat red meat and fatty foods. You should take regular exercise. You should get at least six hours' sleep a night. You shouldn't work more than eight hours a day. You should get plenty of fresh air.

EXERCISE 2

In pairs, the students discuss what they do to stay healthy. Elicit quick feedback from the class.

READING EXERCISE 3

Direct the class to the title of the article and the picture. As a class, discuss the questions. Write students' ideas for question 3 on the board. Then they read the article quickly to confirm their ideas. Encourage students to discuss their answers in pairs and then discuss as a class. If you wish, you can tick the words/phrases on the board which are mentioned in the article.

EXERCISE 4

Refer the students to the questions and ask them to read the article again. Encourage them to compare answers with their partner and then check as a class. Finally, the students discuss in pairs or as a class if they agree with the opinions expressed in the article.

KEY

1 Not expressed: . . . many adults take regular exercise . . .
2 Expressed in the article: . . . do the under-fives need exercise routines? . . . The author, Lucy Jackson, believes that they do not get enough exercise.
3 Expressed: . . . parents should begin exercises with very small babies.
4 Expressed: They would not be overweight if they ate healthier food.
5 Not expressed in the article.

EXERCISE 5

Write the heading YOUNG CHILDREN on the board and refer the class back to the article. Ask *What is the first word or phrase in the article that refers to young children?* Elicit *the under-fives* and write it on the board under the heading. The students then read the article to find the other phrases. Encourage them to compare answers in pairs. To check their answers, draw this scale on the board:

```
0  6mths  1  18mths  2        3        4      5+
└──┴────┴──┴─────┴──┴──┴────┴──┴────┴──┴───┘
```

Elicit their answers and write them on the scale from the youngest to the oldest with the students' help.

KEY

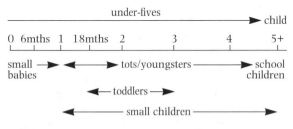

DEVELOPING VOCABULARY EXERCISE 6

Copy the three words in the exercise onto the board and ask the students to find them in the text. Discuss as a class what they mean and then elicit the meaning of *-able* and *over-*. Next, refer the students to the sentences and copy the words in italics onto the board. The students work in pairs and discuss the meanings of the words in the sentences. Encourage them to write definitions. Check as a class and write the definitions next to the words on the board.

KEY

over- = too much. *Overweight* – weighing more than is expected or is usual (e.g. children become overweight) *-able* = you can do this. *Disposable* – can be used once and then thrown away (disposed of), *washable* – it can be washed
1 (an evening) you can enjoy
2 (a business) you can make money or get good results from
3 (staff) you can depend on
4 (teachers who) work too much
5 (there are) too many people living in the areas
6 (the bus is) carrying too much

DISCOVERING LANGUAGE EXERCISES 7 AND 8

Notes:

1 Conditional sentences that begin with *If* have a comma after the first clause, e.g. *If it rains, I'll stay at home.* Conditional sentences with the *if* clause second do not have a comma, e.g. *I'd apply for the job if I spoke Italian.*
2 In second conditional sentences, *if* is followed by a past simple form. However, *were* is often considered more correct than *was* in the first and third person singular. In spoken English, the use of *was* instead of *were* is becoming very common, e.g. *If I **was** you, I'd go on holiday.* It is acceptable in informal discourse.
3 Your students may be reluctant to use the contracted forms of *will* or *would* with subject pronouns, e.g. *I'll, you'll.* They may find the pronunciation of the negative contractions *won't* /wəʊnt/, *wouldn't* /wʊ(də)nt/ and *weren't* /wɜːnt/ particularly difficult and will need drilling.

Alternative presentation

Copy this job advertisement onto the board:

> # SUMMER CAMP USA
>
> *urgently needed to work on a summer camp for 8 weeks this summer:*
>
> Young person (18–21) with international driving licence. Must like outdoor sports, teenagers and be fluent in [+ students' language].

Display or draw a picture of a young man/ woman playing tennis and ask *Is she young?* (Yes) *Does she like outside sports?* (Yes) *Is her [+ students' language] fluent?* (Yes) *Is she very good at tennis?*

(Yes) *Is it possible for her to apply for the job?* (Yes) *Does she want to go?* (Yes) *What will she do if she's offered the job?* Elicit *If she's offered the job, she'll take it.* To check the concept of the first conditional, ask *Is it possible for her to apply for the job?* (Yes), *Why?* (Because she's got the right experience, etc.), *Do we know if she'll definitely get the job?* (No). Drill the sentence chorally and individually, concentrating on the contraction of *she'll* /ʃiːl/. Then ask *What will she do if she takes the job?* Elicit *She'll go to the States if she takes the job. She'll work with teenagers, she'll teach tennis,* etc. The students practise the exchanges in pairs.

Next, ask *What about me? Can I apply for the job?* (No) *Why not?* (Because you're too old). Ask *But if I were younger, what would I do?* Elicit *You'd apply for the job if you were younger.* To check concept, ask *Can I apply for the job?* (No) *Why not? Are we talking about the past, present or future?* (present – future). Drill the sentence chorally and individually, concentrating on the contraction of *you'd* /juːd/ or /jəd/.

Finally, ask *What's the difference in meaning between the two situations?* and get the students to discuss the difference in pairs and then as a class. (The first situation is *possible*; the second is *unreal*.)

The students work in pairs to discuss the questions. To check their answers, write the example sentence from Exercise 7 on the board and use it to highlight the form and meaning (questions 1 and 2). Use the board to check their answers to question 3 (see Key). Follow the same procedures for Exercise 8. See the Key below for a suggestion of boardwork.

KEY FOR EXERCISE 7

1 *If* + present simple, +　　*will*
   If small children *take*
   no regular exercise,　　bad habits *will continue* . . .
2 *If* clause = a condition　　main clause = a consequence
3 If toddlers do exercises, they'll stay fit.
4 The first conditional expresses a likely condition.

KEY FOR EXERCISE 8

1 *If* + past simple, + *would* + infinitive *(– to)*
2 *If* clause = a condition
   main clause = a consequence
3 *Were* is used with third person (*the world*) instead of *was*.
4 If there were no cars, children would play in the streets.
5 The second conditional expresses an unreal or unlikely condition.

EXERCISE 9

Direct the class to the eight prompts in the exercise. Ask a student to read out the first one and to complete it. Elicit ideas from other students for the first one. They then work in pairs and discuss the other prompts. If you wish, they can write their answers. Discuss their answers as a class and write example sentences on the board with the students' help.

If you wish to practise question forms with the second conditional, ask a student *What would you do if you had a small child?* Elicit their reply and then indicate that the student should ask you the question. Reply and drill the exchange chorally and individually. The students then work in pairs and write questions for prompts 1–4. Elicit their questions and write them on the board.

SUGGESTED KEY

1 If I had a small child, I'd employ a nanny.
2 If children didn't watch television, they'd play with each other.
3 If they played in the streets, they'd get more exercise.
4 If parents didn't listen to experts, they'd worry less about their children.
5 Children would be fit and healthy if they took more exercise.
6 They wouldn't have a bad diet if their parents cooked more often.
7 Teenagers would be healthier if they switched off the television occasionally.
8 If I found my child with a cigarette, I'd explain the dangers of smoking.

SPEAKING EXERCISE 10

Divide the class into 'smokers' and 'non-smokers'. Tell the 'non-smokers' to make a list of reasons why the 'smokers' should stop smoking and the 'smokers' to make a list of reasons why it wouldn't be good for them to stop. They can read the example excuse in the Students' Book for their first idea. Then regroup the students to work in pairs if possible (one smoker who must make excuses and one non-smoker who must persuade). They could work in groups of three if necessary with two non-smokers/one smoker or vice versa. Tell the students that the winner of the argument is the student who keeps going the longest. Monitor and note down any errors you hear with conditional sentences. Use the board to correct them at the end of the activity.

Treatment

Focus

TOPICS
- Doctors and dentists
- Medical treatment
- Fear

GRAMMAR
- *Should* + infinitive
- *Ought to* + infinitive

FUNCTIONS
- Giving advice
- Expressing fear
- Calming and reassuring someone

SKILLS
- Listening: a medical consultation, a monologue
- Speaking: role play

VOCABULARY DEVELOPMENT
- Adjective + preposition collocation

SPEECH PATTERNS
- Intonation of calming and reassuring someone

GETTING STARTED EXERCISE 1

Note: A **pharmacist (druggist** in American English) is a trained person who works in a pharmacy dispensing medicines. An **acupuncturist** treats diseases by placing needles in certain parts of the body. A **herbalist** uses herbs to treat illness. A **psychiatrist** is a doctor who is trained to treat people with disorders of the mind. (**Psychologists** are trained in the study or science of the mind. They are not doctors and are not able to prescribe medicines or treatment.)

If you wish to check the concept of the second conditional quickly, ask the class *Do you have toothache?* (No) *Who would you see if you had toothache?* (I'd see a dentist if I had toothache). Drill the second conditional sentence as necessary. Refer the class to the seven jobs and ask a student to read out the example sentence. They work in pairs and write second conditional sentences for the other medical situations. Check their answers as a class and drill for correct pronunciation of the jobs.

KEY

b) If I needed an operation, I'd see a surgeon. /'sɜːdʒn/
c) If I were extremely unhappy, I'd see a psychiatrist. /saɪˈkaɪətrɪst/
d) If I had bad eyesight, I'd see an optician. /ɒpˈtɪʃn/
e) If I wanted natural medicines from plants, I'd see a herbalist. /'hɜːbəlɪst/
f) If I wanted treatment with needles, I'd see an acupuncturist. /'ækjə,pʌŋktʃərɪst/
g) If I needed medicine for a minor problem, I'd see a pharmacist. /'fɑːməsɪst/

EXERCISE 2

Note: *A pain* is a sharp, intense feeling. *An ache* is a continuous, but not violent pain. *-ache* is often combined with *head, stomach, ear, tooth, back*. *Headache* is always a countable noun. The others are often uncountable nouns if they refer to a condition, e.g. *I often have terrible backache.* If you are talking about a single attack, the nouns can be countable or uncountable, e.g. *I've got (a) terrible backache.* In American English, they are more often used as countable nouns. *Painful* and *sore* are both adjectives. They both refer to physical pain, though *painful*, like *pain*, is more intense. *Sore* includes the idea of aching from a wound or infection, e.g. *I've got a sore throat. My legs are sore from doing aerobics yesterday.* The verb *to hurt* can be used for all types of aches and pains.

The aim of this exercise is to check that the students understand the different symptoms by matching them with an appropriate ailment, then with expressions which describe the ailment. Direct the class to the four pictures and match the health problem to each picture. Then ask *What is the person in picture 1 saying?* and elicit *A bee's stung me./It hurts./It's painful.* The students then work in pairs and do the same with the other three pictures. Check as a class.

SUGGESTED KEY

A A bee's stung me. It hurts. It's painful. It's sore.
B I've cut myself. I've broken my arm. It's sore. It's bleeding. It hurts. It's painful.
C I've got a headache. It aches.
D I've got a pain in my side. It hurts. It's painful.

COMPARING CULTURES EXERCISE 3

Direct the class to the picture. Discuss the questions as a class or in groups. The artist is suggesting that you have to wait a long time in doctors' surgeries in Britain. This is, of course, not true of all surgeries, but some operate without an appointment system and there may be a long queue. Doctors may also be called away to deal with emergencies.

🔲 LISTENING EXERCISE 4

There are three separate parts to this listening text. First, divide the students into pairs. Explain that first they are going to listen to a doctor and patient, and then they must write down the questions that the doctor could ask the patient about his 'illness'. Play the first part of the conversation. The pairs then make their list of questions. Elicit some of their questions as a class and write them on the board.

Next, play the second part of the conversation for the students to check which questions the doctor asked. They compare answers in pairs and then as a class. Add the doctor's questions to the ones on the board. Leave them there for Exercise

6. Then ask the pairs to discuss what advice the doctor will give, and elicit advice from some pairs. Play Part 3 of the conversation. Finally, discuss question 4 as a class.

KEY AND TAPESCRIPT

The answers to Exercise 4 are in **bold**.

Part one.

DOCTOR: Good morning. Sit down.

PATIENT: Thank you.

DOCTOR: Now then, what's the problem?

PATIENT: I feel terrible. I feel tired all the time ... and I get headaches.

Part two. (with answers to question 1)

DOCTOR: **How long have you felt like this?**

PATIENT: Oh ... for a few weeks, now.

DOCTOR: **And how old are you now?**

PATIENT: Sixteen.

DOCTOR: **Do you do much exercise?**

PATIENT: Er ... well, no, not really.

DOCTOR: I see. Sports? Cycling? Swimming? Nothing?

PATIENT: Er ... I walk to school. That's about it.

DOCTOR: What about sleeping? **Do you sleep well?**

PATIENT: No, not really. I wake up in the night a lot.

DOCTOR: **Why do you think you wake up?**

PATIENT: Well, I worry a lot – mainly about school work. I'm getting behind and I can't seem to catch up.

DOCTOR: Oh dear. **What time do you usually go to bed?**

PATIENT: Oh, about midnight in the week ... and later at the weekends.

DOCTOR: I see. **And do you drink anything before you go to bed?**

PATIENT: I have a cup of coffee, yes. And I'm always hungry in the evening. I usually have something to eat before I go to bed.

Part 3 (with answers to question 3)

DOCTOR: OK. Well, I'm not surprised you can't sleep. I'm not going to give you anything at the moment. I want you to go home and change a few things about your routine. Then I'll see you again in a few weeks and see how you're doing. OK?

PATIENT: OK.

DOCTOR: Right. First of all, you're probably tired because you're not getting enough sleep. People of your age ought to sleep for at least seven hours a night, all right? So **try to go to bed a little earlier.** Secondly, **you should start to take some exercise.** Go for a short run every day or go swimming. Anything that gives your body some exercise. Right? Then there's the eating. **It's not a good idea to eat just before sleeping and you certainly ought not to drink coffee before going to bed.** Coffee contains caffeine ... and caffeine will keep you awake.

PATIENT: OK.

DOCTOR: **And you shouldn't worry so much.** All this can be solved quite easily. If you do take my advice, you'll sleep better. If you're sleeping well, you won't be tired in the day ... and then your school work will improve.

FOCUS ON FUNCTIONS EXERCISE 5

Ask the class to read the four example sentences. Write the verb phrases on the board: *ought to sleep, should start, ought not to drink coffee, shouldn't worry.* The students then discuss the questions in pairs. Then discuss as a class and highlight the form on the board.

KEY

1 They give advice.
2 a) *should* is followed by the infinitive without *to*
   b) *ought* is followed by the infinitive with *to*
3 *not* is added, e.g. *should not/shouldn't, ought not to/oughtn't to*

SPEAKING EXERCISE 6

Divide the students into As (patients) and Bs (doctors) and ask them to read their roles. Refer the class to the questions on the board from Exercise 4 and the question prompts in the Students' Book. If you wish, brainstorm possible questions and write them on the board. Also, remind the students of the symptoms in Exercise 2. As they role play their conversations, monitor and make a note of any errors. Make sure they change roles. Before you use the board to correct the errors, find out which 'doctor' gave the best advice.

🔊 Documentary

📼 LISTENING EXERCISE 7

Note: You can be *nervous* (= rather afraid) before or during an event, e.g. if you have to make a speech in public. A person can have a *nervous* character. *Anxious* usually means worried about something that might happen. *Worried* also expresses anxiety but is a little stronger than *anxious. Nervous, anxious* and *worried* are all similar in intensity.

Discuss questions 1 and 2 as a class. Then copy the adjectives from question 3 onto the board and draw a scale like this:

LEAST ◄━━━━━━━━━━━━━━► GREATEST
　　uneasy

Ask *Which is the least frightened?* and elicit *uneasy*. Write it on the scale. The students work in pairs and do the same with the other adjectives, using their dictionaries to help them. Elicit their answers and write the adjectives on the board. Drill for correct pronunciation. Then discuss question 4 as a class.

KEY

1 He's a dentist.
2 He's talking to a patient.
3 uneasy, anxious*, nervous*, worried*, frightened, terrified, petrified
   *These three are very similar.
4 open answers

EXERCISE 8

Refer the class to the questions and check that the students understand *local/general anaesthetic* and *tranquilliser*. Play the cassette once (there are two interviews). Encourage the students to compare answers with their partners. If necessary, play the cassette again and then check as a class.

KEY

1 Because they have had a bad experience in the past.
2 c, e
3 You should brush your teeth every night before bedtime. You shouldn't eat a lot of sweets. You shouldn't eat anything straight after brushing your teeth.

TAPESCRIPT

MUBARAK SAMJI
People are, even in this day and age, frightened of going to the dentist, and it is generally because they've had a bad experience in the past. If a patient turned up who was very frightened, you would have to go through the various stages. First of all I would try doing treatment with just a local anaesthetic, but because people are frightened of needles, I would ask them to take a tranquilliser by mouth, which in most cases makes them feel a little better. But you do also get patients who are beyond that, and for them they would have to have a tranquilliser admin, ... administered in their vein. And you unfortunately also get the final category of patient who would need to be ... actually be put out completely, by means of a general anaesthetic.

PRESENTER: Now listen to a conversation between Mr Samji and one of his younger patients.
MR SAMJI: Do you eat a lot of sweets?
PATIENT: Only on Saturdays.
MR SAMJI: That's good, so not, not so many.
PATIENT: No.

MR SAMJI: That's ever so important. You should eat as few as possible, because it's sweets that give you holes in your teeth. All righty?
PATIENT: Yes.
MR SAMJI: And how about brushing, how often do you brush your teeth?
PATIENT: In the mornings and sometimes in the evenings.
MR SAMJI: Excellent. Brushing in the evening is ever so important; you should brush every evening before bedtime. And remember not to eat anything straight after you've brushed your teeth. All right?

FOCUS ON FUNCTIONS EXERCISE 9

Copy the expressions in the Students' Book onto the board. Play the dialogue until *I'm afraid of needles* and elicit which expression they hear. Tick it off on the board. Then play the complete dialogue. Encourage the students to compare answers and then check as a class on the board. Next, ask *'Don't worry' – is it describing fear or calming someone?* Elicit *calming someone* and write (b) next to *Don't worry* on the board. The students then work in pairs and classify the expressions in the same way. Check their answers as a class on the board. Leave the 'fear' ones on the board for the next exercise.

KEY

1 The students should tick: I'm afraid of . . . Don't worry. It'll be all right. I'm frightened of . . . Relax.
2 a) I'm afraid of . . . I'm worried about . . . I'm frightened of . . .
   b) Don't worry. Don't cry. Don't be afraid. Calm down. It'll be all right. Relax.

TAPESCRIPT

DENTIST: Right. Open your mouth. I'm just going to give you a little injection.
MAN: Er, no! No! Sorry ... er ... I don't like injections . . . . I'm afraid of needles.
DENTIST: Don't worry. It'll be all right. You'll hardly feel a thing. It's quite bad, that tooth. I have to fill it.
MAN: No, really . . .
DENTIST: All right. Here we go then . . .
MAN: Stop! No, sorry, I really can't. I'm frightened of drilling too. I'd better go.
DENTIST: No, sit down again. Relax. You're not the only one, you know. Why don't we just talk about it for a moment . . .

DEVELOPING VOCABULARY EXERCISE 10

Refer the students back to the three 'fear' expressions on the board from Exercise 9 and as a class highlight the preposition used and the *-ing* form. Then refer the students back to Exercise 7 and ask them to dictate the adjectives to you as you write them in a list on the board like this:

$$I\ am \begin{cases} \text{frightened +} \\ \text{terrified +} \\ \text{nervous +} \\ \text{petrified +} \\ \text{uneasy +} \\ \text{worried +} \\ \text{anxious +} \end{cases}$$

Together, write in the preposition which follows *frightened* (*of*). The students then work in pairs and discuss the prepositions which follow the other adjectives. Elicit their answers and write them on the board. Each student then writes at least seven sentences about their own fears, using the expressions. They work in threes and tell each other about their fears. Monitor and correct any errors you hear.

KEY

2 frightened + of   terrified + of   nervous + about/of
  petrified + of   uneasy + about   worried + about
  anxious + about

Extra practice

To revise these adjectives + prepositions, write a *Find someone who . . .* on the board, e.g.

FIND SOMEONE WHO   NAME
– is nervous about taking exams   Susanna
– is frightened of being alone at night
– is petrified of snakes/mice/spiders
– is worried about war in the world
– is anxious about travelling alone
– is uneasy about smoking in
  restaurants
– is terrified of having an operation

The students copy the questions into their notebooks and mingle to find people in the class, e.g.
A: *Susanna, are you nervous about taking exams?*
B: *Yes, I am.*

🔊 SPEECH PATTERNS EXERCISE 11

Direct the class to the two groups of expressions in the exercise and draw two arrows on the board, like this:

A

B

Play the first expression, stop the cassette and elicit whether the intonation goes up or down at the end of the expression. Write the expression

next to the correct arrow. Play the rest of the expressions. Encourage the students to compare their answers with their partner. Then check as a class on the board. Play the expressions again, pausing to allow the students to repeat them.

KEY AND TAPESCRIPT

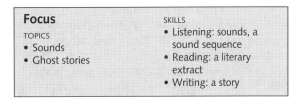

A: Don't worry.
B: It'll be all right.
C: Don't be afraid.
D: Don't cry.
E: Calm down.
F: Relax.

SPEAKING EXERCISE 12

To demonstrate the task, tell the students about something that you are worried about doing, e.g. giving a lecture. As you talk about it, indicate to the students that they should reassure you and give you some advice. Then ask the students to think of something that they are worried about. Divide the class into pairs. They role play the conversation: the As have the problem and the Bs reassure. Make sure they change roles. Monitor and make a note of any errors you hear. If you wish, ask volunteer pairs to role play their conversation for the whole class and then use the board to correct any errors you heard.

Short of time?

If you wish, you can omit Exercise 3 from this lesson. Exercise 10 can be done for homework.

CREATIVE WRITING: Creating a mood

Focus	SKILLS
TOPICS • Sounds • Ghost stories	• Listening: sounds, a sound sequence • Reading: a literary extract • Writing: a story

🔊 COMPARING CULTURES EXERCISE 1

Direct the class to the cartoon, then the introduction in the Students' Book and ask the students to read it. Discuss if they use 'bang' in their language(s), and, if not, what they use. Next, they work in pairs and say the words in question 1 together. Then write 1–12 on the board. Play the first sound and decide as a class which word it matches. Write *rumble* next to 1 on the board and get the students to copy this in their notebooks. Play the complete sequence of sounds. Encourage the students to check their answers in pairs. Discuss the answers as a class and write them on the board. Leave them there for Exercise 9. For question 2, if you do not have access to dictionaries, play the cassette again and elicit what is making the sound, e.g. *a dog is growling, thunder is rumbling*, etc. Then discuss if the words are the same or different in the students' own language. If you have a multilingual group, the students can discuss the exercise in groups of different nationalities/languages.

KEY AND TAPESCRIPT

1 rumble (i)   2 smash (h)   3 growl (f)   4 crack (d)
5 cough (l)   6 rustle (g)   7 scream (a)   8 drip (j)
9 bump (e)   10 creak (b)   11 whisper (c)
12 splash (k)

READING: A LITERARY EXTRACT EXERCISE 2

Ask the students to think of a ghost story that they have read or a play/film that they have seen and then to think of a scene where a person is terrified. Make sure they have all thought of a story, then refer them to the prompts in the exercise and ask them to make three lists of words or phrases. If necessary, read out the example prompts. When students have written their lists, they compare notes with their partners and add any words/phrases that they have not thought of. If you wish, elicit their words and collate them on the board. Leave them for the next exercise.

EXERCISE 3

Tell the students that they are going to read an extract from a famous English novel called *The Woman in Black*. Find out if they have heard of it. If you wish, they can read the notes about the author at the end of the text. Then refer them back to their list of expressions in Exercise 2 and explain that they should read the text quickly and tick the expressions that they find on their list from Exercise 2. Encourage them to compare lists with their partner after they have finished reading. Tick the answers off the board if you wish.

EXERCISE 4

Refer the students to the questions about the text. They read it again. Encourage them to compare their answers and then check as a class.

KEY

1 a dog
2 Because the dog was standing at the door, growling.

3 In the bedroom. The narrator was in bed.
4 Because they could hear a noise in the house, not far from the bedroom.
5 They listened for the sound.
6 It was still outside, there was no wind coming through the window (casement).

EXERCISE 5

Write the first three words in the exercise on the board and ask the students to find them in the text. Then discuss what the students think they mean. They work in pairs and do the same with questions 2 and 3. Discuss as a class.

KEY

1 standing upright, straight up
2 *paralysed/frozen*: you cannot move because you are so frightened; *tense*: very nervous, holding your body stiff because of your fear
3 they are all quiet noises:
   a *faint* noise: a quiet, distant noise
   a *muffled* noise: a noise which is not very clear
   the *moaning* of the wind: a low noise, as if made by a person in pain
   the *snuffling* of a dog: a sniffing noise, as if the dog is smelling something

EXERCISE 6

Direct the class to the first question and ask the students to read the first sentence of the text. Elicit the words *at first* and write them on the board. The students then read the rest of the text and make a list of the other words and phrases. Encourage them to compare their list with their partner. Check as a class and elicit other words that could be used. Finally, the students use expressions from the list to sequence the events in question 3. Encourage them to compare their answers and then discuss as a class.

KEY

1 At first, and, Then, suddenly, And then
2 Examples: first, afterwards, after that, when . . . , next, finally, to begin with
3 Example: First, the dog went to the door. Then the man woke up and he sat up in bed. At first/To begin with, he couldn't hear anything, but then he heard the sound for the first time.

EXERCISE 7

Copy the example sentence onto the board, highlight *like* and discuss what it means in this sentence (to compare one thing with another but in a literary rather than factual sense). Then ask the students to read the other two examples. If you wish to check understanding further, ask

What is this classroom like? and elicit ideas, e.g. *This classroom is like a prison cell,* etc. Next, direct the class to the four prompts in the exercise. In pairs, they think of comparisons. If you wish to make this a competitive activity, divide the class into teams and write some more prompts on the board, e.g. *The sky was like . . ./The day was like . . ./ Her skin was like . . . /The journey was like . . . .* Encourage the students to complete the sentences as imaginatively as possible. You then award points for each sentence: one for correct grammar and one for the most imaginative sentence for each prompt.

EXERCISE 8

Divide the class into pairs and refer the students to the questions in the exercise. They then discuss the questions in relation to the extract from *The Woman in Black.* Discuss their ideas as a class.

SUGGESTED KEY

1 a) very big: the depths of the house
   b) probably in an old-fashioned way, and sparsely: floorboards, casements
   c) short-haired: every hair was on end
   d) open answer
2 open answers
3 open answers

🔲 LISTENING EXERCISE 9

Refer the students back to the noises from Exercise 1 on the board. Explain that they are going to hear the next part of the story and they must write down the sounds they hear. Play the first sound for students to write, pause, and tick it on the list on the board. Then play the complete sequence. Check their answers. Next, repeat the whole sequence, part by part, pausing to allow the students to make notes about what happened. Encourage students to compare their notes with their partner and check as a class. Ask the students to think about the man's feelings and this time play the complete sequence straight through. Discuss as a class.

Note: The sequence of noises is on the cassette twice. The first time it is divided into parts, with pauses between each section. The second time it is played straight through.

KEY (TO QUESTION 2)

1 man – got out of bed, floorboards creaked, man coughed and spoke to dog
2 man creeps to door, dog pants and growls, man opens door, door creaks
3 dog stops in corridor, growls, man walks along and opens door

4 man closes door: nothing in room
5 bump sounds again, man frightened
6 man and dog walk to room where sound comes from
7 dog sniffs and growls at door, man opens door . . .

TAPESCRIPT

Sound sequence only.

WRITING EXERCISE 10

The aim of this exercise is for students to use their notes from Exercise 9, the vocabulary from Exercises 1, 5 and 7, and the sequencing words from Exercise 6. Explain to the students that they are the narrator in the story and they are going to finish the story, using their notes from Exercise 9 and their imagination. Refer them to the guidelines for their writing in the Students' Book. Monitor and help. If you wish, they can write the story in pairs and swap their stories with another pair who can correct it. If you have time, ask two or three pairs to read out their endings (as dramatically as possible). You could then tell them how the story actually continues and ends:

The man discovers the room is a fully-equipped but deserted nursery. The sound is of an empty rocking chair rocking next to a child's bed. He eventually finds out that the house is haunted by a woman who went mad after her child was drowned in front of her. Her ghost, and the noises that she makes, terrify visitors to the house. However, her greatest revenge is that after someone has seen her ghost, a child dies. Soon after the man visits the house, he gets married and has a son. One day, the three of them go to a park in London. His wife and son take a ride in a horse and cart. The ghost of the mad woman appears and terrifies the horse. The mother and child are thrown to the ground. The child dies immediately; the mother dies ten months later.

Short of time?
Exercise 10 can be done for homework.

Talkback

Urban survival

This is a fluency activity, based on discussion and negotiation. Students may use conditionals and passives, but will need to draw on their whole language resource.

To introduce the topic, tell the students about

John Wiseman and his ideas of a 'City Survival Kit' to help in an emergency. Discuss as a class what students always carry with them – you could get them to guess what you carry in your bag/pockets and then show them.

1 Direct the students to the items John Wiseman suggests, and check that they know the names of the objects and their uses. Discuss situations in which they would be useful.

2 Then divide the class into groups of four or five and appoint a group secretary to make notes. The groups make a list of the things they would put in the kit.

3 Each group then reports to the whole class. Write the lists on the board.

4 The class then discusses the items and makes a final list of no more than 15 items.

5 Finally, tell the class what was in John Wiseman's list for them to compare what they have put in their kits.

KEY

needle and thread   paper and pencil   phone card
paper money (enough for a taxi)   coins   safety pins
tweezers   aspirin/paracetamol   lens   plasters
whistle   tiny torch   tiny scissors   blade

7 *Away from home*

An unusual break

> **Focus**
>
> **TOPIC**
> • Places to stay
>
> **GRAMMAR**
> • Defining relative clauses
> • Relative pronouns: *who, which, that, whose*
>
> **SKILLS**
> • Reading: a magazine article
> • Speaking: asking questions about vocabulary

GETTING STARTED EXERCISE 1

To introduce the topic, brainstorm the places that you can pay to stay in and write them on the board. Refer the students to the places in the Students' Book and compare them with their ideas. Add any that are missing and drill for correct pronunciation as necessary. If you wish, find out which ones the students have stayed in. Next, they work in pairs and discuss the questions. Discuss their ideas as a class.

KEY

1 a) guesthouse, youth hostel, hotel, B & B

b) guesthouse, youth hostel (some), hotel
c) youth hostel (some), caravan park, campsite, self-catering flat
d) caravan park, campsite

2 a) hotel
b) guesthouse, self-catering flat
c) youth hostel, caravan park, campsite, B & B

3 open answers

READING EXERCISES 2 AND 3

Direct the class to the title of the article and the picture. As a class, discuss what the students think the article is about. Then each student makes a list of words they think are in the article. They compare lists with their partner. If you wish, write their ideas on the board. Then the students read the article quickly to confirm their ideas. Encourage them to discuss their answers in pairs and then discuss as a class. If you wish, you can tick their words/phrases which are on the board.

EXERCISE 4

Check that the students understand *melt* and *igloo*. Refer the students to the questions and get them to read the article again, more carefully this time. Encourage them to compare answers with their partner and then discuss as a class.

KEY

1 The wooden front door.
2 The hotel melts, and Nils holds a contest to predict when it will happen.
3 A survival certificate.
4 It's made of ice and everyone sleeps on ice beds. It has an ice theatre, a radio station and an ice bar. The rooms have no doors, furniture or heating.

EXERCISE 5

Ask the students to think about the questions and discuss them in pairs. Make sure they realise there are no correct answers.

SUGGESTED KEY

1 It is a play on the words *Arctic* and *art*. The hotel is in the Arctic Circle. Each hotel is a work of art, and the owner also organises art exhibitions.
2 There are no doors, no furniture, no heating.
3 an architect/an artist/a hotel manager/an exhibition organiser
4 open answers

DISCOVERING LANGUAGE EXERCISE 6

Note: This unit deals only with defining relative clauses. Non-defining relatives are presented in *Look Ahead Upper Intermediate*.

The students discuss the questions in pairs and then check as a class. If you wish, copy the five extracts onto the board and use them to highlight the form and use of defining relative clauses. If your students have problems with this structure, explain with the following:

The defining relative sentence either makes no sense or needs further definition when the relative clause is removed, e.g.

*The man **who runs the hotel** is Nils.* – This makes sense.

The man . . . . is Nils. – No sense. Which man?

*The paintings **that hang on the hotel walls** are for sale.* – This is complete.

The paintings . . . . are for sale. – Needs further definition. Which paintings?

KEY

1 a) which, that   b) who, whose, that
2 a) false   b) true
    c) true – they usually *define* a person or thing
3 that
4 The relative pronoun can be omitted when it is the object of the verb in the following relative clause, but not when it is the subject:

subject →		
The paintings	that hang on the hotel walls	are for sale.
object →		
The paintings	[that] Nils hangs on the hotel walls	are for sale.

EXERCISE 7

Write 1–7 on the board and refer the students to the sentences in the Students' Book. Encourage them to compare answers with their partner. Elicit the correct answer and write it on the board. Establish which sentences do not need the relative pronoun and check the students understand why.

KEY

1 that/which   2 that/which   3 that/who   4 that/which – can be omitted   5 whose   6 that/which – can be omitted   7 that/which – can be omitted

SPEAKING EXERCISE 8

The aim of this exercise is for one student to ask questions which elicit a defining relative clause as a response. To demonstrate the task, read out the example exchange with a student. Then divide the class into pairs of students and direct the As to their list of words on page 57 and the Bs to their list on page 128. Monitor and make a note of any errors you hear with defining relative clauses. When they have guessed the words in

the exercise, ask them to think of another three words (at least) for their partner to guess. Finally, use the board to correct any errors you heard.

Extra practice

Divide the class into teams and give each group a different list of three nouns, e.g. *a screwdriver, Britain, Princess Diana*. The students write at least two sentences using defining relative clauses about each noun, without saying who or what the subject is, e.g. *She's a person who is famous because of the man she married.* They then read out their sentences, one by one. The other teams must guess who/what the subject is. If they guess after one sentence, they get 5 points, if they guess after two sentences, they get 4 points, etc. If they do not guess, the original team gets 10 points.

Short of time?

You can omit Exercise 5 if you wish. Exercise 7 can be done for homework.

Facilities

Focus	SKILLS
TOPIC • Hotel facilities GRAMMAR • Causative: *have something done* FUNCTIONS • Polite requests • Asking if something is possible • Expressing satisfaction	• Listening: interviews, a hotel dialogue • Speaking: discussion, role play SPEECH PATTERNS • Expressing satisfaction/sarcasm

GETTING STARTED EXERCISE 1

The names of these hotel facilities should be revision for the students. However, if you are concerned that they might not know some of the phrases, refer them to the list and ask which ones are new. Write them on the board. First, see if any of the other students can explain the phrases and, if not, explain them yourself. The students work in threes and discuss the questions. Then discuss as a class and drill for correct pronunciation.

SUGGESTED KEY

1 a) fax machines, a high-quality restaurant, meeting rooms, secretarial services, mobile telephone hire, photocopiers, a laundry service, a dry-cleaning service, car hire
    b) a swimming pool, a fast food snack bar, cartoon film shows, a children's playground, a babysitting service, a laundry service

c) a disco, tennis courts, a swimming pool, a fast food snack bar, (cartoon film shows), horse-riding, a sports centre, satellite television

d) a disco, tennis courts, a swimming pool, horse-riding, a room with a balcony, a room with a view, a sports centre, tour guides, car hire

e) a swimming pool, a high-quality restaurant, a room with a balcony and view, tour guides, car hire

Documentary

LISTENING EXERCISE 2

Direct the students to the pictures, remind them of the ice hotel and explain that this is another unusual hotel. Discuss why people would want to stay at this kind of hotel.

EXERCISES 3 AND 4

Note: The phrase *horseback riding* is used on the cassette. This is American English. The usual British English phrase is *horse riding* or just *riding*.

Direct the class to the questions. Play the interview and encourage the students to compare answers with their partner. Then check as a class. Follow the same procedure for Exercise 4.

KEY FOR EXERCISE 3

1 New Mexico
2 two tennis courts, a swimming pool with a sun deck, horseback riding
3 a) the horses   b) the tennis courts

TAPESCRIPT FOR EXERCISE 3

JOHN EGAN

We have two tennis courts at Rancho Encantado that are of a very good surface called plexipave. And the individual that we have taking care of them we refer to as the recreation director. We have a swimming pool, which has a sun deck around it, where the guests can sit back and just enjoy the beautiful sunshine of New Mexico. Horseback riding is a very important feature of Rancho Encantado and it's certainly one of the reasons that people come from around the country to, to stay at the ranch. The person in charge of our stable operation we refer to as the head wrangler. 'Wrangler', of course, is a term that is common in the south-west and it just means the person who takes care of the horses.

KEY FOR EXERCISE 4

1 No, most of the guests have never ridden before.
2 The beautiful scenery and the important history of the area of cowboys and Indians.

TAPESCRIPT FOR EXERCISE 4

WRANGLER

Most of our riders have never been on a horse. We're happy to take them out and give them an opportunity to see the land and the beauty of New Mexico, by horseback, not by car.

JOHN EGAN

I think the reason that people come to the south-west is not only because of the scenery itself – the vast spaces and the beautiful colours of the country – but also the important history and the legends that surround the south-west, insofar as cowboys are concerned, and Indians and so on. This is a uniquely American sort of legend, but at the same time it's something that I think people throughout the world really identify with and, and love to be a part of.

SPEAKING EXERCISE 5

The students can discuss the exercise in pairs or as a class.

DISCOVERING LANGUAGE EXERCISE 6

Write the question *What is the relationship between the two speakers?* on the board. Play the conversation with the students following it in their Students' Book. Discuss their answers to the question. Next, ask the students to read questions 1 and 2 in the exercise and play the conversation again. Elicit their answers. Once you are sure they understand the concept (that someone else is going to do the action), the students can discuss questions 3 and 4 in pairs. Then check their answers as a class. If you wish to highlight the form further, copy the four examples in question 4 onto the board and highlight the form and word order in each one (see Key).

KEY

Mr Johnson is a hotel guest and B is the receptionist. The polite language used by B and the general context make this clear.

1 someone else
2 someone else

3

HAVE +	OBJECT +	PAST PARTICIPLE
I'll have	the car	washed today.
I need to have	my bike	mended.
Do you want to have	your hair	cut?
Have they had	their order	taken?

4 We use this structure when someone else performs a service for us.

EXERCISE 7

Refer the class to the situation in the Students' Book. Check the students understand the situation by asking *Did the hotel owner do the work or did someone else do it?* Elicit *someone else.* You may need to check the tense, e.g. ask *Is the fire now or in the past?* (in the past). The students write complete sentences in their notebooks. Encourage them to check answers with their partners. Then elicit their answers and write them on the board under the headings below.

KEY

	HAVE	OBJECT	PAST PARTICIPLE
1	They had	the walls and ceilings	painted.
2	They had	the carpets	cleaned.
3	They had	the windows	repaired.
4	They had	the doors	mended.
5	They had	the pictures	changed.
6	They had	smoke alarms	fitted.

Extra practice

Students work in groups and list all the things that they have done by someone else, e.g. house cleaned, car washed, windows cleaned, eyes tested, newspapers delivered, hair cut, shoes heeled, clothes dry-cleaned, etc. The students then combine with another pair, compare lists and add things that they hadn't thought of. Elicit their ideas as a class and discuss which ones all the students have done and which they do themselves. Make sure that they realise that this structure is usually used for services which are paid for.

FOCUS ON FUNCTIONS EXERCISE 8

Note: Students can find the replies to *Would you mind . . . ?* confusing. If you want to agree to the request, the reply is usually *No, not at all.* If you wish to refuse the request, the reply is usually *Well, yes, I would, because . . .* The opposite reply is given ('no' to agree and 'yes' to refuse) because *mind* carries a negative meaning.

Refer the class back to the dialogue in Exercise 6 and ask the students to discuss question 1 in pairs. Elicit their answers and write the three expressions on the board. Discuss question 2 as a class and highlight the form on the board. The students then work in pairs and practise making the polite requests. If you wish, they can also write the polite requests.

Alternative presentation

If you wish to teach the students the appropriate replies (see Note 1 above), indicate a student to ask you the first prompt. (s: *Would you mind paying your bill now?*) Reply by agreeing. (T: *Not at all*). To check the concept, ask *Am I agreeing or disagreeing?* (Agreeing) *But what do I say to agree?*

(Not at all). Do the same with another student and refuse (e.g. *Well, yes, I'd rather pay later*). Check the concept again in the same way and explain the negative connotation of *mind*. The students then practise the two exchanges in open and closed pairs. Make sure they are aware of the intonation pattern (see Note 2). They then role play similar exchanges using the prompts in question 3 in the Students' Book. Monitor and correct any errors you hear. To check their answers, ask pairs to role play the exchanges for the whole class.

KEY

1 a) Would you mind filling in this form, please?
   b) Can I have my suit cleaned, then?
   c) Excellent!
2 Would you mind + -*ing.*
3 a) Would you mind paying your bill now, please?
   b) Would you mind signing this, please?
   c) Would you mind letting me see your card, please?
   d) Would you mind showing me your passport, please?
   e) Would you mind completing this questionnaire, please?

SPEECH PATTERNS EXERCISE 9

Refer the students to the expressions in the Students' Book. Explain that they will hear each expression spoken twice by two different people and they must decide which speaker (A or B) is satisfied. Write 1–9 on the board. Play the cassette, stopping after the first expression. Elicit which speaker was satisfied and write A on the board next to 1. Play the complete sequence. Encourage the students to compare answers with their partner and then check as a class. If necessary, play the sequence again. Discuss how the other speaker reacts (sarcastically) and how the intonation pattern changes (low fall rather than the high fall of satisfaction). Play the sequence again, pausing for the students to repeat with the correct intonation pattern.

KEY

The sarcastic intonation carries a low fall.
The satisfied intonation carries a high fall.
1 A   2 B   3 B   4 B   5 A   6 A   7 B   8 A   9 B

SPEAKING EXERCISE 10

The aim of this exercise is to practise the language from Exercises 6, 8 and 9. Divide the class into As (hotel guests) and Bs (receptionists) and ask the students to read the information about their roles in the Students' Book. They then role play their conversations. Monitor and make a note of any errors you hear with causative *have*, polite requests or intonation. Follow the same procedures for the second role play. If you wish, two volunteer pairs can role play their conversations for the whole class. Finally, use the board to correct any errors you heard.

Alternatively, if you have a large class, organise the pairs into groups of four. One pair role plays the first conversation while the second pair notes down any errors (see above). They then swap roles and do the same with the second role play. Finally, they correct the errors together.

Short of time?
If you wish, you can omit Exercise 5 from this lesson.

SPEAKING: Telling stories

FOCUS	SKILLS
TOPIC	• Reading: a literary text
• Experiences abroad	• Listening: an anecdote
	• Speaking: telling, and retelling stories

GETTING STARTED EXERCISE 1

To introduce the exercise, tell the students to think of a country which is very different from their own. Elicit a few examples. Then ask each student to make a list of the problems they could have if they visited that country. If necessary, elicit an example from a student to demonstrate the task. Monitor while they write their lists and help with any vocabulary problems. The students then work in pairs and compare their lists. Discuss as a class and find out which fears are common and which ones are realistic.

READING: A LITERARY EXTRACT EXERCISE 2

Background note
Gerald Durrell is an English writer of travel books and books about the natural world. He is also known for his work as the Director of Jersey Zoo.

Point at the picture of the insect at the bottom of the page and elicit what it is (a scorpion). Find out what the students know about scorpions (e.g. they live in hot climates; some kill you with their sting). Then ask the students to read the introduction to the story. In pairs, they predict what happens next by sequencing the pictures in the Students' Book. If you wish, compare their ideas as a class. Then they read the text to check their answers.

KEY
The order is: C, B, D, A

EXERCISE 3

Refer the students to the questions about the passage. They decide if they are true or false and correct the false ones. Encourage students to compare their answers and then check as a class.

KEY
1 true   2 false – He's a young man.   3 true
4 false – It hit Gerald's mother.
5 false – It hid under Leslie's plate.

EXERCISE 4

Draw two columns on the board like this:

NOISE	MOVEMENT

Direct the students to the verbs in the Students' Book. To demonstrate the task, ask them to find *uttered* in the text and together write it in the correct column. Decide the type of noise: a short, sudden, human noise (in this context). The students then work in pairs and do the same with the other verbs. Check as a class on the board. Then the students discuss question 3 in pairs. To check their answers as a class, write the letter of the definition next to the correct verb on the board.

KEY
1 Noise: uttered, barking, thumped
2 Movement: scattering, sped, quivering, leapt, flicked, peered, hurled, drenched, swarm
3 a) leap   b) quiver   c) hurl   d) peer
   e) flick   f) drench

SPEAKING EXERCISE 5

Divide the class into pairs. Direct the As to the picture and Bs to the text. Explain that the As are going to retell the story using the pictures and the Bs can help with vocabulary from the text. Monitor and make a note of any serious errors. Make sure they change roles after A has described the first two pictures. Use the board to correct any errors you heard.

EXERCISE 6

Discuss as a class or in pairs what the students think happened next. Then tell them the ending of the story:

When everyone finally calms down, the baby scorpions are hiding under the plates and cutlery on the table. Leslie suggests that all the scorpions should be killed, but Mother supports Gerry's plea for mercy. So, after the rest of the family has left the room, Gerry carefully puts each baby scorpion onto the mother scorpion's back using a teaspoon. He then carries them all outside on a saucer and returns them to the garden wall where he found them. Gerry and Roger spend the rest of the afternoon well away from the house in the hope that the episode will be forgotten.

📼 LISTENING EXERCISE 7

Tell the students that they are going to listen to someone talking about an experience that they had on holiday. Write the questions on the board and students listen with their books closed. Encourage them to compare answers with their partner and then check as a class.

KEY

1 It was a camping safari.
2 She stopped each night and put up her tent.
3 Because the coach broke down.
4 There was an infestation of mice – there were mice everywhere.
5 When she opened her suitcase, about six mice leapt out.

📼 EXERCISE 8

Direct the class to the three questions in the exercise. Play the cassette again and the students follow in their books. Allow them a few minutes to think about the questions and then discuss as a class.

KEY

1 It's less complicated with fewer different verbs and adjectives. It's also more informal, e.g. *gear* instead of *equipment*, *stuck there* instead of *unable to travel further*. She also uses *you know* and *sort of*, which are features of spoken colloquial English.
2 With simple linkers such as *and, so, but.*
3 There is repetition to create dramatic effect and she uses her voice (intonation) to show her feelings, e.g. *There were mice everywhere, everywhere you looked.* She doesn't speak in complete sentences and doesn't always finish them.

EXERCISE 9

Refer the students to the questions. Tell them that it can be a real or imaginary story. They can make notes if they wish. Monitor and help with any new vocabulary.

SPEAKING EXERCISE 10

Ask the students to read the information about their roles in the Students' Book. First the As use their notes from Exercise 9 to tell their story to

their partner. The Bs listen and make notes of the important words and ask questions for clarification. Then they change roles. Next, explain that they are going to tell their partner's story to the class and that they must use their voice to make it dramatic. If you have a large class, they can retell their partner's story in groups of six.

Short of time?
Exercise 5 can be omitted.

Progress check: Units 6–7

Grammar and functions

EXERCISE 1

1 What would you do if you failed your exams?
2 When will you/we leave if there are no seats on the 14th?
3 How will he travel if the coaches are full?
4 Where would you shop if there weren't any local shops?
5 How would you feel if she needed a major operation?

EXERCISE 2

1 which – blank   2 which   3 who   4 who – blank
5 whose   6 which   7 which – blank

EXERCISE 3

1 She had the letters typed.
2 He has his shopping done.
3 I'll have the fence painted.
4 They're having/going to have some business cards printed.
5 We're going to have our picture taken.

EXERCISE 4 (SUGGESTED ANSWERS)

1 Students shouldn't study all day. They ought to enjoy themselves.
2 People oughtn't to try to change their looks. They should accept them.
3 We shouldn't have children at twenty. We ought to wait until we are thirty.
4 You should talk about your fears. You oughtn't to keep quiet.
5 We shouldn't stay at the ice hotel. We ought to go somewhere hot.

EXERCISE 5

1 Can I have my suit cleaned?
2 Calm down!

3 Would you mind closing the door, please?
4 I'm very nervous about speaking in public.

Vocabulary

EXERCISE 6

1 overconfident   2 acceptable   3 predictable
4 oversleep

8 Paths to success

••

Job options

Focus	FUNCTIONS
TOPICS	• Talking about ambitions
• Jobs	**SKILLS**
• Qualifications	• Reading: case studies
• School subjects	
GRAMMAR	
• Present perfect simple	
• Adverbs: *for* and *since*	

GETTING STARTED EXERCISE 1
Draw three columns on the board like this:

a) UNIVERSITY QUALIFICATIONS	b) QUALIFICATIONS BUT NOT UNIVERSITY	c) NO QUALIFICATIONS

Make sure the students understand all the jobs in the list in their books. They work in pairs and categorise the jobs according to the qualifications needed in their countries and discuss which ones they think they would be good at. Elicit their answers and write them on the board.

KEY (FOR UK)

a) dentist, engineer, teacher, journalist, librarian, pharmacist
b) carpenter, chef, nurse, plumber, firefighter, hotel receptionist, window dresser, lorry driver, police officer
c) cleaner, postman, waiter

Note: It is becoming increasingly common to find an alternative for -*man*/*woman*, e.g. *firefighter* rather than *fireman*, *police officer* rather than *policeman*/*woman*. It is still common to use -*man*/*woman* with jobs such as *postman*/*milkman*.

READING EXERCISE 2
Direct the class to the pictures. The students discuss the exercise as a class or in pairs. Do not confirm their ideas yet.

KEY
A is putting clothes on dummies in a shop window.
B is making something out of wood.
C is giving an injection to a horse.

EXERCISE 3
The students read the text about the three jobs to check their ideas from Exercise 2. Encourage them to compare their answers and to discuss what surprises them about the jobs.

KEY
1 C   2 A   3 B

EXERCISES 4 AND 5
Refer the students to the questions and ask them to read the three texts again. Ask students to compare answers with their partner and then discuss as a class. Follow the same procedures for Exercise 5.

KEY FOR EXERCISE 4
a) Diana, Paul and Liz   b) Liz   c) Diana   d) Paul

KEY FOR EXERCISE 5
a) 'A' levels   b) degree   c) diploma, certificate

EXERCISE 6
Check that the students understand the different subjects. Then write *Diana*, *Paul* and *Liz* on the board. To demonstrate the task, ask *Which subjects do you think Diana liked best at school?* Discuss their ideas and write the subjects next to *Diana*. The students then work in pairs and do the same for *Paul* and *Liz*. Discuss as a class. Drill the subjects for correct pronunciation, write them on the board and then mark the stress. Divide the class into pairs to discuss which subjects the students prefer/red and why. If you wish, discuss as a class.

SUGGESTED KEY
Diana: 'chemistry, bi'ology
Paul: art, craft, de'sign and tech'nology
Liz: ˌmathe'matics, craft, de'sign and tech'nology

COMPARING CULTURES EXERCISE 7
Background note
Advanced level examinations ('A' levels) are the entrance qualification for universities (and higher education in general). In the UK **higher education** refers to universities and other institutions offering academic courses, which usually lead to **degrees. Further education** refers to colleges offering more vocational qualifications.

Ask the students to read the short text about the British educational system and to complete the grid in pairs. Elicit their answers and together complete the grid on the board. The students then work in pairs and interview each other about the educational system in their countries. They use the grid to collate their answers. If you have a monolingual class, they can discuss the questions together and complete one grid. If you have a multilingual class, they can work in mixed nationality pairs. Monitor and correct any errors you hear. With a monolingual class, discuss their educational system as a class. If you wish, with a multilingual group, the students can give short presentations about their partner's system.

🔊 FOCUS ON FUNCTIONS EXERCISE 8

Write 1–3 on the board and refer the students back to the jobs in Exercise 2. They listen with their books closed and match the people talking with the jobs. Check as a class. Then play the cassette again, pausing to allow the students to complete the sentences in the book. Encourage them to compare answers with their partner and then check as a class.

KEY

1 1 window dresser   2 vet   3 carpenter
2 a) My ambition is to become a manager.
   b) I've always wanted to work with animals.
   c) In the future, I'd like to work for myself.

TAPESCRIPT

One.
You've got to make them look as beautiful as possible because that's your job. You're there to make the customer think: I want to look like that – exactly the same as models on the catwalks in Milan or Paris. My ambition is to become a manager so that I can decide on the themes for displays instead of just dressing the mannequins. It *is* possible to get a job doing this kind of work without qualifications, but lately it's become difficult. I'm glad I've got a proper qualification.
Two.
I prefer dealing with domestic pets because I like these smaller animals. I think the problems are more interesting; er, I like talking to all the different people who bring them in. I don't have any other ambitions, really. I've always wanted to work with animals and now I do!
Three.
You have to provide all your own tools. Saws are quite expensive, and you have to replace them every couple of months, because they wear out. The most irritating thing about the job is when I get stuff in my hair that I have to cut out, and of course my hands and clothes are

always dirty. In the future I'd like to work for myself . . . to be self-employed and run my own carpentry business.

EXERCISE 9

To demonstrate the task, get the class to interview you about your ambitions using the questions in the Students' Book. Then the students do the same in pairs. Make sure they make brief notes about their partner. Monitor and make a note of any errors you hear. The students then use their notes to tell the class about their partner. If you have a large class, they can give feedback in groups of six.

DISCOVERING LANGUAGE EXERCISE 10

Note: This exercise should be revision for your students. If it is not, see Units 11–14 of *Look Ahead 2* for presentation and practice ideas.

Refer the class back to the texts in Exercise 3 and ask the students to note down all the examples of statements with the present perfect. Do the first one together and write it on the board. The students compare their statements with their partner. Then elicit them and write them on the board. Do question 1 together and write some of their examples on the board. The students then discuss questions 2 and 3 in pairs. Ask them to decide which uses in question 2 are reflected in the examples from the text. Discuss as a class, using the statements on the board to highlight the different uses (question 1) and the difference between *for* and *since* (question 3).

KEY

Examples from the texts:
Diana Stapleton, 28, has been a veterinary surgeon for three years. (use c)
She has always loved animals. (use c)
Since then she has obtained a basic skills certificate. (use b)
1 Examples: *She hasn't been to America. What have you done in your life?*
2 a) false – past simple   b) true   c) true
   d) false – past simple
3 *For* and *since* are used to describe actions that began in the past and continue up to the present time. *For* + a period of time, e.g. a year, three seconds; *since* + exact time, e.g. yesterday, 1976.

EXERCISE 11

Direct the class to the interview in the Students' Book and write 1–9 on the board. Complete the first gap together as a class and write the answer on the board next to 1. Point out that 2 does not require a verb. The students then do the same for the rest of the conversation. Encourage them to check answers with their partner. Then discuss their answers as a class and write them on the board.

KEY

1 have you been   2 For   3 Has the company employed   4 has not   5 Have you taken
6 finished   7 Did you enjoy   8 loved
9 haven't used

Extra practice

Write these sentence stems on the board:

_____ *recently.*

I have never _____ .

I once _____ .

_____ *for the past three years.*

_____ *for a month.*

I have always _____ .

The students complete them about themselves/ their families. They tell their partner or mingle with other students in the class.

Preparing to work

Focus	SKILLS
TOPIC • Arts and crafts GRAMMAR • Present perfect progressive • Linkers	• Listening: an interview • Reading: an article • Writing: a brief biography

🎞 Documentary

LISTENING EXERCISE 1

Note: *Bunnell* is pronounced /bəˈnel/.

Direct the class to the pictures and explain that Katie does something rather unusual. The students discuss the questions in pairs. Discuss as a class but do not confirm the students' answers yet.

📼 EXERCISE 2

Background note
The Royal College of Art (RCA) is a leading art college in London and is well-known for its annual show of students' work.

Play the interview once for the students to check their answers from Exercise 1. Check as a class. Then refer the students to the comprehension questions in Exercise 2 and play the interview again. Encourage them to compare answers with their partner and then check as a class.

SUGGESTED KEY FOR EXERCISE 1

1 She's an art student.   2 a sculpture
3 'A' levels in arts subjects

KEY FOR EXERCISE 2

1 at the Royal College of Art
2 2 years
3 almost 2 years ago
4 almost 2 years
5 A show of the students' work. They also talk about their work for an hour.
6 at the beginning of September

TAPESCRIPT

KATIE BUNNELL

I'm studying for an MA in ceramics at the Royal College of Art. I've been studying for nearly two years now – this is my final year. The first year we do quite a lot of project work, and then throughout the summer holidays after the first year we have to write a thesis. And then in the second year we have a final exam, where we have to put up a show and talk about our work for an hour. And then we have a big show where the public come to see what we've made. I'm working on a project at the moment which is basically making a large piece of sculpture. I've been working on it now since the beginning of September. And I started the project by making large collages from drawings of myself. And the sculpture is made up of a pair of arms and a pair of legs; and they're very large and curvaceous; and they're going to be in very, very bright colours; and they will be set against a stripy coloured background. In the end I will present it for my MA. It'll be part of my show.

📼 EXERCISE 3

The aim of Exercise 3 is to make the students aware of the four verb + noun collocations. Direct the class to the chart and copy the two columns onto the board. Play the interview again, stopping after 'thesis' and complete the columns for the first definition as a class. Then play the complete interview. Encourage the students to compare answers with their partner. Elicit their answers and complete the chart on the board. Drill as necessary for correct pronunciation.

KEY

NOUN IN INTERVIEW	RELATED VERB
a thesis /ˈθiːsɪs/	write
a project /ˈprɒdʒekt/	work on, start
a sculpture /ˈskʌlptʃə/	make
a collage /kɒˈlɑːʒ/	make

EXERCISE 4
Direct the class to the exercise and play the

interview again if necessary. Encourage the students to compare answers in pairs and to use their dictionaries. Elicit their answers as a class and write them on the board. Drill for correct pronunciation as necessary. Alternatively, the students can answer Exercises 3 and 4 at the same time.

KEY

a) final   b) large and curvaceous   c) bright
d) stripy, coloured

DISCOVERING LANGUAGE EXERCISE 5

Note: The students may find the form and pronunciation of the present perfect progressive difficult to manipulate and so will need choral and individual drilling.

Alternative presentation
Think of three or four things that you have been doing recently, e.g. *learning to . . . , planning your garden, writing a book*. Tell the class that you've been doing some interesting things recently. Encourage them to ask you what (don't worry if the question form is not accurate or if they use the present perfect simple) and reply *I've been writing a book for nine months.* To check the concept, ask *Am I still writing the book?* (Yes), *Have I finished writing it?* (No) *Did I start writing it in the past?* (Yes). Once you're sure they understand the concept, ask *What have I been doing?* and drill the reply chorally and individually, concentrating on the pronunciation of *you've been* /juːvbɪn/. Indicate a student to ask you the question and elicit *What've you been doing recently?* Reply and drill the question form. Repeat the same procedures for two other recent activities. To elicit the third person question form, indicate one student to ask another one about yourself (*What's she been doing recently?*). The students then practise the exchanges in open and closed pairs. The students can then work in pairs and ask and answer each other about their activities.

Write the example sentence in the exercise on the board and refer the students to the questions. They discuss them in pairs and then as a class. Highlight the forms on the board.

KEY

1 AUXILIARY *HAVE*	+ *BEEN*	+ *-ING* VERB FORM
2 She has You have We have They have	been	studying for nearly two years.

3 How long have you been studying?

4 She hasn't been studying at Manchester University. (She's been studying at the Royal College of Art.)

EXERCISE 6

To demonstrate the task, write the example prompt on the board. Elicit the question form and write it on the board. Do the same with the short answer (*For three years*). The students work in pairs and do the same with the other prompts. Check as a class, drilling the exchanges for correct pronunciation if necessary.

KEY

1 How long have you been studying economics? For about a year.
2 How long have you been doing the computer course? Since January.
3 How long have you been working in the library? Since two o'clock.
4 How long have you been waiting for your interview? For half an hour.

DISCOVERING LANGUAGE EXERCISE 7

Direct the students to the exercise and ask them to think about the two questions. They discuss their ideas in pairs and then check as a class.

KEY

1 the present perfect simple (Sentence A)
2 There is no difference in meaning.
Note: Verbs like *work, live, drive, smoke* can be used in either tense and the choice depends on the speaker.

EXERCISE 8

Refer the class to the exercise and establish that they should only use the present perfect simple and progressive. To demonstrate the task, read out the first situation. Elicit the answer and write it on the board. The students then work in pairs and do the same with the other situations. Check answers as a class and if you wish, write them on the board.

KEY

1 I've been living/I've lived in this house since 1980.
2 I've been studying/I've studied English since 1990.
3 I've been writing this essay since 10.00/for five hours.
4 I've played three games of tennis this morning./I've been playing tennis since 11.00 a.m.

EXERCISE 9

The aim of this exercise is to practise the present, past and present perfect (progressive) tenses rather than to practise reading skills. Refer the class to the title of the text and establish the students know the meaning of *solicitor*. Discuss what they think the text might be about. Then direct the students to the statements about Philip Hughes before they read the text. Tell them to concentrate on changing the tenses. After they've read the text, encourage them to compare answers with their partner and then check as a class. Elicit full sentences to check that the students can manipulate the different tenses accurately.

KEY

1 False. He has been a student./He was a student.
2 False. He worked as a lawyer for less than a week.
3 true
4 true
5 true
6 False. He wore a suit for less than a week.
7 False. He has been making furniture in a studio for a few years.
8 true

Extra practice

Think of six statements about yourself using the present perfect simple and progressive, the past simple and present simple. Three should be true and three should be false but it shouldn't be obvious which are which, e.g. *I've been living in my flat for six months*, *I've never been to Canada*, *I met the Prime Minister six years ago*, etc. Write the six sentences on the board. Explain that three are true and three are false. The students must ask you questions to find out which ones are false. Explain that you will only answer questions which are grammatically correct. The students can then do the same for themselves. They work in groups of four and ask and answer questions. Monitor for errors.

DISCOVERING LANGUAGE EXERCISE 10

Check that the students understand *anthropology*, *Fiji* and *Sri Lanka*. Refer the students back to the text in Exercise 8 and ask them to write down all the expressions that refer to 'time'. Do the first one together to demonstrate the task. Elicit their answers and write them on the board. Next, write 1–5 on the board and direct the students to the text. First they read the text to understand the general meaning. Then they complete the gaps, using the words on the board. Encourage the students to check answers with their partner and then check as a class and write them on the board.

KEY

After, then, eight years later, finally, when, before, now
1 After   2 before   3 later   4 then   5 After/when

WRITING EXERCISE 11

The students can write about their own career or their friend's. Direct the class to the outline in the Students' Book. If your students have jobs (and so have more experience), you may wish them to write about their partner. First, use the headings in the outline to brainstorm questions for them to interview their partner. Write them on the board. Then they interview each other and make notes. They use the notes to write three paragraphs. They can then exchange texts with their partner and correct them for factual or language errors.

Short of time?

Exercises 3 and 4 can be omitted from this lesson and Exercise 11 can be done for homework.

Speaking: Personal interviews

Focus	
TOPIC	SKILLS
• Personal information	• Reading: job advertisements
FUNCTIONS	• Listening: a job interview
• Asking for repetition	• Speaking: interviews
• Asking for clarification	SPEECH PATTERNS
• Correcting yourself	• Using intonation to introduce a new topic
• Showing interest	

READING EXERCISE 1

Background notes

1 **Hampstead** is an area in London, about five miles north-west of the centre. It is an expensive place to live and is considered to be a desirable area.
2 **Au pair** is pronounced /əʊˈpeə/. They are usually young women who go abroad and live with a family, normally in order to learn their country's language, in return for doing light work in the house or looking after children.

Direct the students to the job advertisement and questions in the Students' Book. Encourage the students to compare answers and then check as a class. Check that they understand *contract*.

KEY

1 a live-in au pair
2 Hampstead, London
3 between 18 and 25
4 No, but they must speak good English.
5 £100 per week
6 Their own room with a television. Their fare home will be paid at the end of the contract. They may have use of a car.

LISTENING EXERCISE 2

Direct the class to the picture and discuss what the students think is happening. Establish that the young man is applying for the job in Exercise 1. Ask *What will the woman ask him?* and elicit the first topic. Write it on the board. The students then work in pairs and list the other topics that could be discussed. Elicit their ideas and write them on the board. Do not confirm them yet.

📼 EXERCISE 3

You may wish to tell the students that the interview is long but reassure them that the first time they listen, they only have to check and expand on their answers to Exercise 2. Play the interview once and encourage the students to compare their list of topics in pairs before you check as a class.

KEY

3 family   4 school/education   5 work experience
6 interests   7 experience with children

📼 EXERCISE 4

Refer the students to the questions in their books and play the interview again, pausing if necessary to allow the students to make notes. Follow the same procedure for checking their answers.

KEY

1 He's from Helsinki, Finland.
2 He's twenty years old.
3 He came one month ago.
4 He's been visiting friends in Scotland and Wales, and looking for a job.
5 He's got two brothers and one sister.
6 His brothers are ten and eight and his sister is eighteen.
7 He's a student at Helsinki University.
8 He's studying English, French and Business Studies.
9 He's been studying there for two years.
10 He's worked in a paper factory, he's been a cleaner, he's worked in a shop and at EuroDisney.
11 Yes he has. He worked with children at EuroDisney and he's been a helper at a youth centre in Finland. He's also looked after his brothers.

TAPESCRIPT

MRS SANDERS: Hello, I'm Margaret Sanders. You must be Emil.
EMIL: Yes, Emil Aalto.
MRS S: How do you spell that?
EMIL: Emil's E-M-I-L. And my surname's Aalto ... A-A-L-T-O.
MRS S: And where are you from, Emil?
EMIL: From Finland – Helsinki.

MRS S: Oh really? How old are you?
EMIL: Twenty.
MRS S: Sorry?
EMIL: I'm twenty years old.
MRS S: So how long have you been in Britain?
EMIL: Oh ... about a month.
MRS S: And did you come specifically to find a job?
EMIL: No, not really. I arrived a month ago and I wanted to travel, you know ... and improve my English ... but then I thought it would be a good idea to try to find work.
MRS S: And what have you been doing in the last month? Travelling around?
EMIL: Er ... yes ... a little. I've been visiting friends in Scotland and Wales. And I've been looking for a job.
MRS S: Yes, of course. Right. Can I ask about your family? Have you got any brothers and sisters?
EMIL: Yes. I've got two brothers and one sister.
MRS S: I see. And how old are they?
EMIL: Oh, well, my brothers are quite young. One is ten and the other's eight. My sister's closer to my age ... she's ... er ... eighteen now.
MRS S: So you're the oldest ...
EMIL: Yes, of course. I don't live at home any more, but I often see them at weekends.
MRS S: Right. What about school? You went to school in Helsinki?
EMIL: Yes, that's right.
MRS S: And what were your favourite subjects?
EMIL: Oh, well ... I liked languages, geography ... and music. They were my favourites I think. And then I decided to study languages at university.
MRS S: Oh. Which university?
EMIL: In Helsinki. I started there two years ago. I'm doing English, French and Business Studies.
MRS S: I'm afraid I don't understand. You haven't finished your course yet?
EMIL: No. I decided to take a year off to improve my English before the final exams.
MRS S: Oh, I see. Good idea. OK. What about work? Have you got any work experience?
EMIL: Yes. I had a job in a paper factory for a few months after I left school. Then while I was a student I worked in the summer holidays ... first as a cleaner, then in a shop ... then I got a job at EuroDisney.
MRS S: Near Paris?
EMIL: Yes, that's right. It was good because I was able to use my English and my French.
MRS S: What was the job exactly?
EMIL: I had to dress as a bear ... and entertain children.
MRS S: A bear? That must have been fun.
EMIL: Oh yes. I really enjoyed it. But it was quite hot in the costume sometimes.

MRS S: I can imagine. OK ...Do you drive? Have you got a driving licence?

EMIL: Yes, I have. A Finnish licence and an International one.

MRS S: That's fine, then. So, what kind of interests do you have?

EMIL: Interests? Well, I like travelling ...I play a lot of sports ...and I play the piano.

MRS S: What sort of sports do you like?

EMIL: Football, tennis and swimming. I ski as well.

MRS S: Right. And what sort of music do you play on the piano?

EMIL: Oh. A lot of different types. Classical, jazz, blues ...

MRS S: Really? Are you a good pianist, then?

EMIL: Well ...not as good as I'd like to be!

MRS S: Right. The most important questions now. What experience have you had with children?

EMIL: Well, I've looked after my brothers, as babies and as young children. I've also worked with children in a youth club.

MRS S: A youth club?

EMIL: Yes. I've been working as a helper at a youth club in Helsinki since I started at the university ...as a sort of volunteer ...with teenagers ...you know, helping them to organise things they're interested in.

MRS S: That's wonderful.

EMIL: And then, of course, I've worked with younger children as well – at EuroDisney. I haven't looked after children in a family before, but I'm sure I'll enjoy it.

MRS S: Good. Now, have you got any questions you'd like to ask?

EMIL: Er ...yes. What are the times?

MRS S: The times?

EMIL: Er ...sorry. I mean, what are the hours ...the working hours?

MRS S: Well ...they'll have to be a bit flexible, but usually while we're at work, Monday to Friday ... about eight in the morning till six in the evening.

EMIL: I see. And the pay is £100 ...

MRS S: Yes, £100 a week ...and ...er ... accommodation and food are included, of course. You'll be able to use a car during the day and sometimes in the evenings. Then, as it says in the advertisement, we'll pay your fare back to Helsinki at the end of the contract.

EMIL: Right ...could I ask a few other things?

MRS S: Of course.

EMIL: The contract is for a year ... what about holidays in that time? Will I be able to ...

🔲 SPEECH PATTERNS EXERCISE 5

Draw the two arrows (↗↘) on the board and direct the students to the exercise. Play the first extract on the cassette and elicit if the woman's voice goes up or down on *so*. Write the word under the correct arrow on the board. Then play the other words. The students compare answers with their partner. Play the cassette again, stopping to check their answers. The students then practise saying the words with the correct intonation, chorally and individually.

KEY AND TAPESCRIPT

We generally use a falling tone when using a word to change topic.

MRS SANDERS: So, how long have you been in Britain?

MRS SANDERS: Right. Can I ask about your family?

MRS SANDERS: OK. Do you drive?

MRS SANDERS: Now, have you got any questions you'd like to ask?

🔲 EXERCISE 6

Note: Depending on their L1, the students may find the rising intonation at the end of the responses difficult but it is an important way in English of showing your listener that you are interested and following what they are saying.

Copy this chart onto the board:

INTERESTED AND FRIENDLY	UNINTERESTED AND COLD

Direct the students to the statement and four responses. Play the cassette, stopping after the first response and ask *Is the person interested or uninterested?* Elicit their answer and write *a* under the correct column on the board. Play the other responses. The students check answers in pairs and then check as a class on the board and discuss how the intonation is different. Drill the two intonation patterns. The students can then work in pairs and practise the four exchanges.

Next, refer the class to the eight responses in the Students' Book. Play the cassette, stopping for the students to repeat. Make sure their intonation rises at the end of each response.

KEY AND TAPESCRIPT

A sentence ending in a low fall (e.g. a and b) can sound uninterested. A high fall or a rise at the end sounds interested and friendly.

a) A: I've got a brother who lives in New York.
   B: [uninterested] Really?

b) A: I've got a brother who lives in New York.
   B: [uninterested] Oh.

c) A I've got a brother who lives in New York.
   B: [very interested] Have you?

d) A I've got a brother who lives in New York.
   B [very interested] New York?

e) That's interesting.   f) That's terrible.   g) Do you?

h) How fantastic!   i) How nice!   j) How awful!

k) I see.   l) Oh dear.

EXERCISE 7

Divide the class into pairs and direct them to the exercise. Check that they understand *to make a fortune*. To demonstrate the task, say the first sentence to a student and elicit one of the expressions to show interest. They then work in pairs and role play the conversation. Make sure they change pairs. If you wish, a pair can role play their conversation for the whole class.

FOCUS ON FUNCTIONS EXERCISE 8

Direct the class to the three functions in the exercise. To check that students understand them ask *What do you do if you make a mistake?* (Correct yourself) *What do you do if you don't hear what someone says?* (Ask for repetition) *What do you do if you don't understand what someone says?* (Ask for clarification). Play the cassette, stop after (a) and elicit which function it is. Then play all the sentences. The students compare answers in pairs and then check as a class. Play the sentences again, stopping for the students to repeat.

KEY

1 a, b, f
2 c, e, g
Note: It is possible to use *Sorry?* or *Pardon?* to ask for clarification but usually in conjunction with a question, e.g. *Sorry? What do you mean?*
3 d

LISTENING EXERCISE 9

The aim of this exercise is to help prepare the students for the interview in Exercises 10 and 11. Copy the five topics onto the board and discuss as a class which tenses Emil used to talk about them. Write their ideas on the board next to each topic. Then play the cassette, stopping after each extract to check if their ideas were correct. Write the correct tenses on the board for the next exercise.

KEY

a) present simple   b) present simple   c) past simple
d) past simple and present perfect simple
e) present simple

TAPESCRIPT

A I'm twenty years old.

B Oh, well, my brothers are quite young. One is ten and the other's eight. My sister's closer to my age . . . she's . . . er . . . eighteen now.

C Oh, well . . . I liked languages, geography . . . and music. They were my favourites I think. And then I decided to study languages at university.

D Yes. I had a job in a paper factory for a few months after I left school. Then while I was a student I worked in the summer holidays . . . first as a cleaner, then in a shop . . . then I got a job at EuroDisney. I've looked after my brothers, as babies and as young children. I've also worked with children in a youth club.

E I like travelling . . . I play a lot of sports . . . and I play the piano.

SPEAKING EXERCISE 10

This is quite a complicated role play to organise. You might find it helpful to give each student a letter (A, B, C) to help them find the other students with the same role.

Direct the class to the advertisement and check that they understand *courier*. Divide the students into threes and allocate each one a role (A, B, C). Then reorganise the class into As, Bs and Cs. The As and Bs look at the advertisement and write down questions that they would like to ask about the job. The Cs look at their advertisement and notes and write down the questions that they want to ask. Monitor and help.

EXERCISE 11

The students return to their original groups of three (A, B, C). Explain that they are going to do two role plays and make sure that they understand their roles: C is the interviewer in both role plays, in the first one A is the candidate and B makes notes of any language errors. In the second role play, B is the candidate and A makes notes. Explain that they can use their imagination for information about themselves. The students then do the two role plays. Next, they decide in their groups if A or B should get the job. To round off the activity, you can elicit as a class who got the job in each group and why.

Short of time?

Exercise 9 can be omitted if your students can manipulate the tenses well.

Talkback

Happy endings

This is a fluency activity which allows students to use their imagination to create a story from a few visual prompts. They are likely to need the language of sequencing, relative clauses, present perfect and story-telling skills.

1 The students work in threes and describe each scene, using their imagination to build up the background to the story.
2 Then they decide on an order for the pictures. They must be able to justify their order.
3 In the third stage, they tell the story orally but do not need to write it.
4 In the fourth stage, the students write what the people are saying in each picture. They also need to write 'background' comments, e.g. *Inside the café, Liz and Simon are sitting at a table.* Make sure they write the script following the format suggested in the Students' Book.
5 Finally, they act out the story in front of the class. If you have a large class, they can act it out in groups of six, nine or twelve.

As a follow-up, the students could write their story as a simple narrative.

9 *Skin deep*

First impressions

Focus

TOPIC
• People's appearances

GRAMMAR
• *Look* + adjective
• *Look like* + noun

FUNCTIONS
• Certainty and probability in the future

SKILLS
• Listening: a discussion
• Speaking: a discussion
• Writing: a short report

VOCABULARY DEVELOPMENT
• Adjectives describing people

GETTING STARTED EXERCISE 1
Direct the class to picture A and the questions. The students discuss the exercise as a class or in pairs.

⌨ EXERCISE 2
Tell the class that they are going to hear two people talking about the man in Picture A. Write *Do they recognise him? How do you know?* on the board and play the dialogue. Encourage the students to compare answers with their partner and then discuss as a class.

KEY

Yes, they do recognise him. The first speaker says, 'He looks awful these days' comparing his appearance to the way he used to look. Comments like 'He's his own person' and 'He's got so much money' show that they have read or heard about him.

TAPESCRIPT

JENNY: Look at him! He looks awful these days, doesn't he?
GAIL: No, he doesn't. He looks nice. I like him. He's his own person.
JENNY: Oh, come on. He looks middle-aged, and his clothes ...
GAIL: What's wrong with them?
JENNY: Well, he looks like an old tramp ... and he's got so much money.

DISCOVERING LANGUAGE EXERCISE 3
Write A – D onto the board and direct the class to the questions, which they discuss in pairs. Elicit their answers and write *age*, *appearance* or *personality* next to the appropriate letters. Then use the sentences to highlight the form of the two constructions (question 2) with the students' help.

KEY

1 a) age – C
   b) appearance – A, (B), D
   c) personality – B
2 *He looks* + adjective
   He looks like + noun

DEVELOPING VOCABULARY EXERCISE 4
Alternative presentation
If you think the students will have problems with the adjectives of appearance and personality, check they understand them in the following way. For the adjectives of appearance, write these on the board:

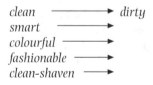

clean ⟶ dirty
smart ⟶
colourful ⟶
fashionable ⟶
clean-shaven ⟶

Together as a class, brainstorm the opposites. Then get the class to check their answers in the Students' Book. If necessary to check understanding, ask the students questions about their own appearances, e.g.

T: Are you unshaven?
S: No, I'm clean-shaven.
For the adjectives of personality, copy these headings onto the board:

POSITIVE	NEGATIVE	IT DEPENDS

First, the students categorise the adjectives they know in pairs. Then they mingle and find students who can help them with some of the unknown words. They return to their partner and complete more of the grid. Finally, you can explain any remaining new vocabulary. To check concepts, you can use questions such as:

Is someone who behaves childishly mature? (no, immature)

What's the opposite of interesting? (boring, uninteresting, dull)

What's the adjective for someone who wants to enjoy themselves? (fun-loving)

If you don't remember things, you are . . . (forgetful)

If you obey your parents, you aren't . . . (rebellious)

Is the royal family unconventional? (no, conventional and traditional)

Drill the adjectives chorally and individually and mark the stress on the board.

Copy this grid onto the board (without the adjectives/phrases):

	HIS AGE	HIS APPEARANCE	HIS PERSONALITY
A	about 25	clean, (drab), clean-shaven	mature, relaxed, intelligent, serious, boring
B	about 14	clean, smart, young, clean-shaven, old-fashioned	innocent, conventional
C	about 22	scruffy, colourful, unshaven	rebellious, crazy, interesting, fun-loving, unconventional

Refer the students to the first three questions in the exercise. The students work in pairs and describe the man in the different pictures. Monitor and correct errors you hear with the language from Exercise 3. Elicit their ideas about the man under each heading and drill the adjectives as necessary for correct pronunciation. The students then discuss questions 4 and 5 in pairs or as a class.

SUGGESTED KEY

See chart above for questions 1–3.

4 open answers

5 He's had his ear pierced. He's started to wear glasses. He's started to dress more casually.

COMPARING CULTURES EXERCISE 5
Background note

Nigel Kennedy is a famous British classical violinist, who became well-known for his punk appearance when playing classical pieces.

First, ask the students to read the information about when people in Britain wear smart clothes. Then they discuss the exercise in pairs or as a class. You may need to drill the clothes vocabulary for correct pronunciation, e.g. *bow tie, suit, dinner jacket.*

LISTENING EXERCISE 6

This exercise revises *have something done* from Unit 7. Direct the class to the pictures of the two people. Discuss what they look like and check the students understand *wig, tattoo* and *pierced.* If necessary, write the example sentence on the board and check the meaning and form of the construction. Drill for correct pronunciation. The students then work in pairs and use the expressions to describe the two people. Monitor and correct any errors you hear. Check their answers as a class. The students then work in pairs to discuss other ways of changing their appearance. If you wish, discuss as a class.

KEY

The man has grown a beard and his hair. He's had his hair dyed and he's bought a wig. He's had his ear pierced. (He's had his teeth straightened.)
The woman has grown her nails. She's had her head shaved. She's had her arm tattooed and her nose pierced.

EXERCISE 7

Direct the class to the questions in the exercise and play the dialogue on cassette. Encourage the students to compare answers with their partner and then check as a class.

KEY

1 a) Pam   b) Lucy   c) Jenny
2 a) Lucy   b) Pam   c) Jenny
3 Yes, they are very familiar with each other and use expressions used amongst friends, e.g. *You must be joking!*
4 She's probably in her late teens/early twenties: she has been dyeing her hair for a few years, but is still influenced by her parents (*Your mum'll go crazy!*).

📼 FOCUS ON FUNCTIONS EXERCISE 8

Copy 1–3 onto the board and refer the students to the expressions on the right. They listen to the conversations again and match the meanings with the expressions. Then they check their answers in pairs and as a class on the board.

KEY

1 *I'm certain (I will)*: I'll definitely
2 *There's a strong chance (that I will/won't)*: I probably won't, I'll probably
3 *There's a small possibility (that I will/won't)*: I think, I'm not sure, it's possible

TAPESCRIPT

Part One.

JENNY: What about you, Lucy? Will you ever dye your hair?

LUCY: Oh yes. I do dye it sometimes, and I'll definitely dye it again.

JENNY: Oh, I didn't know that.

LUCY: It was bright red a few years ago, then I was blonde for a while. Now I'm my natural colour again.

PAM: I'll probably dye my hair when I'm older – when I start going grey. I'm sure lots of middle-aged women do. Won't you, Jenny?

JENNY: Mm ... I'm not sure. It looks so artificial. You can always tell when someone's hair isn't natural ... no, I probably won't have mine dyed.

Part Two.

LUCY: I've decided to have a tattoo.

JENNY: Lucy! You must be joking! You'll regret it ... And your mum'll go crazy!

LUCY: Well ... maybe. But that's her problem. I've thought about it for a long time and now I'm sure I want one. Just a small one.

PAM: What sort of tattoo?

LUCY: I'm not sure at the moment ... maybe a butterfly. Something colourful, anyway.

PAM: Where are you going to have it?

LUCY: On my shoulder, I think. Or on my arm.

JENNY: Would you have yourself tattooed, Pam?

PAM: Well, ... it's possible. They can look quite good but they're so difficult to remove after you've got one.

JENNY: Well, there's one thing I'm certain about ... you're both mad!

EXERCISE 9

Divide the class into fours and ask one student in each group to copy the chart in the exercise into their notebooks. Make sure they write all the expressions from Exercise 6 in the chart. To demonstrate the task, ask a student *Would you dye your hair?* and elicit their answer (they should use one of the expressions from Exercise 8). Make sure the group secretary writes the student's name in the correct place in the chart. They then work in their groups and discuss how they would change their appearance. Monitor and correct any errors you hear with the language from Exercise 8.

WRITING EXERCISE 10

Ask the class to read the example text. The students stay in their groups of four and, using the information about themselves from the chart in Exercise 9, they write a similar text. They can then swap texts with another group to find out what the other students would or wouldn't do.

Extra practice

The students work in groups of four. Give each group a set of prompts like this: *do your homework tonight/watch television/get married/have children/travel abroad/live abroad/learn another foreign language/live in a palace/travel to the moon/meet the queen*, etc. The students place the prompts face down on the desk. The first student picks up a prompt and makes a sentence about their plans, e.g. *I'll definitely do my homework tonight*. The others let them keep the prompt if the response is grammatically correct and if they think the student is telling the truth. If not, the prompt is returned to the bottom of the pile, and the second student picks up the next prompt. The student who collects the most prompts 'wins'.

Short of time?

Exercise 5 can be omitted from this lesson. Exercise 10 can be done as homework as long as all the students have copied the chart.

A professional interest

Focus	FUNCTIONS
TOPIC	• Guessing
• Models and model agencies	• Making deductions
GRAMMAR	SKILLS
• *Must, can't, might, could + be*	• Listening: a monologue, sound sequences
	SPEECH PATTERNS
	• Running words together

📖 Documentary

LISTENING EXERCISE 1

Direct the class to the pictures in the Students' Book. The students discuss the questions in pairs. If you wish, discuss as a class.

KEY

1 It is given to prospective models by people who work for the Elite agency.
2 They are models.
3 open answers

EXERCISE 2

The aim of this exercise is to pre-teach some vocabulary that the students will need for the listening in Exercises 3 and 4. Refer the class to the expressions and their definitions in the Students' Book. The students work in pairs to match them and use dictionaries to check any they are not sure of. Alternatively, if the students do not have access to dictionaries, ask them to match the ones they know, and then discuss the others as a class. Drill the phrases for correct pronunciation and, using the phrases, discuss as a class how people can become models. Write some of the students' ideas on the board. Leave them there for the next exercise.

KEY

1 f 2 g 3 b 4 e 5 d 6 a 7 h 8 c

📼 EXERCISE 3

Refer the class to the information and questions about Chris Owen and the model agency. Play the first part of the interview. Encourage the students to compare answers with their partner and then check as a class. Tick off the students' answers to Exercise 2 on the board.

KEY

1 They use a scouting programme. Each booker carries cards to give to people who may be suitable models. These contain information about present models and show that the agency is bona fide. The agency operates an open-door policy and all potential models have an expert assessment to see if they are suitable.
2 symmetrical features, height of about 5 ft 8 inches, nice eyes, nice mouth, a great personality and good professional attitude

TAPESCRIPT FOR EXERCISES 3 AND 5

CHRIS OWEN

We have a, quite a good scouting programme. A lot of the bookers will constantly, when they go home in the tube or, or if they're going away on holiday somewhere – you know, it's part of their job – and they look for a look that they think might or might not be worthwhile. This is a card that all the bookers take around with them – they keep it in their handbags. So, if they see a girl on the street that they think is particularly interesting, you know, they can take it out of their pocket or their purse (whatever it is). And it gives the would-be model a feeling of reasonable security that it is a bona fide

agency, with pictures of girls on and a telephone number that they can call afterwards. And that's just one of the little things that we use to help us scout.

And we have an open-door policy: I mean, if anyone wants to come in, they come in; we can assess them; they don't need an expensive portfolio; they don't need anything really but themselves, and perhaps their mother or father to reassure them. And they can come in and they'll have an expert assessment, basically. I can show you a book of a very new girl to give you an idea of the sort of pictures that come just from testing; and then gradually she'll start doing shots for *Looks* magazine, for example, *19*; young girl magazines. We look for a girl around 5ft 8, who's got symmetrical features – you know, nice eyes, nice mouth; and girls with great personalities as well; and, you know, good professional attitudes.

📼 EXERCISE 4

Refer the students to the exercise and establish that the information describes three models (Susie, Cathy and Joanna). Play the second part of the interview. Encourage students to compare answers in pairs and then check as a class.

KEY

Susie: b, c   Cathy: a, c, d   Joanna: b, e, f
The picture on the right shows Cathy.

TAPESCRIPT

This girl here, Cathy, is, is half-Chilean and half-English. And she was scouted in a, a shoe shop in, in the Kings Road – she was working there. And she has a very exotic Latin look. She's a very beautiful girl and again has a good personality. She's, you know … she's got a dark coffee skin, dark hair, and she looks great with her hair up – nice neck. She has a good profile, and photographers will like that. I mean, it creates a nice image, and I think that, you know, she is going to do very, very well, this girl, very nice.

This is another girl here, Joanna Rhodes, who's, was discovered in a model competition with *Company* magazine, and she's one of the top English models. I think a lot of English models don't necessarily look English. For example, Susie Big; she might be Spanish, she might be Italian, she might be, er, South American, you know, in fact, she's very English.

📼 EXERCISE 5

Ask the students to read the questions in the exercise and then play the first part of the interview again. You do not need to rewind the cassette to listen again; the first extract is repeated here. The students discuss their ideas in pairs and then discuss as a class. You may wish to omit question 4 if this is a sensitive subject with your students.

FOCUS ON FUNCTIONS EXERCISE 6

Direct the class to the picture of the two women in the Students' Book and discuss what country the students think the women could be from. Then ask two students to read out the dialogue in the exercise. Ask the class *Are the two speakers sure they know where the women come from?* (No) *So what are they doing?* (Guessing).

EXERCISE 7

Note: The students may have problems with the concept of *can't be* being the opposite of *must be*. They may try to use *mustn't be* instead of *can't be*, which is only used in dialects, not Standard English.

Copy the chart onto the board and refer the students back to the dialogue in Exercise 6. The students find the four verb phrases and write them in the appropriate column. They compare answers in pairs and then check as a class.

KEY

Possible: might be, could be
Certain (+): must be
Certain (-): can't be

EXERCISE 8

Refer the students to the picture in the Students' Book and use it to teach *horns* and *reindeer*. The students then use the four verb phrases from Exercise 7 to complete the dialogue. Encourage them to compare answers with their partner and then check as a class.

KEY

1 can't be   2 might be, could be   3 must be
4 could be, might be

📼 SPEECH PATTERNS EXERCISE 9

Copy the four sentences onto the board and ask the students to read the introduction to the exercise. Play the cassette once and discuss what happens to the end of the first word in each verb phrase (the final *t* or *d* is dropped). Use the board to highlight this. Then play the cassette again, stopping to allow the students to repeat.

KEY

a) *t* is not pronounced /'mʌsbɪ/
b) *d* is not pronounced /'kʊbɪ/
c) *t* is not pronounced /'maɪbɪ/
d) *t* is not pronounced and *n* sounds more like an *m* /'kɑːmbɪ/

📼 EXERCISE 10

Tell the students that they are going to hear three groups of sounds. After the first sound in each

one, they must guess where the place is, then try again after the other sounds. If necessary, direct the students to the expressions below the exercise. Play the first sound. Elicit the students' guesses. Do the same with the other sounds. Then tell them the correct answer. Repeat the procedure with the other two groups of sounds.

Alternatively, the students can do this exercise in teams. Play the sounds in the same way but write each team's guesses on the board after each sound. When you tell them the correct answer, the team who guessed first gets 3 points, the team who guessed second gets 2 points and so on.

KEY

1 underground station   2 café   3 swimming pool

Extra practice

Bring in about ten objects and a large plastic bag. Divide the students into teams. Put the first object into the bag and allow each team to feel the object for three seconds. They then guess what they think it is using the language from Exercise 10. Award points for the correct guess. Do the same with all the objects.

Short of time?

If you wish, omit Exercise 5 from this lesson.

WRITING: Describing appearances

Focus	
TOPICS	SKILLS
• Unusual models	• Reading: an article
• Ordinary people	• Writing: descriptions of people
• Ideas of beauty	VOCABULARY DEVELOPMENT
	• Compound adjectives and prepositional phrases

READING EXERCISE 1

Direct the students to the pictures and the questions in the Students' Book. They discuss in pairs or as a class. Do not check answers until students have done Exercise 2.

KEY

1 D, E and F are professional models.
2 – 4 open answers

EXERCISE 2

The students read the article to check their answers to question 3 in Exercise 1. Check as a class.

EXERCISE 3

Refer the students to the questions and the article. They read it again more carefully. Encourage the students to compare answers in pairs and then check as a class.

KEY

1 False. Some models can be ordinary looking.
2 False. In the world of fashion modelling, ordinary people look out of place.
3 False. They get more work than ugly women.
4 True.
5 False. There is an agency offering models that look like real people.

COMPARING CULTURES EXERCISE 4

The students can discuss the exercise in pairs or as a class.

DEVELOPING VOCABULARY EXERCISE 5

Copy the first chart onto the board. Ask the students to close their Students' Books and then copy the chart into their notebooks. To check that the students understand the headings in the chart, ask *Where does 'short' go?* Elicit their answer and write *short* under the correct heading on the board. Do the same with *ordinary-looking* and *with broken teeth*. Then direct the students back to the article and ask them to complete the chart with words and phrases taken from it. Monitor and help. Elicit their answers and complete the chart on the board. Drill the vocabulary as necessary.

Next, to revise the different ways compound adjectives are formed, copy the following onto the board:

ONE-WORD ADJECTIVES:
(ADJECTIVE) + NOUN + -ED:
ADJECTIVE + PRESENT PARTICIPLE:
ADVERB + PAST PARTICIPLE:
PREPOSITIONAL PHRASES:

Refer the students to their chart from question 1 and elicit the examples of the adjectives. Write some of them next to the headings on the board with the students' help. Highlight the form:

one-word adjectives: ordinary, ugly, short, etc.
(adjective) + noun + -ed (past participle): e.g. sun-bleach*ed*, muscle-*bound*
adjective + present participle: unusual-look*ing*, strange-look*ing*
adverb + past participle: e.g. well-oil*ed*
prepositional phrases: with broken teeth, with perfect skin, etc.

Next, direct the students to the second chart. If you wish, they can copy it into their notebooks. They then work in pairs and think of other phrases that describe ordinary people and fashion models. If they find the exercise difficult, you can refer them to the adjectives on page 72, Exercise 4, and brainstorm others that they know and write them on the board. Monitor and help. Elicit their ideas and write them on the board next to the headings.

KEY

1

	ONE-WORD ADJECTIVES	COMPOUND ADJECTIVES	PREPOSITIONAL PHRASES
Real people & UGLY models	ordinary, ugly, short, fat, tall, thin, dull	unusual-looking strange-looking	
Fashion models	slim, beautiful	sun-bleached well-oiled muscle-bound	with perfect skin with perfect teeth

2

	ORDINARY PEOPLE	FASHION MODELS
One-word adjectives	plump, pretty, skinny	elegant, stunning
Compound adjectives: a) adjective + noun + -ed	old-fashioned greasy-haired	lightly-tanned smooth-skinned golden-haired
b) adjective + present participle	dull-looking easy-going	good-looking fun-loving
c) adverb + past participle	badly-groomed	well-dressed
Prepositional phrases	with greasy hair with crooked teeth with large ears	with manicured nails with translucent skin

WRITING EXERCISE 6

This is a writing activity with four stages. First, divide the students into pairs. Write on the board *A man stood on the platform* and ask the students to visualise the person and situation. Then they discuss their ideas with their partner. Highlight the different points in the sentence where words and phrases can be added, using the example on the board, e.g.

ADJ. PREP. PHR. ADV. ADJ.
a ⟋ man ⟋ stood ⟋ on the ⟋ platform.
(PREP. PHR. = prepositional phrase)

Elicit possibilities from the students, or use the expanded sentence from the Students' Book to illustrate. You could point out that some adverbs and phrases can be placed at the beginning and/or end of the sentence. Ask one student to describe his/her 'picture' of the situation and expand the sentence on the board again as a class. Ask the students to add some descriptive phrases to the sentence but make sure they only write one sentence. Follow the same procedures with the other two sentences in question 1. Monitor and help but do not get class feedback.

Then do the same with the personality/state of mind of each person (question 2) and the situation (question 3). Next, organise the students to work with a different partner. They exchange their three sentences and discuss how they could change or add to their description. Finally, direct them to the instructions for question 5. Monitor and help while they write their description.

EXERCISE 7

As a class, discuss the kinds of mistakes that can occur in writing. With the students' help, write them on the board, e.g. *grammar, vocabulary, linking words, spelling, punctuation, organisation.* Next, the students exchange their writing from Exercise 6 with their partner. Encourage them to check each other's work using the headings on the board. Then they read their descriptions to the whole class. If you have a large class, they can read their descriptions in groups of four.

Short of time?

Exercise 6, question 5 could be done as homework and Exercise 7 would then be omitted. Exercise 4 can be omitted.

Progress check: Units 8–9

GRAMMAR AND FUNCTIONS

EXERCISE 1
1 looks   2 looks like   3 looks   4 looks like
5 looks   6 don't look

EXERCISE 2
1 must be   2 could be, might be
3 could be, might be   4 can't be

EXERCISE 3
1 has been living   2 for   3 has been trying
4 has already had   5 have been   6 has finished   7 for

8 have been doing   9 since   10 haven't achieved
11 Since   12 has been learning

EXERCISE 4
1 She'd like to work in films.
2 She's always wanted to work in films.
3 Her ambition is to work in films.

EXERCISE 5
1 No, I'm not sure. No, it's not definite.
2 Yes, almost certainly. Yes, probably.
3 Yes, maybe. Yes, it's possible.

Vocabulary

EXERCISE 6
Suggested answers:
a) clean, interesting, serious, smart, fit, relaxed, sensitive
b) dirty, scruffy, immature, crazy, aggressive, forgetful, rebellious, untidy
c) boring, clean-shaven, bald-headed, unshaven, good-looking, old-fashioned, fun-loving, rich

10 *Showtime*

Story-telling

Focus	SKILLS
TOPIC • Puppets GRAMMAR • *Be able* + *to* + infinitive • *Manage* + *to* + infinitive FUNCTIONS • Talking about achievement	• Reading: an informative text • Speaking: considering possibilities VOCABULARY DEVELOPMENT • Related words

COMPARING CULTURES EXERCISE 1
Direct the class to the pictures and questions. The students discuss the exercise as a class or in pairs. Do not check answers to question 1 yet.

READING EXERCISES 2 AND 3
Note: *Punch and Judy* is pronounced /ˈpʌntʃənˈdʒuːdɪ/, *Tchantchès* /ˈtʃænˈtʃez/ and *wayang kulit* /ˈwaɪˈjæŋkʊlɪt/.

Draw the outline of this grid on the board, without the answers:

	COUNTRY	NAMES OF PUPPETS	MADE OF
Picture A	Britain	Punch, Judy, Toby the dog, etc.	wood/cloth
Picture B	Indonesia (Java)	——	leather
Picture C	Belgium	Tchantchès	wood

Ask the students to read the text to check their answers to question 1 in Exercise 1 and to complete the grid. Encourage them to compare answers with their partner. Then check as a class. Next, direct the class to the questions in Exercise 3 and follow the same procedure. You may wish to check that the students understand *audience* before they read the text a second time.

KEY FOR EXERCISES 1 AND 2

See grid above.

KEY FOR EXERCISE 3

1 a) puppets from Belgium
  b) puppets from Britain and Java
2 Punch and Judy shows are about 30 minutes.
  Wayang kulit shows can last all night.
3 Tchantchès and Mr Punch
4 open answers

EXERCISE 4

Write 1–6 on the board and tell the students to read the third paragraph to find the six adjectives in the exercise. Encourage the class to check answers in pairs. Then elicit the adjectives and write them on the board. Mark the stress and then drill for correct pronunciation.

KEY

1 'lazy   2 'greedy   3 'simple   4 warm'hearted
5 'quarrelsome /'kwɒrəlsəm/   6 'tender

DEVELOPING VOCABULARY EXERCISE 5

Copy the two grids in the Students' Book onto the board and ask the students to copy them into their notebooks. To demonstrate the task, direct the class to the first paragraph of the text and ask students to find the adjective from *tradition*, Write *traditional* on the board and mark the stress. The students then work in pairs and do the same. Elicit their answers, write them on the board with the correct stress and drill as necessary.

KEY

NOUN	ADJECTIVE		VERB	NOUN
tra'dition	tra'ditional		enter'tain	enter'tainment
wood	'wooden		'vary	vari'ation
'basis	'basic		'argue	'argument
'comedy	'comic		per'form	per'formance
'quarrel	'quarrelsome			
'history	hi'storical			
re'ligion	re'ligous			

DISCOVERING LANGUAGE EXERCISE 6

Copy the three extracts in the exercise onto the board and direct the students to the questions, which they discuss in pairs. Elicit their answers and use the board to highlight the structures.

KEY

1 can
2 *to* + infinitive (*to raise/ to see/ to tell*)
3 . . . the puppeteers *are able to raise* the arms and legs . . .
4 *Will* people *be able to see* the traditional characters for many more years? People *won't be able to see* the traditional characters for many more years.
5 *Does* he *manage to tell* a long and complex story without a script? He *doesn't manage to tell* a long and complex story without a script.
6 She *managed to solve* the problem.
  Manage + to + infinitive is used to talk about possibility or ability when it is difficult to do something.

EXERCISE 7

Direct the class to the sentences in the exercise and ask the students to complete the gaps with *be able* or *manage*. Encourage them to compare answers with their partner and then check as a class.

KEY

1 managed, were able, manages
2 Will you be able, won't be able
3 managed, weren't able

SPEAKING EXERCISE 8

Ask the students to read the instructions for the exercise and use the board to brainstorm their ideas of where they could go. Divide the class into pairs and ask two students to read the example exchange. Establish that *We could . . .* is being used to make a suggestion. The students then role play similar conversations. Monitor and note down any errors you hear with the language from Exercise 6. For feedback, volunteer pairs can role play parts of their conversations for the whole class. Finally, use the board to correct any errors you heard.

Extra practice

Give each student a slip with a prompt on it, like this:

– *We wanted to see the film but it was sold out.*
– *I climbed the hill but it was difficult.*
– *Children can't walk at six months.*
– *I'd like to meet you tomorrow but I've got too much work.*

The students mingle and say their prompt to another student who has to 'transform' it using the language in Exercise 6, e.g. *We weren't able to see the film. I managed to climb the hill*, etc.

Short of time?

Exercises 4, 5 and 7 can be done for homework.

Stages

> **Focus**
>
> TOPIC
> • Theatre
>
> GRAMMAR
> • *Can* and *could*
>
> FUNCTIONS
> • Making requests
> • Expressing ability
>
> • Expressing possibility
> • Giving permission
> • Talking about prohibition
> • Making deductions
>
> SKILLS
> • Listening: an interview
> • Reading: a literary extract
> • Speaking: role play

GETTING STARTED EXERCISE 1

To introduce the exercise, ask the students *Do you ever go to the theatre? What kinds of show have you seen?* and elicit the different types of show. Write them on the board and drill for correct pronunciation. Then direct the class to the types of show in question 1 and compare them to the students' list. The class then discusses questions 2 and 3 in pairs. Elicit the students' answers and write their ideas for question 3 on the board. Leave the language there for Exercise 3.

KEY

1 open answers
2 stage – 6   curtain – 2   stalls – 5   box – 4
   dress circle – 3   upper circle – 1
3 Open answers, but should include phrases like *Can I help you? I'd like two tickets in the stalls ... Which performance ...?*

🖹 Documentary

🔲 LISTENING EXERCISE 2

Refer the class to the questions about the Old Vic

and check the meaning of *live* (adj /laɪv/). Play both parts of the interview. Encourage the students to compare answers with their partner and then check as a class.

KEY

1 It's the oldest theatre in London.
2 1818
3 Queen Victoria
4 48 (major theatres)
5 television; spectacle – outdoor concerts, rock and pop music
6 yes

TAPESCRIPT

ANDREW LEIGH
Part One.
The Old Vic is a theatre, and it's the oldest theatre in London. It was built in 1818. It was called the Old Vic because it was originally the Royal Victoria Theatre – after Queen Victoria, but popularly became known as the Vic, and then the Old Vic. Like most theatres, people sit in rows – in straight rows – facing the stage. And what we have here is the theatre divided into three levels: the stalls, the dress circle, and the upper circle.

Part Two.
There are about 48 major theatres in London with a broad mixture of presentations. Those theatres between them present anything from large-scale musicals – like *Les Miserables* or *Phantom of the Opera* or *Miss Saigon* – to small-scale plays, often new works by new writers. I think theatre styles change. We are, we have been, very influenced by television, for example, in the kind of drama we present and the way we present it. But in recent years we've become more influenced by spectacle, like outdoor concerts, for example, and the world of rock and pop music – all of this has influenced the way we do theatre; so there's now, at this time, an emphasis on spectacular theatre on a large scale. But, given those influences, I believe that the theatre will always – live theatre – will always have a place in ... as part of our British entertainment scene.

🔲 EXERCISE 3

Refer the class to the expressions from Exercise 1 on the board and the questions in the Students' Book. Play the conversation. Allow the students to compare answers and then check as a class. Add any new phrases to the list on the board from Exercise 1. Leave them there for Exercise 4.

KEY

2 this evening   3 two   4 the stalls   5 K14 and K15
6 £30   7 7.45

📼 EXERCISE 4

Write a) – e) on the board and refer the class to the exercise. Play the conversation again, stopping after 'Can I help?'. Elicit which prompt it is for and write *Can I help?* next to a) on the board. Then play the complete conversation. Encourage the students to compare answers in pairs and then check as a class. Elicit the students' answers and write them on the board. Next, refer them to the list of phrases on the board from Exercise 3. Discuss other expressions for saying the same functions. Write them on the board if you wish.

KEY

a) Can I help?
b) Do you have any tickets available for tonight's performance?
c) How many was it for?
d) Yes, that's fine, thanks.
e) It starts 7.45 this evening.

Suggestions for other expressions:

a) Are you being served? Can I help you?
b) I'd like two tickets for ...? Are there any tickets left for ...? Have you got any tickets for ...?
c) How many (tickets) would you like?
d) They're fine, thanks. Yes, I'll take those, thanks.
e) The performance is at 7.45. The curtain rises at 7.45.

TAPESCRIPT

WOMAN: Hello.
TICKET CLERK: Hello, Can I help?
WOMAN: Yes, do you have any tickets available for tonight's performance?
CLERK: Yes, we have: stalls or dress circle, £30 each. How many was it for?
WOMAN: Just two, thanks.
CLERK: Two tickets. I can do two in the stalls: row K, 14 and 15 – that's eight rows back.
WOMAN: Yes, that's fine, thanks, yeah.
CLERK: Two £30 tickets ... that's £60. Thank you.
WOMAN: Thank you.
CLERK: It starts 7.45 this evening.
WOMAN: OK then. Thanks very much. Bye.

📼 EXERCISE 5

Tell the students that they are going to listen to a conversation at another theatre booking office and that they must decide how it is different. Play the conversation and discuss as a class.

KEY

The ticket clerk is impolite. She is irritated by the interruption. The man is also rude. Both use very direct language.

TAPESCRIPT

TICKET CLERK: Yes?
MAN: I want some tickets for tonight.
CLERK: How many? They're £30 each ...
MAN: Two.
CLERK: That's £60.
MAN: Here.
CLERK: Tickets. 7.45. Don't be late.

SPEAKING EXERCISE 6

Divide the students into pairs and direct the As (customers) to the instructions on page 83 and the Bs (ticket clerks) to page 128. Check that the students know who they are and what they want, and establish that they should be polite with each other, using the language from Exercise 4. They then role play their conversations. Make sure they change roles. Monitor and note any errors you hear. If you wish, volunteer pairs can role play their conversations for the whole class. Finally, use the board to correct any errors you heard.

FOCUS ON FUNCTIONS EXERCISES 7 AND 8

Direct the students to the sentences and functions. Match the first one as a class to demonstrate the task. The students then work in pairs to do question 1. Check their answers as a class. Then the students discuss question 2 in pairs or as a class. If you wish, when you check their answers, ask *Which sentences can you add a time phrase to to show it's in the past?* The students quickly discuss their answers in pairs and then check as a class. Follow the same procedure for Exercise 8.

KEY FOR EXERCISE 7

1 a) ability   b) possibility   c) prohibition   d) request
  e) permission   f) deduction
2 All the sentences have the same function. Sentence D is more polite with *could*.
  a, b, c, e are now in the past:
  a) My brother, the actor, could learn lines quickly *when he was younger.*
  b) I'm sorry, I couldn't meet you after work *yesterday.*
  c) She's under eighteen, so she couldn't see the film *at the weekend.*
  e) *In the 1980s,* at eighteen we could see any film at the cinema.

KEY FOR EXERCISE 8

Can is not used to describe a future ability.
Could is not used to describe a single opportunity/possibility in the past. However, *couldn't* is used to describe a single possibility in the past.

EXERCISE 9

Refer the students to the eight sentences in the exercise and the functions in Exercise 7. First, in pairs they decide the function of each of the eight sentences. Check as a class. Then students use the different forms in Exercise 8 to complete the sentences. Encourage them to compare answers with their partner and then check as a class.

KEY

1 possibility – couldn't/weren't able to get
2 ability – could/were able to speak
3 permission – can
4 ability – will be able to use
5 possibility – couldn't/wasn't able to
6 possibility – was able to get
7 request – can/could
8 possibility – couldn't/weren't able to/were able to get

READING: A LITERARY EXTRACT EXERCISE 10

To introduce the extract, first brainstorm what the class knows about William Shakespeare (e.g. 16th century poet/playwright) and ask the students to name some of his plays. They can then check their ideas with the information about him under the text. Then write the question *What comparison is he making?* on the board and ask the students to read the text. Encourage them to discuss their ideas in pairs and then discuss as a class. Next, the students discuss question 2 in pairs or as a class. For question 3, explain the task and write the example for the first line on the board. The students then work in pairs and rewrite the speech in their own words. For feedback, elicit their ideas and write a model speech on the board with the students' help. Finally, they discuss question 4 in pairs or as a class.

KEY

1 Shakespeare is comparing a person's life to a play performed on a stage.
2 *Man* and *his* refer to a human being.
3 And all the men and women are just actors:
   They are all born and they all die;
   And one person in their lifetime has many different roles;
   Their life consists of seven periods.
   Note: *Their* is used here to replace *his*. It is becoming increasingly common to avoid the use of *his/her* if possible and to use the impersonal pronoun *their* instead.
4 open answers
   Shakespeare's seven stages are the infant; the school child; the lover; the soldier; the lawyer; the small, old man; the very old man who has lost everything (e.g.

his teeth, his sight, his taste, his mind, his hearing, etc.).

Short of time?

If you wish, you can omit Exercise 5 from this lesson.

WRITING: Giving opinions

Focus	
TOPICS	SKILLS
• Circuses	• Reading: an article, a letter
• Animal performers	• Listening: monologues
FUNCTIONS	• Speaking: discussion
• Giving opinions	• Writing: a letter
	VOCABULARY DEVELOPMENT
	• Negative prefixes
	SPEECH PATTERNS
	• Using stress to show disagreement

GETTING STARTED EXERCISE 1

To introduce the topic, find out if the students have been to a circus and discuss the types of performer they saw. If you wish, write them on the board. Then direct the class to the list of circus performers in question 1 and see if they are the same. Next, draw this grid on the board:

a) INTRODUCE THE ACTS	b) MAKE PEOPLE LAUGH	c) DO DANGEROUS STUNTS

The students work in pairs and categorise the performers under the different headings. They then discuss question 2 in pairs. Discuss their answers as a class.

KEY

1 a) ringmasters b) clowns c) acrobats, lion tamers, fire eaters, human cannonballs
2 Open answers, but likely to be horses, big cats and elephants, and perhaps sea animals, such as seals.

READING EXERCISE 2

Direct the class to the picture and questions in the Students' Book. The students discuss the exercise in pairs or as a class. Get feedback but do not confirm their answers yet.

EXERCISE 3

The students read the text to check their answers to Exercise 2. Check as a class.

KEY

1 Because he likes them.
2 Yes, it is.

3 They live in small cages – the conditions are not natural for them.
4 They live longer in a circus.
5 Because the animals wouldn't normally do such circus acts in the wild.

EXERCISE 4
Refer the students to the questions and the text. Encourage them to compare answers in pairs and then check as a class. Drill any new vocabulary for correct pronunciation as necessary.

KEY
1 a) lion, tiger, panther, leopard /ˈlepəd/, puma /ˈpjuːmə/
   b) seals, dolphins, sharks
   c) wounds /wuːnz/   d) a cage
2 a) to tame   b) mauled /mɔːld/   c) tickled

DEVELOPING VOCABULARY EXERCISE 5
Note: The six prefixes have the meaning of *not*: *ir-* is used with adjectives which begin with *r*, e.g. *irregular*, *il-* is used with adjectives that begin with *l*, e.g. *illegal* and *im-* is used with some adjectives that begin with *p-*, e.g. *impossible* and with *m*, e.g. *immoral*.

Write *not satisfied* on the board and ask *What can you say instead of 'not'?* Elicit *dis-*. Do the same with *natural* and establish that *dis-* and *un-* are called prefixes. Next, copy the chart onto the board and ask the students to copy it into their notebooks. Use *natural* and *satisfied* to demonstrate the task and establish that all six prefixes have the meaning of *not*. The students work in pairs and complete their charts. Elicit their answers and complete the chart on the board. Drill for correct pronunciation as necessary.

KEY

UN-	unnatural unusual unpleasant unkind	DIS-	dissatisfied dishonest
IN-	insensitive incorrect	IM-	impractical impossible impatient immoral
IR-	irregular irrational	IL-	illegal illogical

READING EXERCISE 6
Direct the students to the letter from Mr Andrews and the questions. They read the letter and answer the questions. Encourage them to compare answers in pairs and then check as a class.

KEY
1 Because a circus is visiting the town and Mr Andrews objects to the use of animals in circuses.
2 a) paragraph 4: Why don't circuses provide . . .? Let's leave
   b) paragraph 2: I feel that, in my opinion, I believe, I am sure

🔊 LISTENING EXERCISE 7
Direct the students to the questions in the exercise. Play the three monologues. Encourage the class to compare answers in pairs. If necessary, play the cassette again and then check as a class.

KEY
1 Speaker 3.
2 Speaker 1 thinks that only domestic animals should be used.
   Speaker 2 thinks that you can't have a circus without animals and that they like performing. They should be well looked after.
3 Speaker 1: Only domesticated animals should be used: people are now used to seeing wild animals on television. Wild animals shouldn't be taken from their natural world. They shouldn't be kept in cages, as it is unkind.
   Speaker 2: You can't have a circus without animals: the animals should be well cared for with big enough cages and plenty of exercise. Animals like to play. Animals have been performing in circuses for hundreds of years.
   Speaker 3: Animals shouldn't be used in circuses at all: you shouldn't keep them in cages. It's wrong to make them perform acts which they don't do naturally in the wild. People don't like to see animals humiliated.

TAPESCRIPT
One.
Circuses are traditional. They've been around for hundreds of years and I'd hate to see them disappear. But they have to change with the times. People used to like seeing wild animals there . . . perhaps because they'd never seen them before . . . I mean before television, and before foreign travel was popular. But some of those animals – the tigers and the lions . . . and even the zebra . . . their numbers are so small in the natural world that we shouldn't take them away from it and put them in circuses for our pleasure. Of course, we're also more aware of cruelty these days, and keeping large animals in cages all their lives is unkind.

But I'm not worried about domestic animals in circuses – certainly dogs and horses are OK. They don't need to be kept in cages all the time and if they're not asked to do dangerous tricks, I don't see the problem. We could make a law banning wild animals from circuses, but let's keep some animals.

Two.

I really don't agree. As far as *I'm* concerned, this protest is all a lot of rubbish! I loved the circus when I was younger . . . and animals are part of the circus tradition. You just can't have a circus without animals – it wouldn't be a circus. By all means, let's make sure that the animals have cages that are big enough . . . and proper exercise . . . and that they're well looked after. I don't see what the problem is about performing. I mean, all animals like to play, and when you're at the circus you can see they enjoy it . . . or at least they don't find it unpleasant. Why don't people just leave circuses alone and let them go on as they have been for the last two hundred years?

Three.

I think it's awful . . . the whole thing. In *my* opinion, any use of animals that involves keeping them in cages is wrong. And then to get them to do things that they never do naturally . . . like lions standing up on their back legs . . . or seals clapping their flippers together . . . I find the whole thing disgusting. I think all circuses with performing animals – even dogs . . . or birds – should be banned. I don't believe most people like to see animals humiliated. It's unnatural and completely inexcusable. Why don't we just leave them alone to get on with their lives? Surely circuses can come up with entertaining shows without this kind of exploitation?

🔲 SPEECH PATTERNS EXERCISE 8

Write the three expressions on the board and decide as a class or in pairs where the main stress is. Play the cassette, stopping to check the students' answers. Establish why the stress is on the pronoun (because you are showing that you disagree with someone else's opinion). Play the expressions again for the students to repeat them.

KEY AND TAPESCRIPT

I think . . . In *my* opinion . . . As far as *I'm* concerned . . .

SPEAKING EXERCISE 9

Divide the students into groups and remind them of the adjectives and expressions in Exercises 5 and 8. They discuss their opinions on having wild animals in circuses, in zoos, or as pets. Monitor and note down any errors you hear and use the board to correct them at the end of the activity.

WRITING EXERCISE 10

Refer the class back to the letter from Mr Andrews in Exercise 6 as a model. The students can write the letter individually or in their groups from Exercise 9. Monitor and help. If you wish, they can exchange letters to check for errors.

Short of time?

Exercise 10 can be done as homework. Exercise 4 can be omitted.

Talkback

Picture clues

This fluency activity is likely to practise the language of speculation.

1 Divide the class into groups and direct the students to pictures A – C. Tell them that they are going to listen to some people playing a game and that they must write down the rules of the game. Play the cassette and ask the students to compare their rules in pairs. Then check as a class and write the rules on the board if you wish.

KEY

There are four people in a team. One person draws a phrase (they have been given) and the other three have to guess the phrase, title of a book, etc. The person drawing the picture can only say *yes* or *no*. When they have guessed correctly, the person who gave the correct answer runs to get the next phrase, and then draws it. The team which wins is the one which guesses all the phrases first.

TAPESCRIPT

PRESENTER: Listen to people playing a game. Picture A.

WOMAN A: What's that? It looks like a potato or something . . . is it a vegetable?

MAN A: No . . . it's . . .

WOMAN A: Hey! Hey! You mustn't say any more!

WOMAN B: Oh look . . . it's got eyes . . . yes, they're definitely eyes. It must be someone's face.

MAN A: Yes.

MAN B: I know . . . it's a famous person! A man . . .

MAN A: No.

PRESENTER: Listen again. Picture B.

WOMAN B: What are those things coming out of his eyes? Is he crying?

MAN A: No . . . oh . . .

WOMAN B: They could be glasses . . .

WOMAN A: No, no, no . . . they're arrows . . .

MAN A: Yes . . . come on . . . oh, sorry.

WOMAN A: He's, he's looking in a particular direction . . .

MAN A: Yes . . . yes . . .

MAN B: Looking . . . is that one of the words?

MAN A: Er…yes…

PRESENTER: Listen again. Picture C.

WOMAN B: What's that? It looks like a picture …

MAN A: No.

WOMAN A: It's a book … Looking, … looking … book. I know. I've got it.

MAN B: What is it then?

WOMAN A: It's *Look Ahead*!

MAN A: Yes, that's it! Well done. Your turn. Quick! Go and get the next one!

WOMAN A: Oh, OK.

2 Direct the class to pictures D and E and the phrases in the exercise. In pairs, students discuss which phrases they illustrate. Then check as a class.

KEY

D – radio station   E – fashion designer

3 In pairs, the students discuss how they could draw one of the other phrases in stage 2. If you wish, the pairs can draw their pictures on the board.

4 Choose five phrases from those below for the students to draw, and write them on separate slips of paper. Make sure you have a set for each team. Divide the class into teams of four or five. One member from each team comes to get the first phrase from you and then the students play the game following the rules.
Phrases you could use include: street market, TV addict, nightmare, snack bar, seat belt, home-made cake, terraced house, caravan park, rock face, open sea, border post.

11 *Looking forward*

Energy

Focus	
TOPICS • Energy sources • Life in the future **GRAMMAR** • *Will* + (adverb) + infinitive • *Going to* + infinitive • *May/might* + infinitive **FUNCTIONS** • Making decisions, promises, predictions • Expressing plans and intentions • Talking about possibilities	**SKILLS** • Speaking: negotiating • Listening: an interview, brief comments • Writing: sentences justifying a decision • Reading: a literary extract

GETTING STARTED EXERCISE 1

Write A – H on the board and direct the class to the pictures in the Students' Book. Ask the students *What kind of energy is used to run a car?* Elicit *petrol* and write it on the board. Students then match the forms of energy with the pictures. Elicit the students' answers and write them on the board. Drill for correct pronunciation as necessary. If you wish, discuss which forms of energy are most common in their country/ countries. If you have a multinational class, the students can discuss this in groups.

Next, check that the students understand *fossil fuels*, *alternative energy*, *renewable* and *non-renewable*: ask questions such as *Which come from things that were living many years ago? Which are in the ground? Can you use it again? How many times can you use it?* Write these headings on the board:

FOSSIL FUELS	ALTERNATIVE ENERGY SOURCES	RENEWABLE	NON-RENEWABLE

Ask the students to copy them into their notebooks. To demonstrate the task, ask *Where can you put petrol?* and write *petrol* in the correct columns on the board, i.e. FOSSIL and NON-RENEWABLE. The students then work in pairs and categorise the sources of energy. Elicit their answers as a class and write them on the board.

KEY

1 solar power – A   coal – G   gas – H
wind power – C   nuclear energy – B   wood – F
petrol – D   hydroelectric power – E

2 and 3

FOSSIL FUELS	ALTERNATIVE ENERGY SOURCES	RENEWABLE	NON-RENEWABLE
coal	solar power	solar power	coal
gas	wind power	wind power	gas
wood	nuclear energy	wave power	wood
petrol	wave power	nuclear energy	petrol

Documentary

LISTENING EXERCISE 2

Direct the class to the pictures and questions. The students discuss the exercise as a class or in pairs. Do not confirm their answers yet.

EXERCISE 3

Play the interview once for the students to check their ideas from Exercise 2. Then direct the students to the four questions and play the interview again. Encourage them to compare answers in pairs and then check as a class.

KEY FOR EXERCISE 2

1 It's a plant for producing electricity.
2 Solar power: the manufacturing of electricity by using sunlight.

KEY FOR EXERCISE 3

1 He provides electricity for the city of Austin in Texas.
2 Photo = light, voltaic = of electricity. It means using sunlight to make electricity.
3 100 – 150 homes
4 We will use fewer non-renewable forms of energy (coal, gas) and more renewable ones e.g. wind power.

Note: If any students are still unsure of the meaning of photovoltaics, ask them to find an expression in Exercise 1 with the same meaning (solar power).

TAPESCRIPT

KEVIN: People who work in the energy industry – making electricity – have to look into the future to predict our needs. Especially people who work in 'alternative energy' – people who look for new ways of making electricity, such as photovoltaics. The man to explain photovoltaics and look into the future is John Hoffner. His job is to provide electricity for the city of Austin in Texas. So what exactly does 'photovoltaics' mean?

JOHN: Photovoltaics simply means converting light into electricity. 'Photo' means 'light' and 'voltaic' means 'of electricity'. So the simple definition is that it converts sunlight to electricity. We in Austin have the second largest photovoltaic plant in the United States. That plant is about 300 kilowatts in size; that's enough electricity for about 100 to 150 homes in Austin.

KEVIN: What will our sources of energy be fifty years from now?

JOHN: Fifty years from now we will see a completely different energy picture: a lot less reliance on traditional forms of electricity such as coal and natural gas and oil, and a lot more reliance on renewable energies such as photovoltaics, wind and hydro power.

EXERCISE 4

Direct the class to the four words in the exercise and play the interview again. The students discuss their ideas in pairs and then check as a class. If there is disagreement about the meanings of the words, play the relevant part of the interview again to check the answer.

KEY

a) to describe something that will happen in the future

based on present knowledge or experience
b) to change from one form/state into a different one
c) a factory or other place where an industrial process is carried out
d) dependence on something

🔊 FOCUS ON FUNCTIONS EXERCISE 5

Direct the class to question 1 and play the short extract. Decide as a class what *will* is used for in the extract. Then the students discuss question 2 in pairs. Elicit their answers and write an example affirmative and negative statement under each heading on the board. Then the students discuss question 3 in pairs. Elicit the two different uses of *going to*.

KEY

1 c
2 Suggested examples:
   a) decision: I'll take the job./I won't take the job.
   b) promise: I'll phone tomorrow./I won't be late.
   c) prediction: It'll be cold tonight./It won't snow today.
3 To make a prediction based on clear present evidence. (first example)
   To state an intention, something which is already decided/planned. (second example)

TAPESCRIPT

KEVIN: What will our sources of energy be fifty years from now?

JOHN: Fifty years from now we will see a completely different energy picture.

🔊 DISCOVERING LANGUAGE EXERCISE 6

Direct the class to question 1. Play the cassette and elicit answers as a class. The students then discuss questions 2 and 3 in pairs. Check as a class. Highlight the form (see Key).

KEY

1 a 3   b 2   c 1
2 & 3 certain: will definitely + infinitive without *to*
        probable: I think ... will + infinitive without *to*
        possible: may/might + infinitive without *to*

TAPESCRIPT

One.
I think we may come back to nuclear power. Perhaps it's dangerous at the moment but scientists might be able to design ways of making nuclear power stations safer in the future.
Two.
I think we'll have to change the way we live soon – unless they find far more sources of oil and gas.
Three.
You and I ... all of us ... we know that fossil fuels will

definitely run out in twenty, thirty years. But we do nothing about it.

EXERCISE 7
Direct the class to the exercise and organise the students into groups of three or four. They discuss the questions. For question 3, you may wish to write prompts on the board to guide their discussion, e.g. food, climate, jobs/lifestyle, houses, animals, technology, transport, illness and population. Monitor and make a note of any errors with the language from Exercise 6. Use the board to correct the students at the end of the activity. Groups can report back to the class, if you wish.

READING: A LITERARY EXTRACT EXERCISE 8
Background note
Ben Elton (1962 –) is one of the most famous alternative comedians in the UK. He writes satirical plays and novels, and has also acted in productions of his books.

Find out if the students have heard of Ben Elton and direct them to the footnote about him at the end of the text. Then refer the class to the three questions and ask the students to read the text. Encourage them to compare answers in pairs and then check as a class.

KEY
1 a) He thinks people are irresponsible and they do not think of the future.
   b) Politicians are only concerned with staying in power and finding short-term solutions.
2 The earth will die.
3 No, she doesn't. She calls his idea 'a pathetic generalisation'.
Note: *Man* is used in the first paragraph of the extract to refer to the human race/human beings. To check that the students understand this use of *man*, ask them to work in pairs and rewrite the first paragraph without using *man* and *he*. Elicit their answers and write a model paragraph on the board with the students' help.

SUGGESTED KEY
It's always been dying, ever since *the human race* began to take from it more than *it* needed. I tell you, Rosalie, Earth as we know it is finished, because *human beings* rule it and *they* are incapable of acting responsibly! Of thinking of anything other than the short-term.

SPEAKING EXERCISE 9
First, ask the students to make a list of all the equipment that uses electricity in the home. Ask them to compare lists in pairs and add any items. Then elicit their lists and write the items on the board. Next, explain that it is the year 2010 and that a new law has been announced and it's very serious. Read out the law. Divide the students into pairs and tell them that they share a house and must decide which four pieces of equipment to keep. Next, the pairs combine with another pair and agree a final list. The students stay in these groups for the next exercise.

WRITING EXERCISE 10
Direct the students to the example sentences in the Students' Book. In their groups of four, they write similar sentences justifying the items they have chosen. Monitor and help. If you wish, they can write their paragraph on a poster for the other students to read. Then discuss as a class which are the most popular items to keep and why.

Extra practice
This is a similar activity to Exercises 9 and 10 but this time the students choose items to put in a time capsule which will be opened in a hundred years. They work in groups of four and choose six items that they think will be important for people to see in a hundred years. Then each group tells the class their list, justifying their decisions by using the future tense, e.g. *We've chosen a video and television because they will show people in 100 years how we live today.* Alternatively, they can work with different groups and exchange ideas.

Short of time?
Exercise 8 can be omitted and Exercise 10 can be done for homework.

Survival

Focus	SKILLS
TOPIC • Life in a closed ecosystem GRAMMAR • Articles	• Reading: an article • Listening: a radio news item • Writing: a paragraph VOCABULARY DEVELOPMENT • The prefix *self-* • Compound adjectives (time and size)

GETTING STARTED EXERCISE 1
Direct the class to the picture and discuss as a class what they think the article is about. Write the students' ideas on the board but do not confirm them yet.

READING EXERCISE 2
Background note
Star Trek is a popular American science fiction television programme made in the 1960s and 70s. It is about the adventures of a space ship (the *Starship Enterprise)* and its crew. There are also several *Star Trek* films. The title of the article is a pun on the commentary which introduced every episode of the TV series. The narrator always says 'to boldly go where no man has gone before'. Here the pun is on *grow*, instead of *go*, and *glasshouse enterprise* rather than the name of the ship *Starship Enterprise.*

Point out the first line of the article and discuss as a class what the students know about *Star Trek.* They may be able to work out the pun in the title if they know the series. Then ask the class to read the text to compare their ideas from Exercise 1. Discuss as a class and tick the correct ideas on the board. Check that the students understand *acre* (/'eɪkə/ – a unit for measuring area) and *sponsor* /'spɒnsə/. Then ask the students to copy the headings in the exercise into their notebooks and to read the article again. Make sure they make notes. Encourage them to compare answers with their partner and then check as a class.

KEY

Location: the Arizona desert
Sponsor: Edward Bass, a multibillionaire from Texas
Cost: $150 million
Number of inhabitants: 4 men, 4 women, 3,800 plant and animal species
Duties: to plant, harvest and process their food on a farm and to conduct experiments
Aims: to establish a self-sufficient community which might be used in a spaceship or on another planet; it would be a self-sufficient 'world' floating in space
Criticisms of the project: Many scientists don't believe it will work because the only closed ecosystem which has survived more than a few days was smaller than a football and only contained shrimp and plant life. Mr Bass has also been criticised for wanting to make money rather than do serious scientific research because he opened the biosphere to the public before the experiment began, and hundreds of tourists paid to visit the place every day, all buying souvenirs.

EXERCISE 3
Divide the class into pairs and refer them back to their notes from Exercise 2. Ask students to close their books. Explain that they are each going to give a short talk on the project, using their notes.

First the As will give the talk and the Bs will help if necessary and then they change roles. Monitor and make a note of any errors you hear.

DEVELOPING VOCABULARY EXERCISE 4
Refer the class to paragraph 3 of the article and question 1 in the exercise. Elicit the students' answers and then discuss the meaning of the prefix *self-* (question 2). The students then discuss question 3 in pairs. Check as a class. Establish that *self-* can be followed by an adjective, a present participle, e.g. *self-locking*, or past participle, e.g. *self-taught* or a noun, e.g. *self-defence.* Finally, the students discuss question 4 in pairs. Check as a class.

KEY

1 a) Mr Bass himself (self-titled)
   b) the community itself (self-sustaining)
2 The subject does the 'action' itself, with no help from anybody else.
3 self-locking – the case locks itself
   self-taught – the expert taught him/herself
   self-defence – you can defend yourself
4 a) a self-cleaning oven   b) a self-employed woman
   c) a self-portrait
Note: The prefix *self-* can have two meanings, i.e. *a self-destruct mechanism* = a mechanism that destroys itself, but *a self-service restaurant* = a restaurant in which you serve yourself.

EXERCISE 5
Refer the students to question 1 and ask them to find the compound adjectives in paragraphs 1 and 3. Elicit their answers and write the adjectives on the board. Discuss question 2 as a class and highlight the form on the board (see Key). To demonstrate question 3, write *a guarantee for ten years* on the board and ask the class to make it into a compound adjective. Write *a ten-year guarantee* on the board. Check that the students understand *lease* then ask them to work in pairs and do the same with the other prompts. Check their answers as a class.

KEY

1 a) two-year (study)   b) half-acre (farm)
2 The form of a compound adjective using a time period or size is:

ARTICLE	+ NUMBER	+ -	+ TIME PERIOD/SIZE	+ NOUN
a	two	-	year	study
a	half	-	acre	farm

The time period is always singular, e.g. not a two-years study. The main stress falls on the number.

3 a) a two-metre high wall   b) a ten-day sale
   c) an eight-storey house   d) a hundred-year lease

Extra practice

Students work in pairs and make sentences about themselves using compound adjectives, e.g. *I've just read a 320-page book, I live in a one-storey house, I've got a ten-day holiday this year.* They then combine with two other pairs and pool their sentences. You can make this a team activity by awarding points to the groups with the most grammatically correct sentences.

DISCOVERING LANGUAGE EXERCISE 6

Write the two headings on the board like this:

THE PEOPLE IN BIOSPHERE 2 | BIOSPHERE 2

Refer the class to question 1 and ask the students to find all the words and phrases from the first paragraph in the text that refer to the two headings. Elicit their answers and write them on the board under the headings. Then do the same with the rest of the article. Encourage them to compare answers in pairs and then check as a class on the board. The students use the article and the examples on the board to discuss question 2 in pairs. Check as a class. Follow the same procedures with question 3.

KEY

1 a) four men and four women, the eight, the team, the crew members, Abigail Alling, a US marine biologist
   b) a giant hi-tech greenhouse, the $150 million structure, the so-called Biosphere 2, the seven-storey glass and metal structure
2 a) the people – no article, the biosphere – a/an
   b) the
   c) no article (but note the so-called Biosphere 2, where the article is needed because of the adjective)
3 The definite article is used when referring to information that is shared by the writer and reader. It is also used when there is only one of something, e.g. the Arizona desert.
   The indefinite article is used when information is introduced for the first time (a self-sustaining community) or when the noun belongs to a class of things (a US marine biologist).
   No article is used when talking about things generally rather than specifically. It applies to both countable (mainstream scientists) and uncountable nouns (algae).

With proper names, the definite article may be used or omitted depending on whether it is part of the name or not, e.g. *Star Trek*, The Tower of London.

EXERCISE 7

Write 1–12 on the board and direct the students to the text. First, ask them to read the text through once to understand the general idea. Then complete the first gap as a class and write the answer on the board next to 1. Encourage the students to compare answers in pairs and then check as a class. If the students are having problems, ask questions to check understanding, e.g. *Is it the first time X is mentioned? Has X been mentioned before? Is X mentioned generally or specifically? Do we know what X is?*

KEY

 1 the (specific – the only one)
 2 a (one of a group not mentioned before)
 3, 4, 5 no article (these items in general)
 6 the (refers back to Edward Bass)
 7 no article (general)
 8 a (first time mentioned)
 9 the (second time mentioned)
10 a (first time mentioned)
11 no article (in general)
12 the (refers back to cowboy boots)

LISTENING EXERCISES 8 AND 9

Tell the students that they are going to find out what happened to the Biosphere project. They discuss in pairs what they think and then discuss as a class. Copy these headings onto the board:

SUCCESSES | FAILURES

Ask students to make notes under the headings as they listen. Play the news item. Encourage the students to compare answers in pairs and then check as a class.

KEY

Successes: The people have lived in an enclosed system for 18 months longer than anyone else has done. They have managed to grow most of their food and to recycle their waste and water.
Failures: Oxygen had to be pumped into the system because the atmosphere was too thin and it was making the people ill. They did not manage to grow all their crops successfully, either.

TAPESCRIPT

BROADCASTER

Almost two years ago four men and four women sealed themselves into a giant greenhouse in the Arizona desert to see whether they could survive in a completely enclosed environment. Next month, the 'Biospherians', as they have become known, will return to a mixed reception in the real world. They believe the enterprise has been a success. They've lived in an enclosed system for eighteen months longer than the previous record, held by Russian astronauts; most of their food has been grown inside the complex and all their waste and water has been successfully recycled.

But many experts have dismissed the project as having no scientific value since oxygen was pumped into the biosphere at the beginning of the year. Crew members were suffering from altitude sickness at the time because the atmosphere was so thin.

For Sally Silverstone, who has been responsible for food systems inside the biosphere, the low oxygen levels and crop failures have been the most frustrating part of the whole experience. She has often wanted to give it all up when she sees crops that have taken so much work to grow ruined. But she would do it all again. When I spoke to her on the phone last night she told me she had no plans to take a holiday on her 24 months salary after 're-entry' but will be spending the next few months preparing a new crew to continue the work in the Biosphere.

WRITING EXERCISE 10

To introduce the writing, discuss as a class if the students would like to spend two years in Biosphere 2, and why/why not. They then write a short paragraph and show it to their partner for comment.

Alternatively, they can do the writing in groups. Divide the class into two groups, those who would like to live there and those who would not. They write their paragraphs in small groups and exchange them with a group with the opposite view to read for content and errors.

Short of time?
Exercise 3 can be omitted, Exercise 10 can be done for homework.

SPEAKING: Discussions

> **Focus**
>
> TOPICS
> * Genetic engineering
> * Life in the future
>
> FUNCTIONS
> * Asking for explanations
> * Introducing examples
> * Interrupting
> * Talking about certainties, probability, possibility, plans and ideas
>
> SKILLS
> * Listening: a conversation
> * Speaking: discussion
>
> SPEECH PATTERNS
> * Using intonation to allow or prevent interruption

GETTING STARTED EXERCISE 1

Direct the class to the cartoon and question in the Students' Book. The students discuss the exercise in pairs or as a class. Find out if they are optimists or pessimists. You could do this by drawing a container on the board, e.g. a box (of chocolates), a bottle (of fruit juice), with only half of its contents inside it. Then ask students to put their hands up according to whether they think it is half-empty or half-full. The former would be pessimists, the latter optimists.

KEY

a pessimist

🎰 LISTENING EXERCISE 2

Refer the class to the two questions in the exercise. If your students' listening skills are good, they can listen to the conversation with their books closed. Otherwise, they listen and read the conversation. Encourage them to compare answers in pairs and then check as a class. Check that they understand *genetic engineering* and *genes*.

KEY

1 They are discussing medical research and genetic engineering; specifically research that will eradicate disease and allow parents to choose the exact qualities of their unborn child.
2 Pat is a pessimist. Alan is an optimist. Tim hasn't really thought about the subject. Sara hasn't thought about the subject in great depth.

EXERCISE 3

Refer the students back to the text in Exercise 2. Write 1–4 on the board. In pairs, they read the conversation again and discuss which people might say the four comments. Elicit their answers and write the names next to the numbers on the board. They then discuss their own views on the subject as a class or in pairs.

KEY

1 Pat (science creates problems . . . line 8)
2 Sara (I intend to have the perfect child . . . lines 29 – 30)
3 Tim (What's wrong with that? line 21)
4 Alan (. . . perhaps that won't happen, lines 36 – 37).

EXERCISE 4

Note: Your students may be confused between *to affect* and *an effect*. *Affect* /ə'fekt/ is the usual verb which means to change or influence someone or something, e.g. *Smoking can affect your health*. *Effect* /ɪ'fekt/ is the noun, e.g. *Smoking can have a bad effect on your health*.

Refer the students back to the text and ask them to write down all the words in italic in the text in their notebooks. Elicit the words and write them on the board. Next, ask *What does 'they' refer to?* and elicit *medical advances*. Write the answer on the board. The students then do the same with the other words. Encourage them to compare answers in pairs and then check as a class on the board. Follow the same procedure with question 2. Establish the difference between *affect* (verb) and *effect* (noun).

KEY

1 they (line 5) – geneticists
them (line 9) – problems
what (line 14) – uses
they   (line 15) – geneticists
ones (line 17) – genes
that (line 21) – identifying genes that affect appearance, sex and intelligence
that (line 33) – the possibility that the world will be full of perfect people with too many men
2 a) cut down (line 3)   b) to get rid of (line 5)
c) hereditary (line 5)   d) finding out about (line 15)
e) affects (line 20)   f) variety (line 35)

FOCUS ON FUNCTIONS EXERCISE 5

Write the three functions in the exercise on the board and refer the students back to the conversation in Exercise 2. They write down examples of the functions in the conversation. Encourage them to check answers in pairs and then check as a class. If you wish, write the expressions on the board. Next, copy this onto the board:

PEOPLE YOU KNOW WELL	MORE FORMAL SITUATIONS

The students categorise the expressions in question 2. Follow the same procedures for checking their answers.

KEY

1 a) What do you mean?   Like what?   What's wrong with that?
b) Well, take (+ noun/-*ing*) genetic engineering, for instance.
c) Wait a moment.   Just let me tell you something.
2 a) Just a minute . . . Hang on . . . Let me say something . . . Listen . . .
b) Excuse me . . . Could I ask a question? Forgive me, but, . . . I'm sorry to interrupt, but . . .

SPEECH PATTERNS EXERCISE 6

Draw two arrows on the board (⤸ ⤴) and write 1 – 4 on the board. Direct the class to question 1 and tell them that there are four pauses in the extract (including the end pause) and they must decide if Pat's voice goes up or down before each pause. Play the extract and elicit their answers as a class. If necessary, play the extract again to confirm answers. Discuss questions 2 and 3 as a class. The students then read the extract out loud as a class, using the same intonation patterns. Alternatively, they can take it in turn to read it out in pairs.

KEY AND TAPESCRIPT

PAT: Well, they're not only finding out about genes that cause diseases . . . they're also going to know which ones give us the colour of our hair and eyes. They already know how to create male or female children . . . and now they're saying there might be a gene that affects intelligence!

2 When the intonation falls: this signals that the speaker has finished an 'idea'.
3 By rising before a pause to show that the speaker wants to continue speaking.

FOCUS ON FUNCTIONS EXERCISE 7

Copy the five verb phrases onto the board. The students work in pairs to discuss the two questions, referring back to the conversation if necessary. Elicit their answers and use the board to highlight the meaning and form of the verb phrases (see Key).

KEY

	QUESTION 1	QUESTION 2
A They might (may)	+ infinitive without *to*	= a possibility
B You can't be certain	*that* + clause	= a certainty
C Science is likely	infinitive with *to*	= a probability
D I intend	infinitive with *to*	= a definite plan
E I'm (not) thinking of	+ -*ing* form	= an idea that is/is not being considered

Extra practice
Each student makes a list of things that they will/may do under the headings of *certain/ probable/possible*. They then mingle and find other students who have written the same things. Make sure they write the names of the students next to their ideas. Discuss as a class. If you wish, they can write a short paragraph about their plans.

EXERCISE 8
Write 1–6 on the board and direct the class to the conversation. Ask the students to read the conversation through once to understand the general idea and then to complete the gaps with expressions from Exercise 7. Encourage the students to compare answers with their partners and then check as a class on the board.

KEY
1 having/taking   2 to do   3 to be   4 write/speak
5 be able   6 that they will (be able to) give you

SPEAKING EXERCISE 9
Divide the class into groups of four, and each group into pairs: As (optimists) and Bs (pessimists), and direct them to the two topics in the exercise. Together they discuss their ideas and make notes. Explain that they are going to discuss the topics in their groups from their optimistic or pessimistic perspective. They should try to use the language from this unit. Monitor and note down any errors you hear. Use the board to correct them at the end of the activity. If you wish to extend the activity, give them other discussion prompts, e.g. global co-operation, the changes in crime in the future, work and lifestyle in the future.

Short of time?
Exercise 8 can be omitted.

Progress check: Units 10–11

Grammar and functions

EXERCISE 1
1 were able   2 couldn't   3 will be able   4 can
5 managed   6 can't   7 could   8 will be able

EXERCISE 2
1 a) We'll definitely move next year.
　b) We're certain/It is certain that we'll move next year.

2 a) The company is likely to leave London.
　b) It is probable that the company will leave London.
3 a) It may move to Manchester.
　b) It is possible that it will move to Manchester.

EXERCISE 3
1 C   2 B   3 D   4 E   5 A

EXERCISE 4
1 When are you going to have the party?
　What time will it start?
2 Where are you going to have it?
　Will it be big enough?
3 How many people are you going to invite?
　Will you invite your parents?
4 How much food are you going to provide?/How much food is there going to be?
　Will it be home-made?
5 Are you going to have a band?
　Will you have your stereo outside?

EXERCISE 5
Tony had his party and **the** party was a great success. There wasn't a band, but there was music and **people** danced to it. Tony's neighbours came too, so the party did not move into **the** house until after midnight. **Tony's** friends were still enjoying themselves at three in **the** morning.

Vocabulary

EXERCISE 6
1 irresponsible people
2 a self-governing organisation
3 an unpleasant experience
4 a ten-mile race
5 self-sacrificing parents
6 an incorrect answer
7 self-educated people
8 a ten-pound note
9 an impractical solution
10 a dissatisfied customer

12 News and views

Making news

Focus		SKILLS
TOPIC		• Listening: a monologue
• Newspapers		• Reading: newspaper extracts
GRAMMAR		
• Past simple passive		

GETTING STARTED EXERCISE 1

Write the eight jobs on the board and elicit which two words mean the same (*journalist* and *reporter*). Then direct the class to the list of responsibilities and ask *Who writes opinions on plays and books?* Elicit *critic* and write 1 next to it on the board. The students then work in pairs and match the other jobs and the responsibilities. Check their answers in the same way and drill for correct pronunciation of the jobs as necessary. If you wish, discuss which jobs are the most important for the success of the newspaper.

KEY

1 critic /ˈkrɪtɪk/
2 foreign correspondent /ˈfɒrən kɒrɪˌspɒndənt/
3 editor /ˈedɪtə/
4 journalist/reporter /ˈdʒɜːnəlɪst/, /rɪˈpɔːtə/
5 sub-editor /ˈsʌbedɪtə/
6 cartoonist /kɑːˈtuːnɪst/
7 deputy editor /ˌdepjətɪ ˈedɪtə/

Documentary

LISTENING EXERCISE 2

Direct the class to the questions. The students discuss the exercise as a class or in groups. Tell the students the answer to question 1.

KEY

1 c
2 open answers

EXERCISES 3 AND 4

Direct the students to the two questions and play the interview. Encourage them to compare answers in pairs and then check as a class. Follow the same procedures for Exercise 4.

KEY FOR EXERCISE 3

1 eight and a magazine
2 news, news review, business, classified advertising, art section, books, colour supplement/magazine

KEY FOR EXERCISE 4

1 a broadsheet newspaper
2 It is the newspaper's comment on the most important event of the week and is written by the editor.
3 the business section
4 *The Sunday Times* is the only newspaper in Britain to have a separate book section.

TAPESCRIPT

IVAN FALLON

It's a, a broadsheet newspaper, as opposed to what we call a tabloid newspaper. This is twice the size of a tabloid newspaper. It's a very large newspaper. It's a multi-section newspaper: we've got eight sections and a magazine. The, the first section, which is obviously the most important section, is what we call the News section; and in that we have home news, we have foreign news and we have analysis of some of the major events of the week. After that, we have more specialised sections; we have what we call the News Review section. This section includes what we call the 'leader', which is the newspaper's editorial comment – our views on what is the most important event of the week. This one here, which will be personally written by the editor – which is an attack on the government's economic policy and its employment policies – this is our contribution to the political debate.

The third section, which is the section I edit, is Business. This is a section that is amazingly well-read; it's the classified advertising section – classified advertisements being specialist small advertisements. Quite often they're tiny ads.

Now we get to our tabloid sections. We have effectively three tabloid sections. The reason for this is that we found that not everybody likes the large broadsheet format. We've developed this particular section as our art section. The book section (we call section six) was the first time in Britain that this type of separate section had been done on books, and is still the only separate book section in Britain. We also have a colour magazine, colour supplement, which is very much a separate part of the paper.

READING EXERCISE 5

Direct the class to the picture and questions and explain that *The Sunday Times* has changed since the interview was recorded. The students look at the picture and answer the questions. Check their answers and discuss question 4 as a class.

KEY

1 11   2 The Culture   3 classified advertising
4 open answers

EXERCISE 6

Write a–j on the board and refer the class to the extracts at the top of the page. Ask *Which extract is about money?* Elicit 2 and write 2 on the board next to 'a'. The students then work in pairs and match the topics and extracts in the same way. Elicit their answers and write the numbers of the extracts next to the letters on the board.

KEY

a – 2   b – 7   c – 3   d – 9   e – 4   f – 5   g – 10
h – 1   i – 6   j – 8

EXERCISE 7

Direct the class back to the extracts in Exercise 6.

Discuss as a class or in pairs which sections of the paper the extracts come from.

KEY

1 Magazine (Funday Times)   2 Business/Personal Finance   3 Style and Travel   4 News   5 Books
6 Magazine   7 Culture   8 Sport   9 Appointments
10 News Review

DISCOVERING LANGUAGE EXERCISE 8

Write the example in the exercise on the board and ask *What is the name of this structure?* (the present simple passive) and *How is it formed?* (present simple of verb *to be* + past participle). Then ask the students to discuss the three questions in pairs. Check their answers as a class and highlight the form of the past passive on the board (see Key).

KEY

1 subject + past of verb *to be (was/were)* + past participle
2 Hopes of an advance . . . **were raised** yesterday . . . The first convoy of evacuees . . .**was cancelled** yesterday . . .
3 Because we don't know the subject/the subject is not important.

EXERCISE 9

Note: The **Chancellor of the Exchequer** is the British government minister in charge of finance. The work of the Chancellor is the same as that of the Finance Minister in many other countries. In some countries, e.g. Germany, the **Chancellor** is the chief minister of the government, equivalent to the Prime Minister in Britain.

Copy the example headline onto the board and as a class expand it into a sentence using the past simple passive. Check the class understand *Chancellor*. The students then do the same with the other headlines in pairs. Elicit their answers and write them on the board with the students' help.

KEY

1 The South of England was hit by a storm yesterday.
2 The factory gates were locked by the bosses yesterday.
3 A head teacher was sacked by the council yesterday.
4 New taxes were announced by the Chancellor yesterday.
5 Liverpool was beaten by Tottenham yesterday.
6 An 8-year-old boy was arrested yesterday.

EXERCISE 10

Direct the students to the picture and headline in the Students' Book. Check that the class understands the headline and ask *What was done to the child?* Elicit an example from the class, e.g. *His clothes were torn.* The students work in pairs and make other sentences. Check their ideas as a class and if you wish, write their sentences on the board.

KEY

His clothes were torn and covered with mud. His bicycle was broken. His bag was broken. His books were taken from his bag and they were drenched/ruined. He was pushed/kicked/hit.

Extra practice

Dictate four different ages to your students to write in their notebooks. Choose ages appropriate to your students, e.g. three months, five years old, sixteen years old and twenty-five years old. Ask them to write down one or two things that happened to them at those ages, e.g. *I was given a car, I was bitten by a dog*, etc. They then mingle and find students who had similar or different experiences.

Reading habits

Focus	
TOPICS • Objectivity and bias in newspapers • Reading habits GRAMMAR • Present perfect passive	SKILLS • Reading: comments for a survey • Listening: short interviews • Speaking: discussion, an interview • Writing: a report SPEECH PATTERNS • Word stress

COMPARING CULTURES EXERCISE 1

Bring in two national newspapers from your country, if possible, one broadsheet and one tabloid, to check the vocabulary in the exercise. Check the students understand *ownership* and *sensational*. Then organise the students to discuss the questions in groups of three. Discuss as a class, making sure the students can pronounce the newspaper vocabulary in the exercise.

READING EXERCISE 2

Copy the chart in the Students' Book onto the board and ask the students to copy it into their notebooks. Ask the class to read the quote about British newspapers and to complete the chart. Encourage them to compare answers in pairs and then elicit their answers and complete the chart on the board. Leave the chart for Exercise 4.

KEY

TYPE OF NEWSPAPER	FREQUENCY	REASONS FOR CHOOSING THIS NEWSPAPER	REASONS FOR NOT CHOOSING OTHERS
serious	Sundays	articles written by well-informed journalists	hates sensational stories and chequebook journalism

EXERCISE 3

Ask the class to read the quote in Exercise 2 again and to choose the best meaning for the words/phrases. Encourage the students to compare answers in pairs and then check as a class. Drill for correct pronunciation as necessary.

KEY

1 b   2 b   3 c   4 c

📼 LISTENING EXERCISES 4 AND 5

Refer the students back to the chart from Exercise 2 on the board. Explain that they are going to listen to three different people and they should complete the chart with the information they hear. Play the three interviews once. The students compare answers in pairs and then check as a class. Complete the chart on the board. If necessary, play the conversations again, pausing to confirm their answers. Direct the class to the three questions in Exercise 5 and follow the same procedure.

KEY FOR EXERCISE 4

TYPE OF NEWSPAPER	FREQUENCY	REASONS FOR CHOOSING THIS NEWSPAPER	REASONS FOR NOT CHOOSING OTHERS
1 none			all biased, most are right-wing
2 tabloid	daily	likes human interest stories and quick to read	they are depressing
3 quality tabloid	Sundays 2–3 times a week	good summary of world events stories about royal family	too respectful

KEY FOR EXERCISE 5

1 not politically biased
2 stories about people rather than wars and disasters

3 the British royal family, e.g. the Queen, Princess Diana; examples of other 'public figures': politicians, film stars, pop musicians

TAPESCRIPT

One.
I don't read newspapers at all. They're all biased. They've been taken over by companies who have political interests. And in Britain most of the papers are right-wing. There are one or two that I think are a bit more objective, but I'd rather listen to the radio.
Two.
Actually, I don't want to know about the details of all the troubles in the world – it's all so depressing. I like human interest stories – stories about people, not wars and disasters. So my daily newspaper is a tabloid. The other good thing about a tabloid is that you can read it in ten minutes on the way to work. That's all I want.
Three.
I get a so-called quality newspaper on Sundays because it gives me a good summary of world events, but I also buy tabloids two or three times a week. People are critical of the pictures and stories of the royals and their problems that have been published in the tabloids, but I don't agree. Why shouldn't we know how they're spending our money? They're public figures, and only the tabloids give you the details – the other papers are too respectful.

📼 SPEECH PATTERNS EXERCISE 6

Write the six words on the board and ask the students to say them out loud in pairs. Then they mark the main stress in each word. Play the words on cassette to check their answers. Discuss question 2 as a class and then play the words again, pausing to allow the students to repeat them.

KEY AND TAPESCRIPT

1 sen'sation   edu'cation   infor'mation   imagi'nation   e'dition   pro'duction
2 The syllable before the *-tion* ending carries the main stress, e.g. con'dition, 'station, radi'ation, centrali'sation.

DISCOVERING LANGUAGE EXERCISE 7
Alternative presentation
Draw picture 1 on the board:

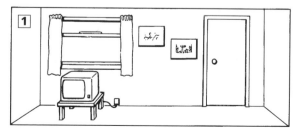

Then draw picture 2. Establish that there has been a burglary. Point to the window and ask *What has happened to the window?* Elicit e.g. *It's broken* and reply *Yes, it has been broken.* To check the concept, ask *Do we know who broke it?* (No) *Can you see the broken window now?* (Yes) *Was it broken in the past?* (Yes) *Do we know when?* (No) *Did the window break itself?* (No, someone did it). Then drill the sentence chorally and individually. Do the same with the pictures (they have been smashed), the television (it has been stolen) and the door (it has been kicked down). The students can practise the sentences in pairs.

Direct the class to the three examples and the questions in the Students' Book. The students discuss them in pairs and then discuss as a class.

KEY

1 the subject + auxiliary *has/have* + *been* + past participle
2 In A and C the passive is used because the subject of the active is long and complex. In B it is used because the subject is obvious or unimportant.
3 an indefinite time in the past, no specific time
4 It is used to talk about an action that happened in the past but we don't know when, or an action that began in the past and continues into the present. It is used when the subject is unknown, unimportant, obvious, or long and complex.

EXERCISE 8

Refer the class to the radio report and ask the students to read it through to get an idea of the general content. Write 1–9 on the board and complete the first gap together to demonstrate the task. Establish that the students can use only the past passive or the present perfect passive. Encourage them to compare answers in pairs and then write the correct answers on the board with the students' help.

KEY

1 were flooded   2 were overturned   3 were torn
4 were killed   5 was blown   6 were injured*
7 have been taken   8 have been damaged
9 have been given
*It is possible to use the present perfect here as the

people are *still* injured. However, its position in the paragraph about *last* night makes the past simple more appropriate.

Extra practice

Divide the class into two groups. Ask each student in group A to put one possession on the desk in front of them, e.g. a watch, piece of paper, book, etc. Group A arranges the items as a collage. Group B does the same, on a different desk. The groups then look at each others' collages for two minutes. Then each group makes changes to its own collage, e.g. changes the time on the watches, shuts the books, etc. and makes a list of the changes. They then show their new collages to each other. Each group has to make a list of the changes, using the present perfect passive (because they don't know who made the changes), e.g. *The time on the watch has been changed.* Group A then reads out its sentences one by one; Group B ticks off each change on the list and awards a second point if the sentence is correct. The groups change roles and do the same with the other collage.

SPEAKING EXERCISE 9

Direct the class to the different types of magazine and newspaper features. The students work in pairs and discuss the kind of features which are popular in their countries, giving examples of articles they have read recently. Monitor and note down any errors you hear. If you wish, discuss their ideas as a class and then use the board to correct any errors you heard.

EXERCISE 10

Copy the question prompts in the exercise onto the board and elicit questions about your reading habits, e.g. *What newspaper do you read? Which features do you like best?* etc. You may wish to write some of the questions on the board to guide the students in their own interviews. Then the students form pairs and interview each other. Make sure they change roles and make notes, which they will need for the next exercise. Monitor and note down any errors you hear and use the board to correct them at the end of the activity.

WRITING EXERCISE 11

Ask the class to read the example model paragraph in the Students' Book. The students then use their notes from Exercise 10 to write about their partner. Monitor and help. If you wish, they can exchange texts with their partners and check for factual or language errors.

Short of time?

Exercise 11 can be done for homework. Exercise 5 can be omitted.

CREATIVE WRITING: Changing perspectives

Focus	
TOPIC	• Writing: a perspective on events; a newspaper report
• Perspectives on events	
SKILLS	VOCABULARY DEVELOPMENT
• Speaking: interpreting events	• Adjectives and their connotations
• Reading: a narrative	

GETTING STARTED EXERCISE 1

Note: Brits is a colloquial expression for the British. **Aussies** is the equivalent for Australians.

Direct the class to the headlines and questions in the Students' Book. The students discuss the exercise in pairs or as a class.

KEY

1 Australia and Britain (Sydney/Brits)
2 the chance to host the Olympics in the year 2000
3 Australia
4 a) B   b) A
5 a) A   b) B
6 They probably felt delighted.
   Olympics delight as Aussie bid wins.
   This focuses on the fact that events can be reported differently depending on the perspective of the person who is doing the reporting.

SPEAKING EXERCISES 2 AND 3

Direct the class to the picture and questions. The students discuss the questions in pairs and then as a class. Follow the same procedures for Exercise 3.

KEY FOR EXERCISE 2

1 They are on a country road.
2 It's evening/night.
3 The elderly couple have broken down.
4 open answers

SUGGESTED KEY FOR EXERCISE 3

• The younger man is having trouble with his own car.
• The elderly couple have called for help on their mobile phone, and the younger man has been sent out by a local garage.
• The couple and the younger man have arranged a secret meeting here to discuss a 'shady' deal (something illegal).

• The couple are the younger man's parents. He has escaped from prison (in a stolen car). His parents have agreed to help him.

DEVELOPING VOCABULARY EXERCISE 4

First, ask the students to read the account to compare it with their interpretation of the scenario. Then copy this grid onto the board:

YOUNGER MAN	THE ELDERLY COUPLE

Ask the students to list the words and expressions which describe the younger man as frightening and the elderly couple as helpless. Elicit the first one as a class (*did not seem to know what to do*) and write it on the board under THE ELDERLY COUPLE. The students then do the same with the rest of the passage. Encourage them to compare answers in pairs and then check as a class.

KEY

YOUNGER MAN	THE ELDERLY COUPLE
huge, ugly-looking	did not seem to know what to do
looked terrifying	
long, greasy hair	lifted his arm weakly
filthy, torn jeans	unsteady steps backwards
big, black leather boots	looked nervously
holding a large metal tool	vulnerable
waved in the air	
walked slowly	

EXERCISE 5

Note: If you think your students will find the vocabulary in this exercise difficult, pre-teach a few of the words that they won't know. Also, encourage the use of dictionaries.

Copy these two columns onto the board:

A FRIGHTENING PERSON	A HELPLESS PERSON

Refer the students to the list of adjectives in the Students' Book. To demonstrate the task, ask *Where does powerful go?* and elicit *a frightening person*. The students work in pairs and categorise the words in the same way. Elicit their answers and write the adjectives on the board with the students' help. Drill for correct pronunciation as necessary.

Next, point to the FRIGHTENING column and ask *Are there any words there which have a similar meaning?* Elicit *powerful* and *strong*. The students then work in pairs and do the same with both columns. Check as a class. Then do the same for words with opposite meanings (question 2). Use the board to collate their answers (see Key).

Copy the five categories in question 3 onto the board and refer the class to the examples for each category in the Students' Book. The students work in pairs and group the words according to the categories. Ask them to make sentences like the examples, if you wish. Alternatively, divide the class into five groups and give each group one of the categories to brainstorm. Then regroup the students so that there is a representative from each of the five categories in the new group and the students exchange their ideas. Check as a class.

For question 4, copy these columns onto the board:

A HELPFUL PERSON	A PERSON WHO IS NOT AFRAID

The students work in pairs and brainstorm adjectives for these two categories. Elicit their adjectives and write them on the board. Drill for correct pronunciation.

SUGGESTED KEY

1 *a frightening person:* powerful /ˈpaʊəfəl/, muscular /ˈmʌskjələ/, angry /ˈæŋgri/, frightening /ˈfraɪtnɪŋ/, sinister /ˈsɪnɪstə/, evil /ˈiːvəl/, strong /strɒŋ/, loud /laʊd/, sharp /ʃɑːp/, aggressive /əˈgresɪv/, threatening /ˈθretnɪŋ/
  a helpless person: powerless /ˈpaʊələs/, defenceless /dɪˈfensləs/, frightened /ˈfraɪtənd/, worried /ˈwʌrɪd/, harmless /ˈhɑːmləs/, innocent /ˈɪnəsənt/, feeble /ˈfiːbəl/, naive /naɪˈiːv/, weak /wiːk/, gentle /ˈdʒentl/, silent /ˈsaɪlənt/, terrified /ˈterɪfaɪd/, confused /kənˈfjuːzd/, trusting /ˈtrʌstɪŋ/, frail /freɪl/

2 a) *similar meanings:* powerful/muscular/strong, frightening/threatening, sinister/evil, loud/sharp/aggressive
  b) *opposite meanings:* powerless/weak/feeble/frail/ defenceless, frightened/worried/terrified, innocent/naive

3 a) muscular (arms), sinister (eyes), strong (legs), feeble/weak (grip), sharp (nose), frail (body)
  b) (feel) powerless/defenceless, frightened, worried, terrified, confused
  c) powerful, sinister, harmless, evil, innocent, strong, naive, weak, gentle, silent, trusting, aggressive
  d) angrily, worriedly, feebly, weakly, loudly, gently, aggressively
  e) angrily, weakly, silently, threateningly
  a helpful person: kind, gentle, sympathetic, sensitive, understanding, practical
  a person who is not afraid: brave, courageous, heroic, assertive, confident, self-assured

Extra practice

1 Bring in pictures of people. The students work in pairs and describe what the people look like and their character. It's more fun if they are famous people.

2 Read out definitions for the adjectives, as in the examples below. The students have to guess the adjectives. This can be done in teams – the first team to shout out the correct adjective gets a point.
  <u>Example definitions</u>
  Someone who is very strong is ...(*powerful*)
  When you are so weak that you can't do anything, you are ...(*powerless*)
  The opposite of strong is ...(*weak*)

WRITING EXERCISE 6

You may wish to give some guidance to your students before they start writing. First, explain that they are going to write a description using some of the language from Exercise 5. Ask them to read the four perspectives and choose the one they want to describe. Then ask them to close their Students' Books. Read out these questions, pausing to allow the students to visualise and make notes:*Who speaks first? What do they say? How do the elderly people feel? How does the man feel?* The students then use their notes to write their descriptions. Monitor and help.

EXERCISE 7

The aim of this exercise is to encourage the students to edit their writing. Read out the questions in the Students' Book and discuss them, then the students make changes to their writing.

Alternatively, if you wish, each pair swaps descriptions with another pair, who tries to improve it.

EXERCISE 8

Ask which students described perspectives 2 or 3 in Exercise 6. Form pairs with one of these students working with someone who described perspectives 1 or 4. Write *a broadsheet* and *a tabloid* on the board and brainstorm the features of reports in these newspapers, e.g. *a broadsheet* – a lot of factual detail, fewer adjectives, more impersonal; *a tabloid* – fewer factual details, more emotive vocabulary, more personal details. The students can decide which type of newspaper report they want to write. Before they start writing, remind the class that it is very common to use the passive form. Tell them also that it is best to write the headline last, as it should summarise the article.

Short of time?
Exercise 8 can be done for homework.

Talkback

....

A critical eye
This is a fluency activity which is likely to encourage the use of passives and the language of possibility, probability and certainty in the future.
1 Direct the students to the pictures that show the development of television and ask them to discuss the questions in pairs. Monitor and note down any errors you hear. If they don't know factual details, they can look these up at home and discuss them in the next lesson.
2 Elicit what objects the students can see in the picture. They discuss the objects using the questions from 1. Make sure they make notes.
3 Regroup the pairs for them to compare notes.
4 The students then return to their original partner to report back on their conversations and to decide if they wish to change their notes.
Finally, if you wish, discuss as a class and use the board to correct any errors you heard.

KEY

The picture shows: an early black-and-white television; a more modern colour television; closed-circuit cameras in shops, which monitor shoppers' actions; an early video game; a very modern flat-screen television with external speakers and an interactive text display on the screen, which allows the viewer to choose items from a 'menu'.

13 *On show*

....

But is it art?

Focus	
TOPICS	SKILLS
• Exhibitions	• Reading: an article
• Art	• Writing: describing an experience
GRAMMAR	VOCABULARY DEVELOPMENT
• Past perfect simple	• *Go* + adjective

GETTING STARTED EXERCISE 1
Start by asking the students to name one or two famous works of art, e.g. *The Mona Lisa* (*La Gioconda*), the *Venus de Milo*, Picasso's *Guernica*. Then direct the class to the questions. The students discuss the exercise in pairs and then as a class. Write all their ideas for question 3 on the board and together write a class definition of art. If you want to discuss question 2 further, you could tell the students about the famous exhibit of a pile of bricks in the Tate Gallery, London, a few years ago.

READING EXERCISE 2
Refer the class back to the pictures and the headline in the Students' Book. The students discuss the question in pairs. Elicit their ideas but do not confirm them yet.

Then direct the students to question 2 and ask them to work in pairs and list some vocabulary. Elicit their ideas and write them on the board. Encourage students to think what *they* would write about the two topics.

KEY

1 Because her work of art was thrown away by mistake.
2 suggested vocabulary:
  a) shiny, red, wobbly
  b) cultural, stimulating, interesting

EXERCISE 3
The students now read the article and check their answers to Exercise 2. Encourage them to compare answers with their partner and then check as a class. Check the class understands *mouldy*.

EXERCISE 4
Direct the students to the questions and ask them to read the article again. Encourage them to compare answers in pairs and then check as a class.

Then ask the students to read the text again and make a list in their notebooks of any vocabulary that they don't understand and which they think is important. They may want to know the meanings of the words in question 5 and others such as *visual metaphor* and *leftovers*. They compare lists with their partners, explaining any words they already know and discuss what the unknown ones could mean from the context of the article. Then they check the remaining ones in their dictionaries.

KEY

1 It was 34 red jellies on 17 plates, laid out in the shape of an arc on the floor of the art gallery.
2 four days
3 The officer in charge of the art gallery removed it

because he thought that it was left-over food from a party.

4 It represented the human body and what happens to it after death.

5 a) jewel-like, very fresh, shiny and red
   b) dull and mouldy, smelling badly

DEVELOPING VOCABULARY EXERCISE 5

To introduce the exercise, ask the class *What happened to the jellies?* Elicit the idea of *They went mouldy.* To check the concept ask *Did this happen quickly?* (No, slowly) *When do we use 'go' + adjective?* (To describe something that happens over a period of time). Then direct them to the five adjectives and questions in the exercise. The students answer the questions using the adjectives. Encourage them to compare answers in pairs and then check as a class on the board. You could ask students if they can think of any other *go* + adjective combinations, e.g. *go deaf, go mad, go wrong.*

KEY

1 it goes grey   2 it goes bad   3 you go bald
4 it goes red   5 you go blind

DISCOVERING LANGUAGE EXERCISE 6

Direct the class to the two bold sections of the sentences from the text and ask *What is the name of this tense?* (the past perfect simple) and *How is it formed?* (past simple of verb *to have* + past participle).

Then ask them to discuss question 2 in pairs. Draw this timeline grid on the board:

Discuss the use of the past perfect as a class and together mark the two tenses on the timeline:

Then discuss question 3 as a class.

KEY

1 subject + past of verb *to have (had)* + past participle
2 b) happened first. The past perfect is used to describe an action which happened before another one in the past.
3 before the jellies were thrown away

Extra practice

The students work in pairs. Read the story (below) out to them, pausing after each prompt for them to write down their answers. Encourage them to be imaginative. Check as a class and write the correct answers on the board, creating a skeleton story. The students then write down what they can remember of the rest of the story. At the end of the activity, the students should have the whole text in their notebooks.

A bad evening

Peter arranged to meet Simon at 7.30. He arrived at 8.00 but Simon . . . (*had already left*). So he went to a restaurant alone and ordered a meal. Twenty minutes later the waiter told him that he couldn't have a meal because the chef . . . (*had walked out*). He went to another restaurant and had a meal. At the end of the meal, he put his hand in his pocket to take out his wallet and found that he . . . (*had left it at home*).

He washed dishes for a couple of hours and then walked home. When he arrived, the front door was open and everything was in a mess because there . . . (*had been a burglary*). Even worse, he couldn't phone the police because the burglar . . . (*had taken the phone*). He went to his neighbour's house and used his phone. It took the police an hour to come because their car . . . (*had broken down*). Peter went to bed after the police . . . (*had gone*) and he didn't get up the next day!

EXERCISE 7

Direct the class to the five questions and the answer prompts. To demonstrate the task, read out the first question. Elicit the students' answers and write the correct sentence on the board with their help. They then do the same with the other questions. Then they take it in turns to ask and answer the questions in pairs. Check as a class and write the answers on the board. Finally, discuss the point of the cartoon as a class.

KEY

1 Because someone had thrown away the jellies.
2 She had planned the sculpture.
3 She had displayed them on 17 plates in the shape of an arc on the floor of the museum.
4 The museum official had thrown them away.
5 Because they were mouldy and smelling badly, and there was no sign.

The cartoon is making the point that, if jellies can be considered art, then anything can, even someone's dinner.

WRITING EXERCISE 8

Ask the students to think of a time when they were very disappointed. If you wish, write these question prompts on the board:

*Why/disappointed?   When/disappointed?
What/do to make yourself happy again?*

The students then work in pairs and interview each other using the prompts. Make sure they make notes. They then use the notes to write about their partner's experience. Encourage the students to exchange their writing to check for factual or language errors. Encourage the students to think of disappointments here rather than periods of great sadness in their lives.

Short of time?

Exercise 8 can be omitted or done for homework.

Learning experiences

> ## Focus
>
> **TOPIC**
> • Museums
>
> **FUNCTIONS**
> • Asking for and giving directions
>
> **SKILLS**
> • Reading: an extract from a brochure
> • Listening: two short talks
> • Speaking: a short talk, a role play

GETTING STARTED EXERCISES 1 AND 2

Direct the class to the pictures and the questions. First, ask the students to guess what the pictures illustrate. They then discuss the questions in pairs and then as a class. Follow the same procedure for Exercise 2.

KEY FOR EXERCISE 1

1 a) C   b) A   c) B
2 open answers

🖻 Documentary

📼 LISTENING EXERCISE 3

Tell the students that they are going to listen to Alison Porter, who is a curator at one of the museums in the pictures. Check they understand *curator*. Direct the class to the questions and then play the cassette. Encourage the students to compare answers in pairs and then check as a class.

KEY

1 The Science Museum, London (Picture A)
2 It's the first of its type in the country.
3 60

4 a) school parties of pupils and teachers
  b) families
5 It's fun and visitors learn a lot from visiting it.

TAPESCRIPT

PRESENTER
Listen to Alison Porter, a curator at the Science Museum in London, talking about a particular gallery in the museum. Answer the questions in your Students' Book.
ALISON PORTER
Launch Pad is, is our largest interactive gallery and, when it opened, it was the first of its type in this country. It has a number of exhibits – as many as 60 different interactive exhibits are, are in the gallery.

During the week you'll see school parties using the gallery with their teachers, but at weekends families come and the whole lot join in. I find the museum a very stimulating place: it's a place that's both a lot of fun and it's also a big learning environment. And I think that anyone that visits here will go away feeling that they've learned something from the experience, and they can take that away with them.

READING EXERCISES 4 AND 5

Refer the class back to Picture B and the two questions. The students discuss the questions in pairs. Direct their attention to the flags in the picture as a clue. Elicit their ideas as a class but do not confirm them yet. The students then read the text quickly and check their answers. Discuss as a class.

KEY FOR EXERCISE 5

1 The International Red Cross/Red Crescent. It helps people who are victims of military conflicts or natural disasters. It was started in 1863.
2 There are two symbols because the cross, although not a religious symbol, was potentially offensive to Muslims.

EXERCISE 6

Direct the class to questions 1–3 and ask the students to read the text again. Encourage them to compare answers in pairs and then check as a class. Discuss question 4 as a class and write the students' ideas for the possible exhibits on the board. Leave them there for the next exercise.

KEY

1 1859
2 There is a red cross on the Swiss flag. This was originally used as a tribute to the Swiss founder of the organisation.
3 Because it is also a symbol of Christianity.
4 open answers

📼 LISTENING EXERCISE 7

Indicate the two questions and check that the students understand *medical kits* and *AIDS*. Play the talk, stopping after 'the Wall of Time' and check that the class have noted this as one of the exhibits she mentions. Then play the complete talk. Encourage the students to compare answers in pairs and then elicit their answers as a class. If necessary, play the talk again for them to check their answers.

KEY

1 a   d   e   g   h
2 original agreements setting up the organisation, computer records of current prisoners of war, sculptures of groups of people who are faceless and have their hands tied

TAPESCRIPT

Well, there are a lot of fascinating exhibits. There's the Wall of Time. This gives details of major world events – wars, conflicts and natural disasters – from 1863 to the present day, and gives details of the Red Cross involvement in each one. It's also got a display of the original agreements setting up the organisation and examples of medical kits carried by volunteers.

Then you can see the kind of records the organisation used to keep. One room has a card index system of all prisoners of war held in thirty-eight different countries during the First World War. Of course nowadays records are held on computers . . . and visitors can consult these if they wish.

There are also films of Red Cross and Red Crescent volunteers in action in the First and Second World Wars, and of its activities in peacetime fighting disease and helping victims of earthquakes, volcanic eruptions, and other natural events. The work of the organisation today is shown on a row of television screens.

Another interesting feature is that a number of sculptures of groups of people are placed throughout the museum. The people are faceless and their hands are tied. They represent the misery of casualties of war and oppressive peace throughout the world.

It's a surprising museum. It leaves you feeling depressed at the amazing scale of human suffering but it's also encouraging to think that organisations like the Red Cross and Red Crescent exist and are dedicated to peace.

📼 EXERCISE 8

Refer the class to the words in the exercise and ask *Which word has a similar meaning to 'exhibit'?* Elicit *display* and write the two words on the board. The students then work in pairs and match the other pairs of words in the same way. Elicit their answers as a class and write them on

the board. Play the talk again so that they can check if their answers are correct, stopping to put the items in context if necessary. Finally, drill for correct pronunciation as necessary.

KEY

exhibit /ekˈsɪbɪt/– display
fascinating – interesting
card index system – records
wars – conflicts
work – activities
casualties /ˈkæʒəltɪz/– victims
misery – suffering

SPEAKING EXERCISE 9

Divide the class into pairs and copy the phrases from the exercise onto the board. To demonstrate the task, use the phrases to tell the class about a museum that you have visited. Encourage the students to ask you more questions about your visit. They then work in pairs and tell each other about a museum they have visited. Monitor and make a note of any errors you hear. If you wish, discuss as a class which museums the students have visited and then use the board to correct any errors you heard.

FOCUS ON FUNCTIONS EXERCISE 10

The aim of this exercise is to check the students know the vocabulary for Exercise 11. Copy the ten prompts onto the board, point to the first one and ask *Where can you get a drink in a museum?* Elicit *a café, restaurant*. The students then work in pairs and do the same for the other prompts. Elicit their ideas and write the places on the board. Leave them there for Exercise 11.

KEY

a) café, restaurant   b) cloakroom
c) souvenir shop, gift shop   d) toilet   e) exit
f) ticket office   g) restaurant   h) picnic area
i) souvenir shop, gift shop   j) library

EXERCISE 11

Divide the class into pairs and direct the As to the instructions and expressions on page 107 and the Bs to page 128. Next, refer them back to the places on the board from Exercise 10 and mark a–e for Student A and f–j for Student B. To demonstrate the task, point to *café* on the board and indicate a Student A to ask a Student B for directions. Student B uses the plan on page 128 to give the directions. The students then work in pairs and role play similar conversations. Make sure they change roles when A has asked about places a–e. Monitor and make a note of any errors.

If you wish, volunteer pairs can role play their conversations for the whole class. Finally, use the board to correct any errors you heard.

Short of time?
Exercises 2 and 9 can be omitted.

SPEAKING: Responding to pictures

Focus	
TOPICS	**SKILLS**
• Children	• Reading: a poem
• Childhood	• Speaking: a discussion, a description
FUNCTIONS	• Listening: a description
• Describing location	**VOCABULARY DEVELOPMENT**
• Describing people	• Words with similar and opposite meanings
• Interpreting/inferring from pictures	
• Expressing opinions and feelings	
• Hesitating	

READING: A POEM EXERCISE 1
Direct the class to the question and ask the students to read the poem. If your students like reading aloud, allow one or two to read the poem to the class. They then discuss their ideas in pairs or as a class. You do not need to explain any new vocabulary now, as this is the aim of Exercise 2.

KEY

Neither of them can look after themselves independently and both need help from other people.

EXERCISE 2
Refer the class to the words and ask the students to find them in the poem. In pairs, they match the words with the explanations in the exercise according to the context of the poem. Check as a class.

KEY

a) beads   b) veins   c) banisters   d) grown-up
e) grand   f) wrinkles

EXERCISE 3
Refer the students to the questions and ask them to read the poem again. Encourage them to compare answers in pairs and then discuss as a class.

KEY

1 She thought they tried to be 'grand'.
2 In a negative way, both physically and in terms of character.
3 She saw a friend of her great-aunt Etty (who was very old) try to pick up the beads from a necklace. It

had broken and the beads were all over the floor. She had difficulty picking them up.
4 Open answers, e.g. no teeth, lose their hair, can't concentrate on things, can't walk far, short memory, physically weak.

SPEAKING EXERCISE 4
Divide the class into groups of four and ask them to choose one of the topics in the exercise to discuss. Make sure that they make notes. Monitor and write down any errors you hear. The students then decide who is going to report back to the whole class.

Alternatively, regroup the students so that they work with students from different groups. They use their notes to report back. Finally, use the board to correct any errors you heard.

EXERCISE 5
Direct the class to the pictures and questions. The students discuss the questions in pairs or as a class.

KEY

1 It is likely to be something on children in different countries.
2 open answers

🔲 FOCUS ON FUNCTIONS EXERCISE 6
Tell the students that they are going to listen to a woman describing one of the pictures. Ask them to read the two questions in the exercise. Play the description once. Encourage them to compare answers with their partner and then check as a class.

KEY

1 C
2 a) describing location
   b) describing people (what you can see)
   c) describing people (what you can guess)
   d) expressing opinions
   e) expressing your feelings

🔲 EXERCISE 7
Write *What expressions does she use when she hesitates?* on the board and play the description again. After they have compared answers in pairs, discuss as a class. If necessary, play the description once more. Finally, discuss whether any of the expressions she uses for hesitating are the same in their language(s).

KEY

let me see   you know   now   so   (also 'sounds', e.g. er, um)

TAPESCRIPT

There are two children in the picture, one in the middle at the front and another behind. I don't know if they're boys or girls ... They look very similar ... perhaps they're twins. They've both got blond hair and ... er ... let me see ... I think they've got blue eyes. They're wearing nappies and they're covered in paint! They've got paint everywhere – in their hair, round their faces and all over their bodies. I guess they're ... em ... probably at a nursery ... you know ... or a playschool, or somewhere like that.

They look about one or two years old ... and they're obviously well-fed ... they're both quite plump. Now ... I think they're probably European ... or American perhaps. Actually, in my opinion this isn't a very natural photograph. It's not likely that both kids would have the dishes on their heads at the same time ... so ... I think the photographer arranged the photo.

Anyway, it's a nice picture. The kids look happy and innocent and secure ... and, you know, they don't seem to have a care in the world. It makes me feel good to see kids so happy and relaxed.

DEVELOPING VOCABULARY EXERCISE 8

Direct the class to the adjectives in the exercise and explain that some of them can make pairs with a similar or opposite meaning. To demonstrate the task, say *Find a word that is similar to 'rich'*. Elicit *wealthy* and write the two words on the board. The students work in pairs and do the same with the other adjectives. They can use the adjectives more than once. Elicit their answers and write them on the board with the students' help. Mark the stress and drill for correct pronunciation as necessary.

SUGGESTED KEY

rich – wealthy (similar)
hungry – well-fed (opposite)
helpless – vulnerable /ˈvʌlnərəbl/ (similar)
neglected – spoilt (opposite)
healthy – ill (opposite)
cheerful – hopeful (similar)
carefree – relaxed (similar)
miserable – cheerful (opposite)
arrogant – proud (similar)

EXERCISE 9

Divide the students into pairs and refer them back to the pictures of the children in Exercise 5. Tell them to choose three adjectives from Exercise 8 to describe each child. They then work with two other pairs and exchange ideas. If you wish, compare the adjectives they have chosen as a class.

SPEAKING EXERCISE 10

Ask the students to each choose a picture from Exercise 5 and remind them of the expressions in Exercises 6 and 7, and of the adjectives in Exercise 8. Next, give them a couple of minutes to think about the picture from the point of view of the headings in the exercise. They then work in pairs. Student A describes his/her picture and B listens and asks A for more information. They then change roles. Monitor and note down any errors you hear and use the board to correct them at the end of the exercise.

Short of time?
Exercise 4 can be omitted.

Progress check: Units 12–13

Grammar and functions

EXERCISE 1
1 What did Jane and Tom do on the last day?
They shopped at the Friendship store.
Had they shopped there before?
No, they hadn't.
2 What did Lenny and Pam do on the last day?
They walked on the Great Wall.
Had they walked on it before?
Yes, they had.
3 What did Tricia do on the last day?
She visited the Summer Palace.
Had she visited it before?
No, she hadn't.

EXERCISE 2
1 when 2 just 3 never 4 already 5 yet
6 by the time

EXERCISE 3
1 Manchester United was beaten by Benfica last night.
2 The pitch was invaded (by the crowd) after the match.
3 Shop windows were smashed outside the ground.
4 Over a hundred people have been arrested.
5 More than fifty people have been treated for minor injuries.

EXERCISE 4
1 of, take 2 on, first 3 there, use
4 How, to the right of, downstairs

Vocabulary

1 Yes, but it's gone cold.
2 He has gone deaf.
3 Everything has gone wrong today.
4 She went crazy.
5 Yes, the nail has gone black.

14 *In touch*

··

Door to door

GETTING STARTED EXERCISE 1

To introduce the topic, show the students a letter and tell them that you must get this to a friend of yours first thing tomorrow morning, and she lives 500 miles away. Ask the students to make a list of the ways they could send this urgent letter. Then they compare lists in pairs. Next, ask *Which is the quickest/slowest/cheapest/most expensive way?* and the students decide in pairs. Discuss as a class and decide which way you should send your letter. If you wish, do the same with a parcel.

READING EXERCISE 2

Refer the class to the headline and the introduction to the article. Discuss question 1 as a class. Then direct the students to the two lists of words in question 2 and write *express* on the board. Ask the class to find a word which goes with it and write *delivery* on the board. Write a definition for the phrase on the board with the students' help, e.g. *a method of sending a letter/parcel very quickly from one place to another.* They then work in pairs to match the words and discuss the meaning of each phrase. Elicit their phrases as a class and write them on the board. Discuss their ideas of the meaning of each one but do not confirm if they are correct yet.

KEY

1 by going as a courier, accompanying documents or packages

EXERCISE 3

Ask the students to look through the article quickly to check their phrases from Exercise 2. Check as a class and tick the right phrases on the board. Add any new ones and check they understand them all. If you wish, write definitions on the board with the students' help and drill for correct pronunciation as necessary.

KEY

express delivery (defined above)
fare-paying passenger (a passenger who pays the correct fare)
customs procedures (checks at the airport for customs purposes)
return flight (a flight back from a destination)
full-fare ticket (a ticket with no reduction in price)
hand luggage (luggage which can be carried onto an aircraft)
last-minute bargain (a flight/ticket which is very cheap because it is bought only a day or two in advance)

EXERCISE 4

Direct the students to the questions and ask them to read the article again, more carefully. Encourage them to compare answers in pairs and then check as a class.

KEY

1 A courier takes urgent documents or parcels from one place to another. In this article, by plane from Britain to abroad.
2 It's a cheap way of travelling abroad and you can get some good bargains. The work doesn't take long and it's easy to do.
3 If you want to use the flight to go on holiday, there isn't a wide choice of destinations and the dates of the flights are fixed so you can't choose when you want to go. If you're travelling as a couple, you usually have to go on separate days because only one courier is needed a day. If you want to travel together, you have to pay for one full airfare. You also have to check in at least two hours in advance and be dressed quite smartly. The representative may only arrive at the airport thirty minutes before the flight, which can make you nervous, and you may have to carry a lot of hand luggage.

EXERCISE 5

Copy the ten adjectives onto the board and direct the class back to the article. Point to *excellent* and ask the students to find the noun it goes with in the article. Elicit their answer and write *meal* on the board. The students then work in pairs and do the same with the other adjectives in the exercise.

Then write two headings on the board like this:

POSITIVE	NEGATIVE

Ask *Does 'excellent' have a positive or negative meaning?* Elicit *positive* and write the phrase under the correct heading. The students then do the same in pairs. Check their answers on the board, drilling for correct pronunciation as necessary.

KEY

POSITIVE	NEGATIVE
excellent (meal)	restricted (range of
steady (nerves) /ˈstedi/	destinations) /rɪˈstrɪktɪd/
fast (service)	fixed (dates) /ˈfɪkst/
low (cost)	anti-social (courier flight)
reliable /rəˈlaɪəbl/ (staff,	/ˈæntɪ ˌsəʊʃl/
courier)	smart (clothes) /smɑːt/
	expensive (staff)

Note: It is worth discussing why some normally positive adjectives may be negative in this context, e.g. *smart* is negative here because *smart clothes* may not be the most comfortable way to travel.

LISTENING EXERCISE 6
Background note
In Britain, some companies operate a **freephone** system. This means that the company will pay for the telephone calls made to it, especially in answer to an advertisement. In the UK the code for these free numbers is 0800.

Ask the class to read the advertisement and answer the questions. Encourage the students to compare answers with their partners and then check as a class.

KEY
1 ICS
2 It delivers parcels to any destination at any time of the day.
3 Freephone 0800 121213
4 They will come and collect your parcel and organise for delivery to New York.

📟 EXERCISES 7 AND 8
Direct the class to the questions in Exercise 7 and play the conversation. Encourage the students to compare answers in pairs and then check as a class. Follow the same procedure for Exercise 8 but pause the conversation as necessary to allow students to note down the information.

KEY FOR EXERCISE 7
1 books

2 from near Oxford to New York
3 less than 24 hours (if the parcel catches the midday flight)

KEY FOR EXERCISE 8
1 the invoice address; the pick-up address if it's different and a contact phone number; the name, address, phone number of the person the parcel is being sent to; the weight, dimensions and value of the parcel and a full description of the contents
2 check the contents and take the invoices
3 the sender's address and the destination address; the contents of the parcel; the weight and value of the contents; a sentence saying that the information is true and the sender's signature

TAPESCRIPT
EMPLOYEE: ICS. Good morning. How can I help you?
WOMAN: Good morning. I'm thinking of sending a parcel to New York by courier next week. Can you tell me what the procedure is, please?
EMPLOYEE: Certainly. When you ring us, we need the following information: the invoice address – that's probably your own address, isn't it? – and then the pick-up address if that's different. And a contact phone number ...
WOMAN: Just a moment ... I'm taking notes. Phone number ... right.
EMPLOYEE: Then we need the full name, address and phone number of the person you're sending the parcel to.
WOMAN: OK. Anything else?
EMPLOYEE: Yes, the weight and dimensions of the parcel – that's height, width and length ... and the value of the goods ... and a full description.
WOMAN: ... value ... description ...
EMPLOYEE: Yes, but don't seal the parcel. You need to leave it open so that the driver can check the contents when he collects it. After the recent bombing, the airlines said that we'd have to check all parcels; they told us we had to do it.
WOMAN: Fine. Now, how long will the parcel take to get to New York?
EMPLOYEE: One to two working days. Just a moment, I'll check with the manager. Yes, the manager says that there are daily flights at midday. If your parcel catches that flight, it'll arrive within 24 hours.
WOMAN: Good. I live near Oxford. What time would you need to collect from here in order to catch the midday flight?
EMPLOYEE: Near Oxford ... What's your postcode?
WOMAN: OX7.
EMPLOYEE: Just a moment. Yes, the manager says we can collect the parcel from you at 10.15 on the morning of the flight. Now, there's one more thing. What are you planning to send?

WOMAN: Books.

EMPLOYEE: In that case, you'll need to write an invoice for customs. We need six copies, and the driver will take them from you when he collects the parcel. On the invoice you need to write your address and the destination. Then you must say what's in the parcel, and specify the weight and the value. Write a sentence declaring that the information is true, and sign each copy.

WOMAN: . . . sign each copy. Right. Thank you very much. You've been very helpful.

EMPLOYEE: Not at all. Goodbye.

WOMAN: Goodbye.

DISCOVERING LANGUAGE EXERCISE 9

Refer the students to the examples in the exercise and ask them to discuss questions 1–3 in pairs. Check as a class and write the airline representative's exact words on the board. Then copy the chart in question 4 onto the board and ask the students to read sentence B again to complete some more of the chart. Check their answers as a class. Follow the same procedures with sentence C.

KEY

1 no
2 Actual words: You will have to check all parcels; you have to do it.

you – we, would – will, have to – had to
3 The reporting verb in A is in the present and so the tenses do not have to change. In B the reporting verbs (said, told) are in the past and so the tenses change.

4

DIRECT SPEECH	REPORTED SPEECH
present simple	past simple
present progressive (are waiting)	past progressive (were waiting)
past simple (left)	past simple/past perfect (had left)
present perfect (have phoned)	past perfect (had phoned)
past perfect	past perfect
will, can, may	would, could, might
must/have to	had to
would, could, should, might	would, could, should, might

EXERCISE 10

Refer the students back to their notes from Exercises 7 and 8 and divide the class into pairs. First the As tell the Bs what the person at the delivery company said about procedures, using reported speech – the Bs listen and correct any errors A makes. Then they change roles and the Bs tell the As. For feedback, elicit as a class what

the delivery person said. If you wish, write it on the board.

EXERCISE 11

First, ask the students to think of something interesting that has happened to them recently. If they can't think of anything, they can make it up. Then divide them into groups of four and give each student in the group a letter (A B C D). First the As and Bs work together and Cs and Ds work together. They take it in turns to tell each other their stories – they are not allowed to make notes.

They change partners (A – C and B – D) and tell each other their first partner's story. Write He/She told me on the board and establish that they must use reported speech. Again, they are not allowed to make notes. Finally, they regroup (A – D and B – C) and repeat the story they've just been told, so D retells A's story to A and A retells D's story to D. They discuss if the story is accurate or not. If it will help your students, write on the board:

Stage 1 A – B C – D
Stage 2 A – C B – D
Stage 3 A – D B – C

Extra practice

Organise the students into groups of three to do a 'running dictation'. Tell the students that A has seen a crime and is going to tell B. B is going to report it to C, and C is going to write it down. Give each Student A a copy of the text below. The student with the text (A) stands on one side of the room, the writer (C) sits on the other side and the reporter (B) goes between the two: so B runs to A who reads them the first part of the text (A cannot show the text to B). B then runs to C and repeats the text to C in reported speech, e.g. He/she said he/she had seen everything. The thief had taken . . . C writes it down. B then runs back to A for the next piece of text. When the first two teams have written down all the text, stop the dictation. The groups then dictate the text to you and you write it on the board exactly as they say it. The teams then have to correct any errors.

Text

I saw everything. The thief took a gold watch and necklace. I can tell you what he looks like. He's quite young and is wearing jeans and a blue T-shirt. He's about 20 years old. Oh, I've been here for about 20 minutes – I'm waiting for my daughter. When my daughter arrives, we'll catch the bus home. Where do I live? In the town centre – I've lived here all my life. Thank you, officer. I hope you catch him soon.

Short of time?
Exercise 5 can be omitted.

Emergency

Focus	
TOPIC	SKILLS
• Emergency services	• Listening: an interview, phone calls, a conversation
FUNCTIONS	• Speaking: a role play, a report of a conversation
• Telephoning	

GETTING STARTED EXERCISE 1
Background note
A **paramedic** is a member of an ambulance crew who is trained to give medical attention in emergencies, but is not a doctor or a nurse. **Ambulance drivers** or **ambulance men and women** are trained to assist people, but they do not have the same level of medical training as paramedics.

Direct the class to the pictures and the questions. The students discuss the questions in pairs and then as a class.

🔖 Documentary

📼 LISTENING EXERCISE 2
Tell the students that they are going to listen to Michelle Redfern, who is the woman in Picture A. Direct the class to the questions and then play the cassette. Encourage the students to compare answers in pairs and then check as a class.

KEY
1 London Ambulance control room
2 999
3 a British Telecom operator
4 what service you need
5 the exact address of where the ambulance needs to go
6 why the caller needs an ambulance
7 advice
8 that a patient had walked to the surgery with a heart attack
9 to get an ambulance to the address as quickly as possible

TAPESCRIPT
PRESENTER: Listen to an interview with Michelle Redfern, who answers the telephone at the London Ambulance control room.
Part One.
MICHELLE: When somebody dials 999, they'll speak to a British Telecom operator. The operator will ask the caller what service they require – either police, fire brigade or ambulance. The caller then will say 'ambulance service'.
Hello, London Ambulance. Can I help you? ... 12 Edrick House, Page Street. Hold on, what, what area of London is that?
The information you, you want from a caller is the correct location – that is very important – you need to know where they actually are.
OPERATOR 2: *Yes, what's the address, sir? 36 where? Larch – L-A-R-C-H Close. And that's where sir? SW ... South West 12?*
MICHELLE: Once you've actually got the correct information, you then find what is wrong, why they need an ambulance, if you can help – give advice over the phone, and get an ambulance to them as soon as you can.
Part Two.
PRESENTER: The interviewer asked about calls that Michelle had received that day. Listen.
MICHELLE: I received a call from a doctor's receptionist and she said to me that a patient had walked to the surgery with a heart attack.
London Ambulance. Can I help you? ... Is this an immediate ambulance? ... And the doctor's name?
The main aim of my job is to help the public and get them the ambulance there as soon as we can – in the shortest time possible.

📼 SPEAKING EXERCISE 3
Background note
Fulham is an area in West London.

Copy this onto the board:

C   – *caller*
BT – *British Telecom operator*
AS – *Ambulance Service operator*

and direct the class to the conversation. Point out the first question (a) and ask *Who says this?* Elicit *the Ambulance Service operator.* The students then work in pairs and do the same with the other lines of the conversation. Check as a class. Then ask *Is the conversation in the correct order?* Elicit *No.* The pairs work together and put the conversation in the correct order. Play the cassette for them to check their answers. Finally, the students read the conversation as a class or in pairs.

KEY AND TAPESCRIPT
BT: Emergency Services. Fire, police or ambulance?
C: Ambulance, please.
BT: I'm putting you through.
AS: Hello. London Ambulance. Can I help you?
C: Yes, there's been an accident ... a boy has been hit by a car.

AS: Can you tell me exactly where you are?

C: In Fulham, outside number . . . 44, Birchfield Avenue.

AS: Can you spell that, please?

C: B-I-R-C-H-F-I-E-L-D. Birchfield.

AS: Is the boy conscious?

C: Yes, but he's losing a lot of blood . . .

AS: OK, we'll have an ambulance there as soon as possible.

EXERCISE 4

Divide the class into threes and give each student in the group a letter (A, B or C). They each read the information about their role in the exercise. Make sure they change roles for the second and third situations so that they all play all three roles. Monitor and note down any errors you hear. If you wish, volunteer pairs can role play their conversations for the whole class. Finally, use the board to correct any errors you heard.

COMPARING CULTURES EXERCISE 5
Background note

In Britain, it is very unusual to answer a private phone by saying your name. People usually say the telephone number, although it is becoming increasingly common just to say *Hello*. It is likely that a business call would be answered with either the company or the individual's name.

Direct the class to the first extract and discuss the question in groups and then as a class. Follow the same procedure with the second question. In a monolingual class, choose volunteer pairs to 'transform' the two conversations into ones typical of their country. In a multilingual class, discuss the differences between nationalities in the class and how they answer the phone.

KEY FOR EXERCISE 2

The man is Mr Naylor. *Speaking* is the short form of *This is (Mr Naylor) speaking.*

FOCUS ON FUNCTIONS EXERCISE 6

Play the cassette for the students to follow the conversation in their Students' Books. Then direct them to the list of functions and ask *Which expressions ask someone to wait?* Make sure they look only at the phrases in italics. Elicit *Hold the line, please.* and *Just a moment.* The students work in pairs and match the functions and expressions in the conversation in the same way. To check their answers, say the function and elicit the expression. Drill each expression for correct pronunciation chorally and individually.

KEY

a 2, 7 b 5 c 4 d 1 e 3 f 6

EXERCISE 7

The students discuss the questions in pairs. Then discuss as a class and write their answers to the questions on the board. Drill the language for correct pronunciation as necessary.

SUGGESTED KEY

1 Hang on. Wait a moment, please.
2 I'm afraid she's out at the moment/she's at lunch/she's away today/she's on holiday/she's very busy at the moment.
3 Because he's making an offer (*I'll put you through*) and a promise (*I'll let her know*). They are both spontaneous decisions.
4 Shall I give her a message? Shall I tell her you rang? Shall I take a message? Could you call back later? Why don't you try again in half an hour?

EXERCISE 8

Divide the class into As and Bs and direct the students to the information about their roles in the exercise. Establish that they know who they are. They role play their conversations. Make sure they change roles for the second conversation. Monitor and note down any errors you hear. If you wish, volunteer pairs can role play their conversations for the whole class. Finally, use the board to correct any errors you heard.

LISTENING EXERCISE 9

Tell the students that they are going to listen to the conversation between the nurse from Exercise 6 and Ms Bayliss. Direct them to the questions. Play the cassette once. The students compare answers with their partner. If necessary, play the cassette again and then check as a class.

KEY

1 Ms Bayliss's son
2 He had a motorbike accident.
3 He's broken his leg and has got cuts and bruises on other parts of his body.
4 No.
5 24 hours
6 She's going to the hospital and is taking some pyjamas and toiletries for him.

TAPESCRIPT

MS BAYLISS: Hello, this is Helen Bayliss.

NURSE: Hello, Ms Bayliss. I'm phoning from the hospital.

MS BAYLISS: Yes? Has something happened?

NURSE: I'm afraid your son has had an accident.

MS BAYLISS: What? Oh no . . . is he hurt?

NURSE: Well, he's broken his leg and he's got cuts and bruises to other parts of his body.

MS BAYLISS: But he's OK?

NURSE:	Yes, he's seen a doctor and he's going to be all right.
MS BAYLISS:	Oh thank goodness! Can I come in and see him?
NURSE:	Yes, of course. And perhaps you could bring some pyjamas and toiletries in for him.
MS BAYLISS:	So you're going to keep him in overnight?
NURSE:	Yes, but don't worry. It's just routine. The doctor wants to keep him under observation for 24 hours. He wants to make sure there are no problems.
MS BAYLISS:	What do you mean? What kind of problems?
NURSE:	Oh ... nothing. Really, it's just routine after an accident like this.
MS BAYLISS:	I see. But ... what happened? What sort of accident was it?
NURSE:	He was riding his motorbike and was hit by a car.
MS BAYLISS:	Oh ... that motorbike ... I've told him to be careful! When did this happen?
NURSE:	Oh ... about three hours ago.
MS BAYLISS:	Right ... er, well, I'll go and get some things for him and I'll be there as soon as I can.
NURSE:	That'll be fine. Come to reception in Accident and Emergency.
MS BAYLISS:	Right. I'll be there soon. Thanks. Goodbye.
NURSE:	Goodbye.

EXERCISE 10

Divide the students into pairs: the As are Helen Bayliss and Bs are her colleague. Explain that Helen is telling her colleague about the phone call. Ask a pair to read out the example exchange and establish that they must use reported speech in their role play. Monitor and note down any errors you hear and use the board to correct them at the end of the activity.

Short of time?

Exercise 5 can be omitted. Exercise 10 can be written for homework.

WRITING: Short reports

Focus	
TOPIC	**SKILLS**
• Home computers	• Reading: an article, a report
FUNCTIONS	• Speaking: a survey
• Use of tenses in sections of a report	• Writing: a report of a survey
	VOCABULARY DEVELOPMENT
	• Verbs for reporting results

COMPARING CULTURES EXERCISE 1

The students discuss the question in pairs or as a class.

READING EXERCISES 2 AND 3

Direct the class to the headline and picture and discuss the question as a class. The students then read the article to check their answer. Next, they discuss the two questions in pairs. Check as a class.

KEY

The headline means that girls want to use computers to learn but boys like playing with computers (*Game Boys*).The reasons for the differences are that fewer girls have computers at home and girls are less enthusiastic about Information Technology at school. They are more interested in the word-processing and database functions of computers than in video games.

The possible effects are that because girls are less confident and enthusiastic about IT at school, they do not do as well as boys do in this subject. Consequently, there are fewer girls than boys on higher-level computing courses in colleges and schools.

DEVELOPING VOCABULARY EXERCISE 4

Copy these two headings onto the board:

SUGGESTS	SHOWS
	prove

Ask the class to find the two verbs in the article and together discuss question 1. Next, ask *Does 'prove' have a similar meaning to 'suggest' or 'show'?* Elicit *show* and write *prove* in the column on the board. If necessary, check the concept by asking questions e.g. *Are you sure?* (Yes/Not very), *How do you know?* (You can/can't see the result). The students then work in pairs and discuss the other verbs in question 2 in the same way. Elicit their answers and write the verbs on the board with the students' help. Drill for correct pronunciation.

KEY

1 Shows

2 SUGGESTS	SHOWS
indicate	prove
imply	demonstrate
provide some evidence	confirm
	provide conclusive evidence

READING EXERCISE 5

Copy the titles in question 1 onto the board and direct the class to the report. Ask *How many paragraphs are there in the report?* Elicit *five* and ask the students to skim the survey quickly and

match the five paragraphs with the five titles.
Encourage the students to compare answers in
pairs and then check their answers on the board.
Next, they discuss questions 2 and 3 in pairs.
Elicit their answers and write a model
questionnaire on the board with the students'
help. Leave it there for Exercise 8. Discuss where
the mistake is in the chart (question 3).

KEY

1 1 introduction   2 carrying out the survey
   3 results 1   4 results 2   5 conclusion
2 How old are you?
   Do you have computers at home?
   How much time do you spend on your computer in
   an average week?
   What do you use your computer for?
3 The bars show the number of young people who use
   computers for:
   a playing games   b word processing
   c keeping addresses and telephone numbers/keeping
   a diary   d programming   e studying
   f consulting databases   g anything else
   The mistake is that both f and g should read zero, not
   one as in the case of f.

FOCUS ON FUNCTIONS EXERCISE 6

Direct the students back to the report and the
questions. They discuss the uses of the different
tenses in pairs and then as a class.

KEY

a) present simple (*this report presents, the results
   indicate, the chart gives*)
b) past simple (e.g. *we questioned, asked*)
c) past simple and past progressive (*used, they were
   learning*)
d) present simple (e.g. *show, dislike*)
reported speech

EXERCISE 7

Direct the class back to the first paragraph of the
survey and ask *What words does the writer use to
refer to the people in the survey?* Elicit the students'
answers and write them on the board. They then
do the same with the other paragraphs. Check
their answers in the same way. Next, discuss as a
class why the students think the writer uses the
different expressions.

KEY

young people   teenagers   users   people questioned
respondents   14 – 18 year olds   adolescents
The writer uses different expressions to give variety.

SPEAKING EXERCISE 8

Refer the students back to the questionnaire on

the board from Exercise 5 and tell them that they
are going to carry out a class survey. Divide the
class into small groups and ask the students to
write down the questions they would like to ask.
Monitor and help. Then tell the students that
they are going to interview everybody in the
class. Divide the class into four groups: the
students in these groups interview each other.
Make sure they make notes. Then reorganise the
groups to create four (or more) other groups,
each containing at least one member from each
original group. The students then interview each
other. The students then return to their original
groups and compare all their results ready to
write their report.

WRITING EXERCISE 9

Students stay in their groups from Exercise 8 and
write their report, following the structure of the
report in Exercise 5. Remind them of the tenses in
Exercise 6 and the vocabulary in Exercises 4 and
7. They should also include diagrams and charts
to illustrate their findings. Monitor and help.

EXERCISE 10

Direct the class to the questions to help the
students edit their work. They discuss them in
their groups. Alternatively, read out each
question, stopping after each one for the students
to discuss their surveys. The surveys could also
be edited by other groups. If you wish, they can
display their report on a wall chart for the other
students to read – you may also have word-
processing facilities that the students can use to
present their report.

Short of time?

Exercises 9 and 10 can be done as group
homework. Exercise 1 can be omitted, or dealt
with very quickly.

Talkback

The truth game

This is a fluency activity that encourages the use
of a variety of past tenses, and of reported speech
in discussing the stories.
1 The students read the story in the speech bubble
   and then, in pairs, write questions to find out if
   the man is lying or telling the truth.
2 Divide the class into groups of three and direct
   them to the topics and the pictures. They match

the pictures with the topics, then each group chooses one topic from the list. Encourage groups to choose different topics. The students in each group prepare three different stories; they must decide who is going to tell the true story. Make sure they realise that the other groups are going to ask them questions, so they must be really convincing.

3 Organise the class so that two groups of three join to form groups of six. The first group in each six tells their three stories and the other group asks questions. Then they change roles. If you have time, regroup the class so that each group of three joins with a second group to tell their stories.

4 Each group decides who they think from the other group is telling the truth. They then tell the other group – if they guess correctly, they get a point.

5 Then they choose another topic and do the same again. The group with the most points wins the game.

   Alternatively, each group can tell its stories to the whole class and each student writes down individually who he/she thinks is telling the truth. The student with most points at the end wins the game.

15 *A change of scene*

Preparing to leave

Focus

TOPICS
• Preparations for travel
• Working holidays

GRAMMAR
• First conditional
• Conjunctions: *if, unless, when, as soon as*

SKILLS
• Speaking: discussion
• Reading: an article

GETTING STARTED EXERCISE 1
Explain the situation to the class or ask the students to read about it in the introduction to the exercise. Next, copy the headings in the exercise onto the board and ask *What documents will you need?* Elicit their ideas and write them next to/under DOCUMENTS. The students then work in pairs and decide what they will need for the other headings. Monitor and help with vocabulary.

   Tell the students that they can't carry their

bag now because it's too heavy. In their pairs, they decide which items on their list are essential. If you wish, you can limit the number to ten. The pairs then work in groups of four and compare their lists. They have to explain any unfamiliar vocabulary and justify the items they include. Finally, discuss as a class and write a class list on the board. Drill for correct pronunciation as necessary.

SUGGESTED KEY

Documents: passport, visas, travellers' cheques, credit cards, driving licence, letter of employment, 'register' of all the teenagers, receipts for camera and other equipment
Clothes: waterproof clothes, socks, hat, sunglasses, T-shirts, underwear, jeans, jumpers, swimsuit, shorts, pyjamas (or nightwear in general)
Toiletries and medicines: toothpaste, deodorant, antiseptic cream, hairbrush, aspirin, plasters, first-aid kit, suntan cream, soap, malaria tablets, nail scissors, shampoo
Equipment: whistle, rucksack, torch, Swiss army knife, water bottle, maps, town plans
Books: maps, phrase books, novels, puzzle books
Other things: pack of cards, pens and pencils, paper, sweets, alarm clock, camera and film, walkman, spare travel bag

READING EXERCISES 2 AND 3
The students discuss the questions about working holidays in threes. Then discuss as a class and write the students' answers to question 2 on the board. They now read the article and compare their answers with Exercise 2. Check as a class and tick the jobs on the board that the article mentions and add any extra ones.

SUGGESTED KEY

1 open answers
2 tour guide, waiter, au pair, grape picker, shop assistant, hotel staff, interpreter, courier

SPEAKING EXERCISE 4
Direct the students to the questions and ask them to read the article again. They discuss the questions in pairs and then as a class.

SUGGESTED KEY

1 Advantages: work abroad, practise foreign languages, visit interesting places, earn money, no special qualifications needed, good experience
Disadvantages: work long hours with little free time, low pay, can be difficult work (e.g. the courier in Europe), no job security
2 patient, resourceful, calm, fond of children, caring, energetic, keen on sports

3 mostly seasonal jobs: grape picking in France, working on a campsite, working on American summer camps for children, being a nanny, washing dishes in restaurants, being a holiday courier for American children visiting Europe, working in a hotel

EXERCISE 5

Ask the class to find *seasonal work* in the text, define it and then discuss the first question together. The students then work in pairs to define the other four phrases and discuss the questions. Monitor and move them on to the next phrase if they don't understand one of them. Elicit their ideas as a class to check they all understand the vocabulary.

KEY

1 work that is only available during a certain time of the year, e.g. jobs in shops at Christmas and during sales, summer jobs
2 the excitement of travel
3 short-term work which is not guaranteed and is needed for a special purpose, e.g. when a company wants to send out a lot of catalogues, it may employ casual labour to put the catalogues in the envelopes and stick on address labels; casual work does not depend on the time of year
4 the rights a worker has, as set down in the law
5 to lose your job because you have done something wrong, e.g. if you have been rude to a customer

DISCOVERING LANGUAGE EXERCISE 6

Direct the class back to the article and say *Find an example of the first conditional in the article.* Elicit the students' answer and write the sentence on the board. Then tell the students to find the other examples. They dictate them to you to write on the board. Ask *How is it formed?* (*if* + present simple + future simple) and ask *Why is it being used?* (Because it is possible that these things will happen in these situations.) The students then do the same with question 2 and dictate their answers to you. They discuss questions 3 and 4 in pairs and then as a class.

KEY

1 If you work as a nanny ..., you'll have to speak Italian. (*lines 16–18*); You'll work if it's convenient for the company ... (*lines 43–44*); If you don't work hard, or if your employer doesn't like you, you'll get the sack. (*lines 47–48*)
2 a) Unless you speak the language of the country well, there will be very few openings. (*lines 13–15*)
   b) When you arrive to wash dishes in a restaurant in Paris, the owner will expect you to speak French. (*lines 18–20*); You'll have a job when the hotel ...

is busy. (*lines 41–43*)
   c) As soon as the holiday season finishes, they'll get rid of you. (*lines 46–47*)
3 a) Both *if* and *unless* are used in conditional forms but *unless* means *if ... not*, e.g. If you *don't speak* the language ...
   Note: If the students ask about the meaning of *unless* as *except if*, refer them to the Grammar reference on page 126.
   b) Both *when* and *as soon as* are time conjunctions. *As soon as* has the meaning of immediately. They follow the same form as conditional sentences, i.e. *when/as soon as* + present simple, *will* + infinitive without *to*.
4 There is no difference. If the sentence begins with *if*, *as soon as*, *when*, *unless*, there is usually a comma between the two clauses. If the conjunction is in the middle of the sentence, there is no comma.

EXERCISE 7

Direct the class to the text 'Advice for Students' and check that the students understand all the vocabulary. Then point out the conjunctions in brackets. Explain that a mother is reading out the advice and her son is responding. Direct the class to the example exchange in the Students' Book and play the mother's first request. Pause the cassette for the students to respond. Drill for correct pronunciation as necessary. The students can write their responses for checking later. Play the other requests, pausing to allow the students to repeat. Then play the complete conversation for the students to check their answers. Finally, the students can role play similar conversations using the advice but with different conjunctions in the responses.

KEY AND TAPESCRIPT

MOTHER: You'll contact your employers immediately, won't you?
SON: Don't worry! I'll contact them as soon as I arrive.
MOTHER: Look after your bags in public places, won't you!
SON: Of course I'll look after my things if I'm in a public place!
MOTHER: Now, remember not to eat unwashed fruit.
SON: It's all right. I won't eat any fruit unless it's been washed.
MOTHER: And make sure you boil water in rural areas.
SON: Yes, yes. I'll boil the water if I'm outside the cities.
MOTHER: You won't forget to take your malaria tablets every morning?
SON: No. I'll take my malaria tablets when I get up.

MOTHER: And you'll let me know your new address . . . .

SON: Don't worry. I'll write to you when I find somewhere to live.

MOTHER: It says here that it's important to start learning the local language immediately.

SON: Yes, I'll start learning it as soon as I get there.

MOTHER: And you won't accept invitations from strangers, will you?

SON: No, Mother. I won't accept an invitation unless I know the person well. Now, is that it? Can I finish packing?

EXERCISE 8

Tell the students that they are going to give advice to a foreign student who wants to work in their area. Ask them to read the example exchange in the exercise. Give them a few minutes to make notes. They then work in groups of four and discuss their ideas. Then, discuss as a class and use the board to correct any errors you heard.

If you have a multinational class, you could extend the activity by getting the students to write up the advice about getting work in their countries to display for other students to read.

Extra practice

Make a set of cards with the following prompts (or ones appropriate to your students):
– *when, if, unless, as soon as*
– *go to Italy/Greece/Turkey, get a job, take my exams, finish school, learn to drive, learn English well, play tennis tonight, go to the theatre,* etc.

Divide the class into groups of four (two pairs in each) and give each group a set of prompt cards which they place face down in two piles (conjunctions and prompts) on the desk in front of them. The first pair turns over one conjunction card and one prompt card and makes a sentence, e.g. *I'll go to Italy when I have enough money.* The other pair gives one point for correct grammar and one point for the sense of the sentence. They then put the prompts at the bottom of the pile and the game continues. Stop the activity when you wish. The team with the most points wins. **Note:** You may find that some of your students use the present perfect instead of the present simple, e.g. *I'll go to Italy when I've saved enough money.* This is usually acceptable.

Short of time?

Exercise 8 can be omitted.

Getting away

Focus

TOPIC
• Holidays

GRAMMAR
• Indirect questions
• Embedded questions

FUNCTIONS
• Asking politely

SKILLS
• Speaking: discussion, role play
• Listening: a monologue, a conversation at a travel agent's
• Writing: form completion

COMPARING CULTURES EXERCISES 1 AND 2

To introduce the topic, ask *What do you think are the most popular holiday destinations for British tourists?* Students answer before they open their books. Quickly brainstorm the students' ideas on the board and then confirm them according to the list. Then divide the students into groups of four to discuss the two questions in Exercise 1. Monitor and note down any errors you hear. Compare their ideas as a class. The students then discuss Exercise 2 in their groups or as a class. Finally, use the board to correct the errors. In a multilingual class, try to ensure that the groups consist of four different nationalities.

Documentary

LISTENING EXERCISE 3

Direct the class to the photographs from the holiday brochure in the Students' Book. The students discuss the kinds of holidays the company organises in pairs or as a class. Do not confirm their answers yet.

EXERCISE 4
Background note
Kuoni is a travel company in the UK which is well-known for its exotic holidays in quite distant places.

Direct the class to the picture of Maria Paul and establish what her job is (travel agent) and who the people are with her (clients). Refer the students to the questions and tell them that they are going to check their answers from Exercise 3, and to answer the questions in Exercise 4. Play the cassette once. Students compare their answers in pairs. If necessary, play the cassette again and then check as a class.

SUGGESTED KEY FOR EXERCISE 3

The photographs show: a hotel in Kurumba in the Maldives, a Caribbean cruise, the Nile and a Thai temple. The students should infer that the company specialises in long-haul, luxury holidays.

KEY FOR EXERCISE 4

1 c   2 b   3 a
4 Thailand, Hong Kong, Barbados, Egypt

TAPESCRIPT

MARIA PAUL

Kuoni offer some very exciting tours. We go to some quite unusual places that possibly people haven't heard too much about: little islands like Koh Samui. We go to places like the Maldive Islands – lots of different islands with very different characters, different things to offer everyone, everything from a particularly deluxe island like Kurumba down to tiny little islands with just very basic accommodation, restaurants with sand floors, that type of thing. And then there's completely the other end of the market: Princess cruises around the Caribbean, the ultimate in, in luxury. The customers can ask for absolutely anything and we'll provide it, but I think probably the most popular destinations overall are Thailand, Hong Kong, Barbados in the Caribbean, although other Caribbean islands also do very well; Egypt is always popular – a lot of people are fascinated by Egypt and the culture; the Nile cruises in particular are always very full. Working in the travel business, you find that every day is different. You don't know what the client is going to want. When they come through the door, they could ask for anything. They could ask for a rail ticket or they could ask for the most wonderful exotic holiday.

EXERCISE 5

Direct the students to the questions and explain that they are going to listen to part of a conversation in a travel agency. Play the conversation and ask the students to compare answers in pairs. If necessary, play it again and then check as a class.

KEY

1 Egypt   2 two weeks   3 by plane and boat
4 three (Cairo, Aswan, Luxor)
5 in the morning (10.45)
6 a, b and c

WRITING EXERCISE 6

If you wish, ask the students to copy the booking form into their notebooks. First they complete the form with the information that they have got from Exercise 5. Then play the complete conversation. Encourage them to compare answers in pairs. If necessary, play the conversation again. Then elicit their answers and write them on the board with their help.

KEY

BOOKING FORM

Names of travellers

Surname	Initials	Mr/Ms
Porter	S. A.	Ms
Porter	G. L.	Mr

Telephone
Home: 386775   Office: 625903

Travel details

Outward	Date	16th April	Time	10.45
	From	Heathrow	To	Cairo
	Airline	Egyptair		
Return	Date	30th April	Time	20.50
	From	Cairo	To	Heathrow
	Airline	Egyptair		

Accommodation

Hotel name Pullman Maadi Towers
            Number of nights 4
Boat name   Osiris
            Number of nights 10

Deposit   2 people at £100 each = £ 200
Insurance 2 people at 41 each = £ 82

TAPESCRIPT

AGENT: OK, so I'll just go through that with you again. Two adults. Two weeks in Egypt from April 16th to the 30th. Flying from Heathrow to Cairo and back with Egyptair. Two nights at the Pullman Maadi Towers in Cairo, then by air to Aswan. A ten-day Nile cruise from Aswan, through Luxor and back to Cairo, followed by two more nights at the Pullman Maadi Towers, flying back to Heathrow on the 30th. And you're in a double room at the hotel and a double cabin on the boat, which is the Osiris.

MAN: Yes, that's right. Um ... do you know what the flight times are?

AGENT: The outward flight from London is, er ... let me see. Yes , 10.45 ... in the morning. And the return is ... I think it's early evening ... yes ... 20.50. Ten to nine in the evening. Local time, that is.

MAN: Right, that's fine.

WOMAN: Oh ... sorry. I can't remember what you include in the price. Is it all meals or just breakfast?

AGENT: Yes, it's full board … so all meals … and transfer from the airport to your hotel … everything's included.

WOMAN: Good.

AGENT: Now, can you tell me if you need travel insurance?

WOMAN: Yes, yes we do.

AGENT: OK, well, that's an extra £41 each. Is that OK?

MAN: Well, there's no choice is there? I mean, we have to have it, don't we?

AGENT: Yes, I'm afraid so.

MAN: Well, all right then.

The conversation stops here in Exercise 5, but continues in Exercise 6.

AGENT: OK. I wonder if I could I take some details now. Right. Could I have your names, please?

WOMAN: The surname's Porter. P-O-R-T-E-R.

AGENT: And your initials, please?

WOMAN: S.A.

AGENT: S.A? And yours, sir?

MAN: G.L.

AGENT: G.L. Right. And can I have your telephone number, please?

MAN: Our home number's 386775.

AGENT: 386775. And do you have a work number – in case I need to contact you during the day?

WOMAN: You can put mine down. It's 625903.

AGENT: Fine. OK. If you could just sign the booking form here. Thank you. And I need a deposit.

WOMAN: Now? Er … can I pay by credit card?

AGENT: Yes, of course, then we'll call you when the tickets arrive from the airline. I don't know when you want to pay the balance of the holiday price, but we will need it before we can issue the tickets. Perhaps you could come into the office some time next week?

WOMAN: Er … yes, I mean, that should be OK.

FOCUS ON FUNCTIONS EXERCISE 7

Note: The students can also use *whether* instead of *if* in indirect and embedded questions which do not start, in direct form, with a question word.

Direct the class to the lines from the conversation and the questions. The students work in pairs and discuss the questions. Check as a class and use the board to highlight the form.

KEY

1 to be more polite or formal

2 A: What are the flight times?
The verb and subject are inverted.
B: Do you need travel insurance?
If is replaced by the auxiliary verb *do*.

3 C, D and E are statements grammatically and questions functionally.

4 C: What do you include in the price?
The auxiliary *do* is added before the subject.
D: Could I take some details now?
The verb and subject are inverted.
E: When do you want to pay the balance of the holiday price?
The auxiliary *do* is added before the subject.

EXERCISE 8

To demonstrate the task, copy the example question onto the board and say *Make the question more polite using 'Could you'.* (*Could you tell me when the plane leaves?*) Elicit the question and drill it chorally and individually. Do the same with *I wonder* (*I wonder when the plane leaves.*) The students then work in pairs. They read the question and then take it in turns to make the question more polite using the prompts. Monitor and correct any errors you hear. Elicit the questions and write them on the board with the students' help.

KEY

1 Could you tell me how much this costs?
I wonder how much this costs.

2 Can you tell me which airport you want to leave from?
I don't know which airport you want to leave from.

3 Can you tell me if you want a luxury hotel?
I can't remember if you want a luxury hotel.

4 Do you know if you would like to hire a car?
I don't know if you would like to hire a car.

5 Do you know when you will be able to pay the balance?
I wonder when you will be able to pay the balance.

SPEAKING EXERCISE 9

Divide the class into pairs and direct the As (the customers) to the information on page 123 and the Bs (travel agents) to the information on page 128. To demonstrate the task, explain that they must be as polite as possible, and choose a pair to read out the example exchange. They then role play their conversations. Monitor and note down any errors you hear. If you wish, they can change roles. For feedback, ask volunteer pairs to role play their exchanges for the whole class and finally use the board to correct any errors you heard.

SUGGESTED KEY

1 Can you tell me what time the outward flight is?
Of course, your plane leaves at 16.45.

2 And I can't remember how much the baggage allowance is.
You're allowed to take 20 kg.

3 Can you tell me when I arrive in Bangkok?
   Yes, certainly. The flight arrives at 05.50.
4 And I don't know the name of the hotel.
   It's the Hotel Caledonian.
5 I can't remember how many days the holiday is.
   It's 10 nights.
6 I wonder if I've already booked the car.
   No, you haven't.
7 Do you know if I have all the meals at the hotel?
   No, you only have breakfast at the hotel.
8 Can you tell me if I need a visa?
   Yes, you do.

Extra practice

Tell the students that a customs officer has stopped a tourist at Heathrow airport and is interviewing him/her. Brainstorm the questions the customs officer could ask and write them on the board, e.g. *What's your name? Where do you come from? How old are you? What do you do? Why do you want to visit Britain? Have you been to Britain before? Where are you going to stay? What are you going to do? How long are you going to stay?* etc. Then tell the class that the tourist has got amnesia and can't remember anything about him/herself and that the customs officer is trying to be very polite and patient. Divide the class into pairs: As are the tourists and Bs are the customs officers. To demonstrate the task, indicate a customs officer to ask you the first question on the board, e.g. *Can you tell me what your name is?* and reply *I don't know what my name is.* If necessary, ask a tourist the same question. The students then role play their conversations. Monitor and note down any errors you hear for correction at the end of the activity. If you wish, they can also write the dialogue.

CREATIVE WRITING: Persuasion

Focus

VOCABULARY DEVELOPMENT

TOPICS
• Persuasion
• Travel brochures

• Adjectives: degrees of intensity

SKILLS
• Reading: persuasive and neutral texts
• Writing: a persuasive description

READING EXERCISE 1

Direct the class to the questions and ask them to read extracts A – C. The students compare their answers in pairs and then discuss as a class.

KEY

1 A is from an advertisement.
  B is from information on the back of a guidebook.
  C is from a personal letter.
2 A is written for potential travellers.
  B is written for travellers to a particular country.
  C is written for a friend.
3 A is to sell flights/to persuade people to fly with a particular airline.
  B is to persuade people to buy the guidebook.
  C is to invite the friend to come to the island on holiday.

EXERCISE 2

If you wish, bring in travel brochures and ask the students *What information would you expect to find in a travel brochure?* Elicit an idea and write it on the board. The students then work in pairs to write their lists, skimming through the travel brochures if you've brought them. Compare their ideas as a class and write them on the board. Leave them there for the next exercise.

EXERCISE 3

Refer the students to Extract D and the questions. Encourage them to compare answers in pairs and then discuss as a class. Tick off the information on the board that they predicted in Exercise 2 and add any other ideas from the text.

KEY

1 someone who was thinking of going on holiday to Bali
2 The qualities mentioned are: the weather, landscape and scenery, resorts and facilities, buildings, entertainment, local handicrafts and culture, the local people.

EXERCISE 4

Copy the four topics in the exercise onto the board and ask the students to read Extract D again. They number the topics in the order they are mentioned in the text. Check their answers as a class and write the topics as headings on the board. To demonstrate question 2 ask *What words and phrases are used to talk about the nature/climate?* Elicit their answers and write them under the heading on the board. The students then do the same in pairs. Check their answers as a class and drill the vocabulary for correct pronunciation as necessary.

KEY

1 The order is b, d, a, c.
2 Nature/climate: radiant sunshine, fresh/verdant landscape, beautiful sunsets, dazzling white beaches,

stunning mountain scenery, clear blue lake and sea waters

Modern facilities: vibrant coastal resorts, high-quality modern hotels, exciting nightlife, bright lights

Local culture: traditional way of life, spectacular temples, colourful ritual dances, shadow puppet plays, vast range of handicrafts, the strength and vitality of the local culture

People: friendly and gentle Balinese will welcome you

EXERCISE 5

First ask the class *Is the language in the brochure colourful or neutral?* Elicit *colourful.* Then tell the students that they are going to do some work on the language in the text. Write *radiant* on the board and ask *What is a more neutral word for 'radiant'?* Elicit *bright.* The students then work in pairs and do the same for questions 1–3. If they do not have access to dictionaries, encourage them to guess the meaning of the words from their context. Elicit their ideas and write the alternatives on the board.

Then ask them to do question 4 in pairs, supplying alternatives if you wish. Check questions 1–4 as a class before doing question 5, helping the students where necessary.

To demonstrate question 5, ask one student to read out the first line of the extract and another one to read out the example in the Students' Book. Write the example on the board. The students then work in pairs to rewrite the extract. To check their answers, elicit their sentences and write a model text on the board with the students' help.

SUGGESTED KEY

1 b) green   c) bright   d) pretty   e) busy
   f) interesting   g) big
2 a) has   b) see   c) has existed   d) enjoy
3 a) countryside   b) pleasures   c) pleasant place
4 is blessed, temples, ritual, paradise (This question focuses on the general 'feeling' given to the text.)
5 Visitors from all over the world come to see the mountains, lakes and sea. In the busy coastal resorts you will find modern hotels and nightlife, but you will also find a traditional way of life which has existed for a long time. You can see the temples, ritual dances, shadow puppet plays and a big range of handicrafts, which show you something of the local culture. The Balinese people will welcome you and you will want to return to this place.

Note: The final sentence above could be considered opinion only and could be omitted.

DEVELOPING VOCABULARY EXERCISE 6

Copy the eight adjectives onto the board and brainstorm the alternatives that the students can think of for *good.* Write them on the board. The students then work in pairs and do the same for the other adjectives. Elicit their ideas as a class and write them on the board. Drill for correct pronunciation as necessary. Next, point to the adjectives for *good* on the board and draw a scale like this:

good ————————————————————▶

Ask the class *Which is the strongest word?* Elicit the answer and write it on the scale. Do the same with the other adjectives. The students then work in pairs and do the same task with the other adjectives. Follow the same procedures for checking their answers.

SUGGESTED KEY

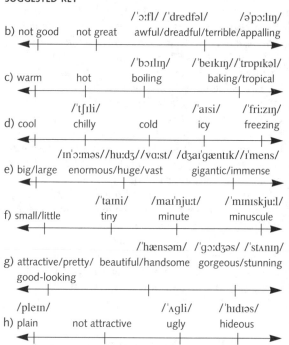

WRITING EXERCISE 7

Direct the class to the brochure pictures and discuss where the place is, what they can see, what the climate is like, what facilities there are, what local culture there is, etc. as a class. The students read the text to see if their ideas were correct. Then ask *Is the language neutral or colourful?* (Neutral) and tell the students that they are going to work in pairs to make it more interesting to the reader. Direct them to the guidelines and ask them to read the example. The students then work in pairs and rewrite the text in the same way, using the language from Exercises 5 and 6. Monitor and help. They can either exchange texts to compare ideas and check for errors or you can discuss their writing sentence by sentence and write a model text on the board containing all their ideas.

SUGGESTED KEY

The visitors who flock to Rio can relax by sailing and swimming in the clear blue sparkling sea which laps gently on the capital's beaches. They also enjoy walking in the spectacular verdant mountain scenery which overlooks the bustling city. Rio is renowned for its vast range of shopping facilities, its delightful and mouth-watering international restaurants, and its vibrant nightlife which will take you through to dawn. A marvellous time to visit is during the fantastic carnival season in February but the colourful local *samba* schools welcome tourists all through the year. The lively and friendly people of Brazil will welcome you with open arms and you will never consider another holiday destination after sampling the delights of this paradise.

EXERCISE 8

Tell the students that they are going to write an extract about a place in their country for a travel brochure. First they make notes under the topics in Exercise 4 and brainstorm words and phrases that they want to use to describe the place as vividly as possible. Monitor and help with the vocabulary. Encourage the students to reread their writing for errors. They then read each others' extracts and write their name at the bottom of the one that they would like to visit as a result of the writing.

Short of time?

Exercise 8 can be done for homework.

Progress check:
Units 14–15

Grammar and functions

EXERCISE 1

1 When   2 arrive   3 If   4 isn't   5 will show
6 unless   7 If   8 take   9 unless   10 want   11 When
12 will need   13 as soon as   14 can   15 if
16 will get

EXERCISE 2

RECEPTIONIST: Good afternoon, can I help you?
CLIENT: Good afternoon. Can I speak to the manager, please?/Could you put me through to the manager, please?
RECEPTIONIST: I'm afraid he's not here at the moment.

CLIENT: Could you tell me where he is, please?
CLIENT: Could you put me through to his secretary, please?
RECEPTIONIST: Could you tell me your name, please?
RECEPTIONIST: Could you just hold the line, please?

EXERCISE 3

1 I don't know if it rains in Morocco in January.
2 I can't remember if you need a visa.
3 I wonder which the best hotel in Casablanca is.
4 I'll find out where you can ski.
5 I know which currency they use.

EXERCISE 4

1 She said it rained in coastal areas but that it didn't rain much in Marrakesh.
2 She said that she had asked the embassy about visas.
3 Last week she asked me if I could check the hotels in my guidebook the next day.
4 She told me that they were planning to go into the Atlas Mountains.
5 Before they left, she said that she would ask about money because they probably couldn't buy Moroccan dirhams here.

Vocabulary

EXERCISE 5

1 How big was the desert?
2 How interesting/nice/pretty were the mountains?
3 How bright was the sun?
4 How good was the food?
5 How cold was the sea?
6 How bad was your sunburn?

Teacher development tasks

Introduction

....

It is easy to be so concerned with the progress of our students that we forget about the importance of our own professional development. We owe it to our students, and especially to ourselves, to be open to new ideas and perspectives, to extend our own awareness of language, to learn from others and to re-evaluate our own procedures. For this reason, a number of worksheets for teacher development have been included here. We feel that they are potentially useful to a wide range of teachers, even those with considerable experience.

The content of these worksheets focuses on both language awareness and classroom practice. All are set in the context of challenges faced when working with intermediate learners.

The worksheet tasks are intended to raise awareness and provoke discussion. Notes on each of the worksheets are provided at the end of the Worksheet section, but these are our comments presented from our perspective and are presented as suggested answers only. You may find that the insights you gain from using the worksheets are different from and/or go beyond what is offered in the notes.

Who are the worksheets for?

1 INDIVIDUAL TEACHERS WORKING ALONE

Although it is always helpful to discuss ideas with other teachers, it is possible to work through the tasks on your own. You may then wish to look at the notes at the end of the section or turn to teachers' handbooks and resource books which focus specifically on areas that you would like to explore further.

2 TEACHER TRAINEES WORKING WITH A TEACHER TRAINER

The worksheets can be photocopied and can therefore be used freely as input or follow-up self-study materials for seminars or courses. Ways of working with the materials are described more fully under 3 below, but one possible procedure is to do the tasks in pairs or small groups and follow this up with a more general discussion led by the trainer.

3 GROUPS OF TEACHERS WHO MEET TO SHARE THEIR EXPERIENCE AND IDEAS

Teachers working in the same institution or geographical area often meet regularly to discuss theoretical and practical teaching issues. Meetings such as these are particularly useful to teachers who are relatively new to the profession and who can be helped by the greater experience of their colleagues. However, more experienced teachers will also find it helpful to reflect on their own knowledge and repertoire of techniques and may be surprised and stimulated by the quite different ideas of some of their colleagues.

You can work through a complete worksheet in a self-development session, or select tasks that are particularly relevant to the group. There are a number of possible ways of preparing for sessions. You can – individually – read and think about either the worksheets themselves or the general focus beforehand, and perhaps do some background reading so that you have more to contribute to the discussion. You can also think about and note down questions that you have in relation to the topics and any problems that you wish to raise at the meeting. Following the session, you may wish to read books and articles that your colleagues have recommended on the subject and these may well lead you to wider discussions on related topics.

Motivating intermediate learners

1 Think about the statement below. Do you agree with it? Why (not)? What arguments might be used by a teacher whose opinion is different from yours?

❝ Intermediate learners are more difficult to teach than beginners. ❞

2 Look at these comments by intermediate learners and their teachers.

1 Do you recognise the problems on the left as ones that intermediate learners often have? Do your students have these problems? If not, why not?
2 Do you share the frustrations of the teachers on the right? If not, why not?

A

I've got no idea how much progress I'm making. There's always so much more to learn.

D

My classes are mixed ability. Some students are bored and others get left behind.

B

I've learnt a lot of different structures and functional phrases, but I don't really know when to use them.

E

Students enjoy communicative classes, but they have to take traditional exams which don't test these skills.

C

I feel silly when I speak because I make mistakes and I can't think of the right word.

F

At this level my students need to be exposed to a lot more English outside the class, but I haven't got time to encourage and monitor this.

3 Consider these suggestions for dealing with Problem A above. Are there others you can add? How could you try to overcome the other problems? Write the aim and two or three strategies for each one.

A *Aim:* to show students what they have achieved
  Strategies:
  Make learning aims clear.
  Give frequent informal and formal tests with quick feedback.
  Praise successful use of language rather than concentrating on correction.
  Repeat activities done at the beginning of the year/course to show how much less challenging they have become.
  When authentic texts have been understood, emphasise that they were written for native speakers.
  Play tapes of real conversations to show that native speakers hesitate, struggle for words and misunderstand each other.

4 Use your experience to complete the following tasks.

1 List other motivational problems that learners may have:
  a) as a group   Example: *Each student in the class has different requirements.*
  b) individually   Example: *Particular needs are not satisfied.*
  Which of these are particularly true of intermediate students?
2 Note down additional problems that you have when teaching intermediate students.
  Example: *They use their first language even when they don't need to.*

5 Consider strategies for dealing with the problems that you identified in Exercise 4.

What's in a written text?

1 **Read the texts below and discuss these questions.**

1 Can you predict how each text is likely to continue in terms of content and overall organisation, grammar and vocabulary?
2 Can you predict more about some texts than others? Why?
3 Where might you find each text?

2 **Consider the ways in which texts are organised.**

1 Match these organising principles with the texts as you expect them to develop.
  a) problem – solution   d) background – instructions
  b) chronological sequence   e) setting – events
  c) question – answer
2 How would you expect these text types to be organised?
  a) a letter of complaint   b) a book review   c) an academic research report

A	B	C	D	E
SO WHAT WOULD £100,000 GET YOU TODAY? Ten years ago, £100,000 would have bought you a three-bedroom flat in Kensington, an old rectory in the country or an island off Scotland. Four years later, when the market peaked in the last quarter of 1988, £100,000 was just below the average price for any house in Greater London and the South-East. That average has now fallen to £77,000. So what would £100,000 buy you today?	Canasta, a game of the Rummy family, originated in South America. In 1949 it spread like wildfire across America, and it has since become popular all over the world. The game is easy to learn and extremely exciting, but at the same time its strategy is sufficiently complex to interest serious card players.	If you are faced with a completely new garden, attached to a house that has just been built and consisting of a bare patch of soil studded with builders' rubble, your first instinct might be to rush off to the nearest garden centre and buy armfuls of plants to cover up the bareness. There are some things in life, however, that can't be rushed, and planning a garden is definitely one of them.	P. D. James was born in Oxford in 1920 and educated at Cambridge High School. From 1949 to 1968 she worked in the National Health Service as an administrator, and the experience she gained from her job helped her with the background for *Shroud for a Nightingale*, *The Black Tower*, and *A Mind to Murder*.	She might have been waiting for her lover. For three-quarters of an hour she had sat on the same high stool, half turned from the counter, watching the swing door. Behind her the ham sandwiches were piled under a glass dome, the urns gently steamed. As the door swung open, the smoke of engines silted in, grit on the skin and like copper on the tongue.

*See page 133 for sources of these texts

3 **What is the overall purpose of Text A? What structural device does the writer use to achieve that purpose? What features of the text make it clear that this is a complete paragraph?**

4 **How do writers link clauses/sentences to make texts flow? Find examples of:**

a) a noun phrase that refers back to another noun. (Text B)
b) a pronoun that refers back to a noun. (Text B)
c) an adverb that refers back to a particular time. (Text B)
d) a noun phrase that refers back to a much longer phrase. (Text A)

5 **How formal is Text C? How does the writer achieve this level of (in)formality?**

6 **Compare Texts D and E.**

1 In which text does the writer have a wider choice of possible lexical items? Why is this so?
2 What is the effect in Text E, the opening paragraph of a novel, of using these words rather than the possibilities given in brackets?
  a) lover (boyfriend)   b) same high stool (omit *same*)   c) swing door (omit *swing*)
  d) steamed (hissed)   e) silted (drifted)
3 Text D begins with 'P. D. James' and Text E begins with 'She'. What different effects do these choices create?

What's in a spoken text?

1 **Without looking at the text on the right, list the features that you feel characterise spoken language.**

2 **The text is the transcription of a real conversation.**

1 What is the relationship between the two speakers?
2 What is the purpose of their conversation?

3 **Study the text in detail and answer these questions.**

1 Which words frequently occur in subject position?
2 In what ways is the organisation different from that of a written text? Look, for example, at lines 10–16.
3 What features do you notice in lines:
   a) 8–10?
   b) 17, and 20–21?
   c) 39–41?
4 What is happening in lines 33–38?
5 What are the different meanings of the words *nice* and *dogmatic* as they are used between line 23 and the end? Are the meanings of these words constant throughout?
6 What do you notice about the range and choice of vocabulary?
7 To what extent are the speakers:
   a) transmitting information?
   b) being co-operative with each other?
   c) being clear and concise?
8 To what extent do you feel the features you have looked at in 1–7 above are characteristic of spoken texts in general?

4 **Which of the features that you noted in Exercise 3 do you think are typical of a service encounter in a shop?**

5 **Look back at your list from Exercise 1. Do you want to amend it in any way?**

NATHAN: We've fought for all this time for the simple reason that you refuse to allow me to have the space in my life to invite people over to stay here.

GLORIA: That's not true. I said I know I'm not -5 gonna feel like this forever – let me think about how I can deal with this. The way I have decided to deal with it is not to be here. I don't want to be here. I just don't want to be here. I -10 don't want to be around someone I'm totally uncomfortable with and I can't be myself around because everything he's gonna say ... and I'm gonna be sitting there like – oh no, I can't -15 believe he said that!

NATHAN: Then why can't you ... Gloria, I feel like your role in life is to react to things that happen around you and that's it, that's all you ever do. Why don't you, -20 I mean, come on, you know, why don't you talk to some people? For one thing you'll be less dogmatic ... it'll be nice.

GLORIA: I don't want to be less dogmatic. I like -25 being dogmatic. I like thinking what I think. I like having strong opinions.

NATHAN: You don't have to change any of those things ...

GLORIA: You want me to be nice and mellow -30 and polite and docile and I'm not willing to be your nice little wife ...

NATHAN: Gloria. Nice, mellow, polite and docile are four words. Three of them mean similar things and one of them is not a -35 synonym. Docile ... you don't have to be nice *and* docile ... that's not the same thing.

GLORIA: Nathan, I'm not nice ...

NATHAN: ... polite and docile are different ... -40

GLORIA: ... I'm just not nice ... and you're gonna have to just live with that if you're interested. I'm just not nice. That's not what I am. I don't walk around buttering people up because -45 I'm supposed to be this nice female type saying – 'Oh yes, let me get you some tea' ... 'Would you like something to drink?' ... I am not nice.

> A If it doesn't rain, the crops will die.   D The crops died if it didn't rain.
> B The crops wouldn't die if it rained.   E The crops won't die if it's rained.
> C If it doesn't rain, the crops die.   F If it were to rain, the crops might not die.

1 Look at the sentences in the box above.

1 Add words and phrases to provide a context for each sentence.
2 Which structures are intermediate students likely to recognise?
3 Which ones can you name?
4 What do we teach intermediate students about the forms and uses of the structures you chose in question 2?
5 What mistakes do students make with the standard form of these structures?
6 Choose a structure from the list above that intermediate students are not usually taught. If a student asked about it, how would you explain its use?

2 Now study the sentences in detail.

1 Which sentences refer to situations which are:
   a) hypothetical?   b) past?   c) future?   d) general truths?
2 Which words or phrases can replace *if* or *if . . . not* in these sentences?
3 In which sentences does *if* mean *whenever*?
4 What are the similarities and differences between:
   a) the basic zero conditional pattern in Sentence C and the variation in Sentence D?
   b) the basic first conditional pattern in Sentence A and the variation in Sentence E?
   c) the basic second conditional pattern in Sentence B and the variation in Sentence F?
5 Which other forms of the verb *rain* can replace:
   a) *doesn't rain* in Sentence A?   b) *rained* in Sentence B?
   What do these verb forms have in common? How does the meaning of the sentence change in each case?
6 Which auxiliaries can replace:
   a) *will* in Sentence A?   b) *wouldn't* in Sentence B?
   What is the effect of these different auxiliaries on the meaning of each sentence?
7 What generalisations can you make that can help you explain variations in the first and second conditional patterns that are taught to intermediate students?

3 Which of the functions in the box can describe the uses of Sentences 1–8 below? Can you generate other *if* sentences for each function? Practise saying them with appropriate intonation.

> a) prediction   b) suggestion   c) threat   d) criticism   e) offer
> f) explanation   g) negotiation   h) polite request

1 'If you do that once more . . . !'
2 'If you could reduce the price, I'm sure we could come to some arrangement.'
3 'Go and lie down if you're tired.'
4 'If I could just ask you to wait for a few minutes . . .'
5 'You can have it if you like.'
6 'If they were your own tools, you'd keep them clean.'
7 'Italy will win if Baggio is playing.'
8 'If you press that switch, the stage lights will come on.'

1 What, in your view, does it mean to 'know' a word in your own or a foreign language? Note down the points that occur to you.

2 Consider the word *honest* as an example of a particular lexical item.

1 What part(s) of speech can it be?
2 Can we add any prefixes to it? Which one(s)?
3 Can we add any suffixes to it? Which one(s)?
4 Are there any features of spelling and pronunciation that you would need to bring to the attention of your students? What are they?
5 Is there a direct translation in your students' language(s)?

Answer the remaining questions with reference to the English word or, if you find this difficult, refer to the word that is most similar in meaning to *honest* in your language.

6 Are there other words that have similar meanings? Are the meanings and contexts of use exactly the same? If not, what are the differences?
7 Are there words that have an opposite meaning?
8 Are there any words that commonly occur with this word? (i.e. what sort of people and things can be *honest*?)
9 Can you think of any fixed phrases or idioms in which the word occurs?

3 Think about the way in which cultural connotations of words can differ.

1 Look at this statement: ❝I was tried by an honest judge. ❞
  a) What exactly does *honest* mean in this case?
  b) What do we learn about the speaker's view of judges?
  c) Which of these characteristics do you associate with judges?
    serious unpredictable sympathetic corruptible wealthy intelligent
    insecure fair pompous privileged
    Do you know of other cultures in which the associations are different?

2 What are the connotations of these words and phrases to you, and to people generally in your culture?
  a) a cup of tea, e.g. *Will it normally have milk in it?*
  b) pride, e.g. *Is this a negative quality?*
  c) politicians, e.g. *Are they representative?*
  d) football fans, e.g. *Are they anti-social?*
  e) to shout, e.g. *Do you do this when you are happy?*

4 'Lexical items' (e.g. *honest*) are often distinguished from 'function words' (e.g. *because, for, can*).

1 Consider the word *so*.
  a) How many different structures can you think of in which it occurs?
  b) How many different meanings of *so* can you identify?
  c) When *so* is used as a conjunction, what are its main functions? Which other words have similar functions?

2 Some lexical items, like *reason*, can also have clear functions.
  a) Which words frequently occur in these positions?
    the reason . . . . *this/that reason*
  b) Contextualise each phrase in one or two sentences. In each case, does the phrase come before or after the reason that is given?

5 Do you want to add anything to the list you made in Exercise 1?

1 Look at these contexts of language use. For each context, list the language that you would expect to occur naturally in terms of:

a) the grammatical structures   b) the functional language

1 A group of people are having a discussion about life in the future. Some are optimistic and others are pessimistic.

2 A family are in a travel agent's to book a holiday. They are not sure of the kind of holiday they want.

3 Two people are standing on a mountain. Below them they can see a town, a number of villages and three or four beaches. Using their map, they are trying to work out what each place is called.

2 One function often suggests another which is likely to follow it in a conversation, e.g. greet – greet; give an opinion – agree/disagree. Which functions would you expect to follow these?

a) compliment –   e) complain –

b) invite –   f) express fear –

c) state a problem –   g) give permission –

d) ask for an explanation –   h) offer –

3 Match the language areas on the left with contexts in which they are likely to occur and which would therefore be useful for language practice. Think of a sample sentence for each context that includes an example of the language area.

1 *used to* + infinitive	a) a conversation at a tourist office
2 past progressive/past simple contrast	b) an end-of-term party
3 present perfect passive	c) a test on common road signs
4 present perfect progressive	d) a verbal report of a meeting with a famous person
5 reported speech	e) an account of childhood
6 giving advice	f) agreeing on a travel itinerary
7 stating obligations and prohibitions	g) a progress report on the building of a new house
8 talking about preferences	h) an annual interview focusing on an employee's performance
9 discussing plans and intentions	i) a conversation with a friend who wants to overcome a phobia
10 asking polite (indirect) questions	j) an eye-witness's report of a crime

4 Can you think of a different context for each of the language areas in Exercise 3 – a context that would interest your particular students?

5 Consider different ways of establishing a context for language practice for your students.

1 Add to this list:
- cards for role play (e.g. Exercise 3 a)
- a simple instruction (e.g. Exercise 3 b: Find out your classmates' plans for the summer)
- picture cards (e.g. Exercise 3 c)

2 Choose a way of introducing each of the contexts that you thought of in Exercise 4.

Notes on the Worksheets

Worksheet 1

Aim: to explore ways of dealing with problems of motivation

1 Examples:
(*Agree*) My knowledge and intuitions are constantly challenged in intermediate classes, so I have less confidence.
(*Disagree*) I don't need to prepare as many different activities as I do for beginners, because students have much more to contribute.

2 open answers

3 B *Aim:* to help students use language appropriately
Example strategies:
Within clear contexts, explore the effects of choosing different language patterns.
Record one group doing a freer practice activity; play it to the class, praise the strengths, and elicit phrasing that would make it even more communicatively effective.
  C *Aim:* to give students the confidence to speak freely
Example strategies:
Be generous with praise, particularly with less confident students.
Teach students ways of rephrasing or paraphrasing if they can't find the exact words.
  D *Aim:* to deal effectively with mixed-ability classes
Example strategies:
Seat more and less able students together, to work in pairs.
Set the better students more complex tasks based on the same input.
  E *Aim:* to reconcile communicative methodology with traditional tests
Example strategies:
Dedicate one class in five to exam practice and techniques, so that students can confidently transfer their skills to other task types.
Ask students to work together on exam-type activities, so that the tasks become more communicative.
  F *Aim:* to encourage students to learn independently
Example strategies:
Ask students to report to you and the class (e.g. via notes on a wallchart) what they have read, listened to, written or talked about in English outside class in the last week.
Place a box in the classroom to which students add articles, advertisements, videos, etc. that they found interesting, so that others can borrow them.

4 1 a) Example: They can see no clear reason for learning English.
   b) Example: Some students resent producing long pieces of writing in their own language – and even more so in English.
   (A particular problem at intermediate level and above, where writing tasks are more substantial.)
   2 Example: Giving feedback after group work is difficult because students have so much language to experiment with that they may have a wide range of problems and questions.

5 open answers

Worksheet 2

Aim: to highlight some key characteristics of written English

The texts on page 128 are from:
A *The Independent*, 23/7/94 (Anne Spackman)
B *The Pan Book of Card Games*, 1960 (Hubert Phillips)
C *Absentee Gardener Spain*, Anaya 1989 (Susan Pendleton)
D *The Children of Men*, Penguin 1994 (P. D. James)
E *England Made Me*, Heinemann 1935 (Graham Greene)

1 1 Open answers, but the following is a suggestion for Text A.
Content: current house prices in different parts of the country
Organisation: answers to the question at the end of paragraph 1 – one paragraph per area – and then a summary or recommendation about when and where to buy for the best price
Grammar: present tenses, first and second conditional structures, prepositional phrases (e.g. with country views, in a quiet area)
Vocabulary: types of property (e.g. semi-detached house), descriptive/evaluative adjectives (e.g. vast, pleasant), etc.
   2 Possible answer:
It is easier to predict the development of a text if:

a) you are familiar with that text type.

b) the conventions that structure the text type are relatively inflexible (e.g. Text D).

c) there are explicit pointers to what is to follow (e.g. Text A).

3 A in a newspaper or magazine

B in a book on card games

C in a book/magazine for amateur gardeners

D on the dust jacket or before the title page of a novel

E in the body of a novel or short story

2 1 a) C b) D c) A d) B e) E

2 Possible answers:

a) general statement of complaint – detail of problem – suggested solution

b) information – introduction – critique – recommendation/summary of views

c) abstract (summary) – introduction – methods – results – discussion/conclusion – bibliography/notes – appendices

3 To introduce the main topic by providing background information. The structure of the paragraph makes it clear that it is complete. Having considered the recent history of price movements, the writer concludes this introduction by repeating the question (also the title of the article), which brings the reader forward to the present day. The use of the word *So* to introduce the question emphasises that the digression to the past has finished.

4 a) *a game* and *the game* refer back to *Canasta*

b) *it* and *its* also refer back to *Canasta*

c) *since* refers back to *1949*

d) *That average* refers back to *the average price for any house in Greater London and the South-East*

5 It is relatively informal – even chatty – for a book extract. Note, for example, the use of *you/your*, *are faced with*, *that has just been built*, *rush off*, *armfuls of plants*; the abbreviation *can't*; the structure of the paragraph, in which the writer takes into account the readers' first instincts before gently suggesting a more sensible alternative.

6 1 Text E, because of the creative potential of fiction

2 The effect of a writer's words obviously vary to a certain extent according to the experiences of the reader. For us the effects are as follows:

a) *lover* suggests secrecy, furtiveness and exoticism; *boyfriend* removes this layer of implied meaning and gives a feeling of openness and banality;

b) the use of *same* emphasises the fact that she has not moved during the time she has been in the cafe;

c) to add *swing* to the word *door* evokes possible sounds, e.g. creaking, and the possibility of a sudden entrance, rather like in a cowboy saloon; it also helps to build up a visual picture of the place;

d) *steamed* suggests something warm, homely and secure; *hissed* is a more violent word that evokes different, harsher sounds;

e) *silted* is an unexpected word here which gives the impression that the smoke-filled air has a certain solidity about it; this solidity is confirmed as the sentence continues. To use *came* would be to imply nothing beyond the fact that a cloud of smoke entered the room.

3 The subject of the text is specified immediately in Text D. Readers of her novel know that relevant biographical information will follow. In Text E, we are onlookers of a scene; the author creates interest in the woman by asking us to imagine who and what she is. As observers we do not know her name.

Worksheet 3

Aim: to highlight some key characteristics of spoken English

1 open answers

2 1 They are husband and wife.

2 To win a battle! Gloria does not want Nathan's friends staying in the house. Nathan wants her to welcome his friends.

3 1 *I, you* and *we*

2 The speech is not organised in paragraphs, nor are there necessarily identifiable, well-structured sentences. Punctuation has been imposed in the transcription, as far as possible, on a sequence of utterances. (Nathan's first speech is better formed, as if it has been planned in advance.)

3 a) Repetition of ideas and particular phrases.

b) Rephrasing ideas, breaking down and restarting utterances.

c) Gloria and Nathan are not listening to each other; both are determined to finish what they want to say, so they interrupt one another.

4 The focus is on language as they analyse and

negotiate the meaning of words.

5 *Nice* is positive in line 24 (it means *pleasant*) and is negative in lines 30 and 32 (*undemanding/submissive*). After that, Nathan uses it to mean *kind* in a positive sense, while Gloria continues to use it as a quality which stereotypes and degrades her as a woman. To Nathan, *dogmatic* means *assertive* in an intolerant sense; to Gloria, being assertive about your views is a positive quality.

6 The vocabulary is quite restricted in range and informal except when the focus is on language itself.

7 a) very little
  b) Nathan is fairly co-operative and open to discussion; Gloria is not.
  c) They are struggling to make themselves clear to a hostile listener; neither is concise.

8 Most features are typical of informal discussions, in which speakers are thinking about their ideas as they speak. However, most conversations are more co-operative than an argument.

4 The features are not at all typical unless the shopkeeper is well-known to you. Speech that is characteristic of service encounters tends to be clear, concise, formulaic and co-operative.

5 open answers

Worksheet 4

Aim: to demonstrate the creative potential of varying a basic structure

1 1 Examples:
  A … doesn't rain *soon* …
  B … wouldn't die *so regularly* …
  C … doesn't rain *by May* … die *each summer.*
  D … died *each summer* … didn't rain *by May.*
  E … die *this year* … rained *by the end of next week*
  F … were to rain *soon* … might not die *this year.*
2–4 A (1st conditional) See *Look Ahead Intermediate* Students' Book p54.
  B (2nd conditional) See *Look Ahead Intermediate* Students' Book p54.
  C (zero conditional) *If* + present simple verb, present simple verb; used to state a general rule.
5–6 open answers

2 1 a) B, F   b) D   c) A, (B), E, F   d) C, D

2 A *Unless* it rains …
  B … *as/so long as* it rained.
  C *When* it doesn't rain …; *Unless* it rains …
  D … *when* it didn't rain; … *unless* it rained.
  E … *as/so long as* it's rained; *provided/providing (that)* it's rained.
  F *Provided/providing that* it were to rain …
3 C, D
4 Structures and meanings are similar, but:
  a) present simple → past simple to generalise about the past
  b) present simple → present perfect with the sense 'by now' or 'by some future date' rather than 'at some future date'
  c) *wouldn't die* → *might not die*, *rained* → *were to rain* for a more tentative hypothesis
5 a) other present tense verb forms: *isn't raining* (now or at some future time), *hasn't rained/hasn't been raining* (see 4b above)
  b) other past tense verb forms: *was raining* (now or at some future time), *had rained/had been raining* (before now or before some future date, especially common with a progressive form: *wouldn't be dying now*)
6 a) *may, might, could* (more tentative); *should* (= are likely to, often with a desired result)
  b) *might not, shouldn't* (more tentative); *couldn't* (wouldn't be able to)
7 open answers

3 1 c   2 g   3 b   4 h   5 e   6 d   7 a   8 f

Worksheet 5

Aim: to explore features of individual words

1 open answers

2 1 adjective (*an honest person*), adverb (*I did do it! Honest!*)
2 dis- (*a dishonest person*)
3 -ly (*I honestly believed her.*), -y (*Honesty is the best policy.*)
4 Examples: stress pattern (<u>hon</u>est), silent *h*, pronunciation of *est* (/ɪst/)
5 open answers
6 Examples:
  a) [= not telling lies] *truthful, straight, open* (person/answer)
  b) [= not cheating, stealing, or breaking the law] *incorruptible, straight, reputable, law-abiding* (person/organisation)
  c) [= not hiding your feelings: neutral] *frank, candid, direct, straightforward* (person/statement)

d) [= not hiding your feelings: potentially rude] *forthright*, *blunt* (person/statement), *outspoken* (person), *bald* (statement)

Longman Language Activator (1993) is a useful resource for teachers and students who are looking for the best way of expressing a particular meaning. Contexts of use are explained and exemplified here for words (and phrases) with the basic meanings 'honest' and 'dishonest' (see 7 below).

7 Examples: *corrupt, crooked, bent, underhand, unscrupulous, fraudulent, devious, sly, untrustworthy, sneaky, disreputable, dodgy*

8 Examples: *an honest answer/opinion/living/ man/face/broker*

9 Examples: *Honest to God . . . , To be (perfectly) honest . . . , scrupulously honest, to make an honest woman/man of you . . .*

3 1 a) incorruptible
   b) that some judges can be corrupted, e.g. bribed
   c) open answers

 2 Open answers, but here is a suggestion for a). In Britain, a cup of tea is generally black tea with milk drunk from a cup (and saucer) or mug. It may well be made from a tea bag (in a mug or teapot) rather than tea leaves (in a teapot), and is drunk at any time of the day, with or without food.

4 1 a)/b) Examples:
   [with the meaning 'therefore'] I invited you, *so I'll pay.*
   ['with the purpose'] She's going to babysit *so that they can both go.* Let's check, *so as to be quite clear* about the implications.
   ['true'] *It just isn't so.*
   ['that' – referring back to something that has just been said] I think/hope *so.* If *so,* I'll help you.
   ['also'] *So do we.*
   ['like this'] *It looked about so long.*
   ['very'] *It was so pretty!*
   ['to such a degree'] *He was so clever that* he took his exams early.
   c) to introduce a consequence, e.g. She's ill, *so she can't come.* Similar words/phrases: *as a result, because of this, therefore.*
   to state a purpose, e.g. I need some extra work *so (that) I can pay for the holiday.* Similar words/phrases: *to (pay), in order to (pay).*

 2 a)/b) The reason why/that I employed you was to improve our general efficiency. (*before*) We need to cut staff in every department. For this/that reason, I am afraid we are forced to let you go. (*after*)

5 open answers

Worksheet 6

Aim: to identify appropriate contexts for language practice

1 1 Examples: a) *will* + infinitive, *going to* + infinitive, adverbs expressing degrees of probability, first conditional
     b) (dis)agreeing (e.g. *So do I, I don't agree*), interrupting (e.g. *Yes, but . . .*)
   2 Examples: a) (polite) questions, question tags, first conditional
     b) asking for/giving advice (e.g. *You could . . .*); giving/accepting thanks (e.g. *It's a pleasure.*)
   3 Examples: a) prepositions of place, adverbs expressing degrees of probability
     b) making logical deductions (e.g. *It can't be . . .*), asking for/giving opinions (e.g. *Which do you think . . .?*)

2 a) thank   b) accept/refuse   c) suggest a solution   d) give an explanation
   e) apologise/present a counter-argument
   f) reassure   g) thank   h) accept/refuse

3 1 e) Example: We used to go to Ireland for our holidays.
   2 j) Example: While she was choosing some frozen food, he put his hand in her bag.
   3 g) Example: The wiring and plumbing have been installed.
   4 h) Example: How much work have you been taking home?
   5 d) Example: She said that she enjoyed working with Woody Allen.
   6 i) Example: If I were you, I'd see a specialist.
   7 c) Example: You have to slow down when you see this sign.
   8 f) Example: I'd rather fly via Singapore.
   9 b) Example: I hope to find some holiday work.
   10 a) Example: Could you tell me how to get to the bus station?

4 open answers

5 1 Examples: eliciting personal experiences/ fantasies (e.g. Exercise 3d), a gap-fill text (e.g. Exercise 3e), a map and tourist leaflets (e.g. Exercise 3f), blackboard drawings (e.g. Exercise 3g), video without sound (e.g. Exercise 3h), a plastic spider (e.g. Exercise 3i), mime (e.g. Exercise 3j)
   2 open answers

Workbook Answer Key and Tapescript

Unit one

LANGUAGE FOCUS

1 Tapescript

JAMES: When are you leaving?

JULIA: Pardon?

JAMES: When are you leaving for Germany?

JULIA: I don't know. Oh, James . . . this is really difficult! I don't know what to do about this flat.

JAMES: Is it yours? Do you own it?

JULIA: No, I rent it. But all the furniture is mine.

JULIA: Hello? Speaking. Mike! Hello. I'm fine, thank you. No, I'm not working for MAP any more. I'm going to Germany – I think. Why? Really? Let me think about it. Bye.

JULIA: Well, well, well . . . That was Mike Roberts of International Promotions.

JAMES: International Promotions ...

JULIA: Yes, I used to work for them. Before I moved to MAP.

JAMES: Oh yes. What did he want?

JULIA: He offered me some freelance work. He thinks I ought to start my own advertising agency.

1 1 c   2 c   3 a   4 b

2 1 T   2 F She's thinking of going to Germany
3 F She rents her flat.   4 F She used to work for International Promotions.

3 Possible answers:
1 How are you, Julia?
2 Are you still working at MAP?
3 What are you doing, then?

4 Conversation 1:
2 Annie to Tom
3 Tom to Annie
4 Annie to Tom

Conversation 2:
1 Diana to George
2 George to Diana
3 John to Diana

5 1 On Tuesday Teresa and Marco are having dinner together at a Thai restaurant in the evening.
2 On Wednesday Marco's playing badminton. Teresa's not doing anything.
3 On Thursday Teresa and Marco are both going to the camera club.

6 1 a   2 d   3 c   4 a   5 d   6 b   7 c   8 b   9 b   10 a

7 1 Where did Mary use to live? She used to live on a farm.   2 Did she use to ride to school? No, she didn't.
3 Did she use to enjoy the lessons? Yes, she did.

EXPLORING VOCABULARY

2 1 3 of: barge   houseboat   (launch)   tug
2 brick   concrete   stone
3 slate   tile
4 5 of: caravan   (cave)   cottage   (estate)   farmhouse   houseboat   tent

3 1 playing cards   2 a watering can   3 a swimming pool   4 a sleeping bag   5 running shoes

4 Tapescript/key
1 community   environment   executive   professional   responsible
2 4 of: area   caravan   industry   left-over   magical   memory   passenger   playing card   relevant

5 1 row   2 launch   3 launch/row/sink   4 launch
5 sink   6 row
The word *row* is pronounced differently depending on its meaning.

SHORT STORY

3 1 T   2 F   (She didn't talk to him about personal things.)   3 F   4 F

4 1 It means that the eyes were wide open, although he was dead.
2 His height and weight were average.
3 Letters that are sent out to thousands of people advertising products.
4 police scientists

Unit two

LANGUAGE FOCUS

1 1 b   2 c   3 a   4 b   5 a   6 b   7 b   8 a

2 1 Would you rather see . . .   2 Would you like to see . . .   3 Do you want to see . . .

3 Tapescript

JAMES: What have you decided to do?

JULIA: Well, I've thought about it a lot, and I've decided to stay in London and form my own company . . . Marsh Advertising!

JAMES: Congratulations!

JULIA: What about you?

JAMES: Me?

JULIA: Are you going to stay at MAP?

JAMES: Yes. Well, I think so.

JULIA: I see ... you'd prefer to live in the country.

JAMES: No ... of course I'd rather live in London, but I can't.

JULIA: Yes, you can. You can stay here and work with me.

JAMES: I prefer working for a bigger company.

JULIA: You haven't tried working for a small one. Look at these. My business plan for the company ... and my first job. It could be *our* first job.

JAMES: Julia ... about this new company of yours ...

JULIA: Yes?

JAMES: I think I'd like to join you.

JULIA: But James ... you prefer working for *big* companies.

JAMES: Yes ... No. I prefer working with people I like. And I'm impressed with this.

JULIA: James, I'm very pleased.

3 1 She's going to stay in London and form her own company.
2 He'd rather live in London.
3 He prefers working with people he likes.
4 He's going to join Julia in her new company.

4 1 Neither/Nor does James.   2 Neither/Nor would Julia.   3 So does James.   4 So is Julia.

5 1 So do I./I don't.   2 So did I./I didn't.   3 Neither have I./I have.   4 Nor can I./I can.   5 So am I./I'm not.

6 Possible answers:
1 It was so funny (that) I fell off the sofa.
2 It was so frightening (that) I had to leave the room.
3 It was so sad (that) I cried.
4 It was so boring (that) I almost fell asleep.
5 It was so exciting (that) I found it difficult to study.

7 1 It's like being in prison.
2 It was like flying.
3 It's like a painting.
4 They were like rocks.
5 It was like reading someone's diary.

EXPLORING VOCABULARY

2 1 nightmare   2 skyscraper   3 earthquake   4 breeze   5 whisper   6 scent   7 chess   8 sliver

3 1 flash   2 flicker   3 sparkle

4 depressing B   satisfied A
ultimate A   brilliant A
production B   seductive B
typical A   runaway A

5 1 seductive (adjective)   2 favourite (adjective)   3 breath (noun)   4 nag (verb)

6 *-ment*, noun, assortment, entertainment
-ly, adverb, hopelessly, happily
-tion, noun, attraction, station
-al, adjective, typical, logical

SHORT STORY

1 The mistakes are in italics:
A friend found the body of an *old* man in his *sitting room*, and called the *ambulance service*. Some *personal* letters were on the table beside the body. Inspector Temple believes that the man's death is the result of a *burglary*.

Sample corrected text:
A friend found the body of a middle-aged man in his kitchen, and called the police. Some junk mail was on the table beside the body. Inspector Temple believes that the man's death is the result of a heart attack.

3 1 To give him her report on how the man died.
2 She tells Temple that the man did not die naturally. A poison – belladonna – had been found in his blood.

5 Cause of death: poison   Murder: yes
Probable time of death: between 7 a.m. and 8 a.m.
Clues: know time of death and cause of death, letters?

Unit three

LANGUAGE FOCUS

1 1 have to   2 don't have to   3 mustn't   4 needn't   5 have to   6 have to

2 1 Must we check in now?
2 He doesn't have to hurry.
3 Does she need to change any money?
4 They needn't worry about food and drink.

3 1 Please don't smoke now./Please put your cigarette out./Please extinguish your cigarette.
The steward told her not to smoke.
2 Could you pass that magazine, please?
The woman asked him to pass her the magazine.
3 Oh, please, can I have one of those, Dad?
He begged his father to buy him a toy.
4 Get off the plane immediately!
The pilot ordered the young men to get off the plane.

4 Tapescript

OFFICIAL: Sir ... would you come here, please? That's all right, sir. You don't need to show me your passport. Where are you travelling from?

KARL: Munich, in Germany.

OFF: And what is the purpose of your visit?

KARL: Business.

OFF: I see. And what's inside the suitcase?

KARL: Oh ... normal things ... clothes ...

OFF: And, er ... what about that?

KARL: The briefcase?

OFF: Yes. Could you open it, please? And what's this – a computer?

KARL: Yes. It's a wonderful machine. My company makes them. Look ... it works like this.

OFF: That's all right, sir, you don't need to give me a demonstration.

KARL: Oh. OK.

4 1 T 2 F 3 T 4 T 5 F

5 I didn't have/need to show   2 didn't ask him to
3 answered/had to answer   4 him to   5 didn't need/have to

EXPLORING VOCABULARY

2 1 dreadful   2 frontier   3 miserable   4 immense
5 marvellous

3 1 hang-gliding – SPORTS   2 porter – HOTEL STAFF/JOBS
3 scared – FEAR ADJECTIVES   4 vision – SENSES

4 1 confident   2 hire   3 illegally   4 relief

5 Pattern A (● ●) Each word contains the schwa
sound /ə/   Sample words: order, builder, painter

6 disappoint, disappointment   disgust, disgust   relax,
relaxation   tolerate, tolerance

SHORT STORY

1 1 Inspector Temple, Ron Elliott, Mrs McCarthy,
Detective Constable Mitchell, the doctor
2 Mr Elliott's kitchen, Inspector Temple's office

2 1 Because he knows there is a murderer who has not
been caught.
2 Because the murder of the second man seems to be
similar to that of the first.

3 1 inquest   2 verdict   3 constable   4 case

4 1 Both men lived alone.
2 Both were in their mid-thirties.
3 Both men died at the breakfast table.
4 There was no obvious cause of death in either case.

6 Tapescript
The heavy curtains were closed and the only light in the
room came from a small lamp on the table next to her old
armchair. Newspaper cuttings filled one of the walls.
SECOND MAN FOUND DEAD. BELLADONNA
MYSTERY CONTINUES. Across a photograph of Copes
was a large number two in red ink.

The woman sat in the chair and glanced lovingly at a
man's picture in a frame beneath the lamp. A tear trickled
down her face. 'Don't worry, my dear,' she whispered.
'I'll get them for you . . . all of them.'

She picked up two small printed labels, turned them
over and placed them carefully on the surface of the
table. Then she reached for a small bottle, opened it
slowly, took out the dropper and squeezed four drops of
the liquid onto the back of each label. She took one of
the brown envelopes from the pile at her feet and placed
inside a folded sheet, another envelope with a printed
address, and the two labels. As she put the labels into the
envelope she looked briefly at the words on the front of
each: *I CLAIM MY PRIZE. My lucky number is 41369.* A
half-smile crossed her face and her eyes narrowed as she
sealed the envelope.

6 1 From poisoning with belladonna. They took the
poison when they licked the back of the labels to
claim their prizes.
2 Because the post had just arrived.

Unit four

LANGUAGE FOCUS

1 Tapescript
JAMES: Morning, Julia.
JULIA: Morning, James.
JAMES: Did you go to the cinema last night?
JULIA: Yes.
JAMES: Did you enjoy the film?
JULIA: Yes, it was very good. But the strangest thing
happened when I got home.
JAMES: What?
JULIA: Well, when I got home, I came up the stairs and
started to put my key in the door . . .
JAMES: Yes?
JULIA: And I heard a noise. A noise like a computer – in my
flat. I thought it was a burglar.
JAMES: So what did you do?
JULIA: I ran into the street and phoned the police from the
phone box on the corner. They came very quickly. But
while we were walking up the stairs, my door opened.
I thought: Oh no! The burglar's coming out! But it
wasn't a burglar.
JAMES: Who was it?
JULIA: It was Karl!
JAMES: Karl?
JULIA: You know, Karl Schiller from Munich.
JAMES: Oh, Karl! Karl?
JULIA: Yes.
JAMES: What was he doing here?
JULIA: He was waiting for me to come home. Imagine . . .
while I was sitting in the cinema, Karl was sitting in my
flat!
JAMES: How did he get in?
JULIA: The porter let him in.

1 1 arrived/got   2 went/walked   3 started/began
4 heard   5 ran   6 phoned/called/rang   7 was
going/walking   8 opened   9 was
10 was waiting   11 was (sitting)   12 was (sitting)

2 1 What was Julia doing yesterday evening?
2 Why did she phone/call/ring the police?
3 What was Karl doing in her flat?
4 What happened while the police were going up the
stairs?
5 How did Karl get into the flat?

3 1 Yes, she did.   2 No, they weren't.   3 Yes, he was.
4 No, she didn't.

4 1 When I saw my friends, I stopped to speak to them.

139

2 While we were having lunch, the door bell rang./We were having lunch when the doorbell rang.

3 He was watching television while she was studying./While she was studying, he was watching television.

5 1 themselves   2 yourself   3 yourselves   4 herself
5 ourselves   6 myself   7 yourself

6 1 agree   2 share   3 don't   4 think   5 disagree
6 wrong/easy

7 1 began   2 drank   3 thought   4 found   5 gave
6 shut   7 wrote   Infinitive: to bring

EXPLORING VOCABULARY

2 1 burglary   embezzlement   mugging   murder
robbery   shoplifting   theft   vandalism
2 burglar   mugger   murderer   pickpocket
robber   shoplifter   thief   vandal

3 1 a detective   2 a witness   3 an enemy
4 a companion

4 1 defend   2 fiction   3 impatience   4 justice

5 Tapescript
'rebel   re'bel   'import   im'port   'export   ex'port
'record   re'cord   'increase   in'crease   'decrease
de'crease

5 1 verb   2 noun
The rule for *rebel* is true for the other words.

6 running   failing   slipping   sitting   swimming
stopping   shopping   sleeping

HELP YOURSELF

1 ENGLISH: trunk

2 A – 6   B – 4   C – 7   D – 3   E – 2   F – 1   G – 5

3 Tapescript
A I'm looking for that white stuff… that white powder with a lovely smell. You know, you put it on your body after you have a bath. What's it called?
B I need to borrow a thing … a metal thing for making holes in the wall. It's got a handle, and you put long pieces of metal in the other end, different sizes, and it works with electricity. What do you call that?
C I want to buy that stuff for … for putting on your hair when you wash it. It's a liquid, and you buy it in bottles. No, not shampoo. It makes your hair soft and shiny. Do you know what I mean?

3 A ENGLISH: talcum powder   B ENGLISH: electric drill
C ENGLISH: conditioner
Uncountable: liquid, stuff, powder
Countable: object, thing

4 Possible answers:
1 It's a strange shape: there's a handle that you hold

and a long round part that spins. The handle is usually made of metal, and the other part is made of a soft material. It can be any colour (but the soft part is often yellow or white). It's for painting with; it's like a paintbrush, but you can paint much faster with it.

2 It's a large round object, like a bowl with holes in it and a long handle. It's made of plastic or metal. It can be any colour. It's for draining vegetables after you cook them, but you can also use it to wash salad and fruit. It's like a sieve, but the holes are bigger.

Unit five

LANGUAGE FOCUS

1 1 Are (the) advisors paid?
2 Where are they sent?
3 What is each advisor asked to do?
4 How are the businesses helped?
5 Are the advisors trained for the job?
6 How is BESO supported?

2 1 Computers for children are designed by Karl's company.
2 Computer software is also developed by his company.
3 The computers are advertised in Britain.
4 Three important features are included.
5 Children are asked to read the screen.
6 Their answers are spoken.
7 Julia and James are offered the job of advertising the product.

3 Tapescript
JAMES: So, Karl, why are you here?
KARL: I'm here to talk about a new business project.
JAMES: What kind of project?
KARL: We are developing a new computer for children to use at home.
JULIA: But surely lots of computers are made for children. And several of them are made for home use. How is your computer different?
KARL: In two ways. First, we are developing a better voice-activation system.
JAMES: A what? What does 'voice-activation' mean?
KARL: I'm sorry. Look at this computer. This one doesn't have a voice-activation system. In order to use it, you have to read the screen, then type your answer. But the new computer speaks to the child. It asks a question and the child answers by speaking to the computer.
JULIA: Hmm. And the other difference?
KARL: Ah. It's educational. Nearly all the computers that are sold to children are for games. Hardly any are made to help children with their studies.
JAMES: But yours will.
KARL: Yes, because we're developing special software – study programs.

JULIA: I see. You're developing the software in order to sell the hardware.

KARL: Yes, you could say that.

JULIA: Hmm. It sounds very interesting.

KARL: It is. And maybe you two can help me.

JULIA: How?

KARL: We need an advertising agency, here in Britain.

JAMES: You mean you want us to advertise your computer?

KARL: Yes.

JAMES: You realise that we're a very small company.

KARL: Yes. So you must work for me to get bigger. What do you think?

JULIA: Yes, Karl. We'd love to.

3 1 T   2 T   3 F   4 F   5 F   6 T   7 T

4 1 all of them   2 none of them   3 neither of them
4 both of them

5 1 c   2 b   3 d   4 a   5 b   6 c   7 a   8 d

EXPLORING VOCABULARY

2 1 distribute   2 design   3 peel   4 employ

3 1 C   2 S   3 S   4 C   5 S/C   6 C   7 S

4 1 fuel tank   2 book-keeping   3 hand-made
4 water tank   5 note-taking   6 home-made

5 advertise   encourage   employ   repay
Employ and *repay* have the same pattern.
advertisement   employment   encouragement
repayment   advertisement (advertise)

HELP YOURSELF

2 A 5   B 8   C 3   D 6   E 1   F 2   G 7   H 4

3 1 Good evening.   2 Sample answer: Thanks very much.   3 Sample answer: By credit card.   4 Cheers!

Unit six

LANGUAGE FOCUS

1 Possible answers:
1 If I lived in a house like that, I'd have a motorbike to drive around it!
2 If I visited Kauai, I'd try to go when it's not raining!
3 If I spoke 58 languages, I'd get a job as a translator.
4 If I received 33 million cards, I'd put an advertisement in the paper to thank people.
5 If I walked that far, I think I'd want to relax for a few years!
6 If I earned that much money, I'd give most of it away.

2 1 What will she do if it rains? She'll go home.
2 How will/would she feel if she sells/sold everything? She'll/She'd be delighted!
3 How would she react if the police came? She'd run!
4 What would happen if the police caught her? She'd have to pay a fine.

3 1 B: I'm terrified of spiders.
A: Don't be afraid.
2 B: I'm worried about (failing) my driving test.
A: Don't worry. It'll be all right.
3 A: Calm down. Don't cry.

4 Tapescript
JAMES: Good morning, Julia.
JULIA: Hello, James.
KARL: Good morning, James.
JAMES: Karl! What are you doing here? Aren't you going back to Germany today?
JULIA: He isn't very well.
JAMES: What's the matter with you?
KARL: I don't know. I have a ... er ...
JULIA: A sore throat.
KARL: Yes, I have a sore throat. And a headache. I feel awful.
JAMES: Have you got a temperature?
KARL: What do you mean?
JAMES: Are you very hot? Do you have a high temperature?
KARL: Oh, yes. I think so.
JULIA: I think you've got 'flu.
JULIA: You ought to see a doctor as soon as possible.
KARL: Here in England? I don't know.
JAMES: I think you should go back to your hotel, and you should call a doctor.
KARL: But I have to be back in Germany tomorrow.
JULIA: Karl, you're ill. I think you ought to stay here for a few days. What do you think, James?
JAMES: No, Julia, he must do what he wants to do. Karl, if I were you, I'd go home tomorrow.
KARL: Listen ... it's all right. I think I should go back to Germany and have a rest for a couple of days. Then I'll be fine. Really.
JULIA: OK, if that's what you want to do.
KARL: Thank you for all your help. Both of you. You've been very kind.
JULIA: Don't mention it. I hope you feel better soon.
KARL: Thank you. I'll call you next week about advertising the new computer.
JULIA: Good.
JAMES: OK. I'll show you out.
KARL: Thank you. Bye bye.

4 1 Today.   2 He's ill.   3 Sample answer: He should see a doctor.   4 ... call a doctor to his hotel and then return to Germany.   5 ... stay in Britain for a few days.   6 ... go back to Germany and rest for a few days.

5 1 He ought to be more polite.
2 He shouldn't use the phone for/make personal calls.
3 He oughtn't to miss appointments.
4 He should ask when he wants to take time off.

EXPLORING VOCABULARY

2 1 pharmacist   2 optician   3 surgeon   4 dentist

5 herbalist   6 acupuncturist

3 1 creak   2 growl   3 drip   4 rustle   5 moan/scream
6 splash

4 1 anxious   2 afraid   3 petrified   4 irritable
5 overweight   6 sore

5 me<u>d</u>icine   <u>p</u>sychiatrist   rus<u>t</u>le   <u>h</u>onest   <u>k</u>nee
lam<u>b</u>   <u>wr</u>ong   coul<u>d</u>   ans<u>w</u>er

6 1 adjective – healthy   2 verb – be the right size
3 verb – put in place   4 noun – sudden attack
5 verb – match

SHORT STORY

1 Possible answer:
She's about 25 and she's got long dark hair. She's
wearing summer clothes and she's got a camera over
her shoulder.

2 1 On a Mediterranean beach.
2 No, she's on holiday.
3 It's probably summer.

3 1 T   2 F   3 T   4 F   5 F

4 It's probably a romance.

Unit seven

LANGUAGE FOCUS

1 1 which/that/–   2 who/that   3 who/that/–
4 who/ that   5 that/which/–   6 that/which/–
7 that/which   8 who/that   9 who/that
10 that/which   11 that/which/–   12 that/which
13 that/which/ –   14 that/which/–

2 1 We visit the cottages that/which Mr James owns.
2 Betty is one of the cleaners who/that works for
Mr James.
3 She does a lot of extra work that/which visitors
create for her.

3 Possible answers:
1 Mr and Mrs James often need to have the curtains
cleaned.
2 They sometimes need to have broken plates
replaced.
3 They have the outsides of the cottages repainted
every year.
4 They have the carpets shampooed.
5 Sometimes they need to have pieces of furniture
repaired.
6 They have the rooms redecorated every winter.

4 1 A: Excuse me. Can I have this dress cleaned, please?
B: Of course. Would you mind waiting a moment?
2 A: Can I have this ice bucket filled?
B: Of course. Would you mind asking the barman?

5 Tapescript and key
Answers to exercise in *italics*.

Part one.
RECEPTIONIST: Good afternoon, sir.
JAMES: Good afternoon.
REC: Terrible weather.
JAMES: Yes.
REC: Excuse me, but ... what happened to you?
JAMES: A car went past and splashed me ... My name is
Brady, by the way. James Brady. I have a reservation.
REC: Oh yes, Mr Brady.
Part two.
REC: You're the person who asked about a conference
room.
JAMES: *That's right. (1)*
REC: Well, our small meeting room is free tomorrow.
JAMES: *Excellent. That's just what I wanted. (2)*
REC: Good. And you're staying for two nights.
JAMES: *Yes. (3)*
REC: Bed and breakfast only.
JAMES: *That's right. (4)*
REC: Would you mind filling in this form, please?
JAMES: *No, not at all. (5)*

5 A car splashed him.
See tapescript above for answers to second part.
I'll take it.   2
Certainly.   5
Yes, I am.   1, 3

EXPLORING VOCABULARY

2 1 annual   2 bewildered   3 proud   4 rapid

3 A swarm   B flick   C roll   D scatter   E leap   F hurl

4 cheap /tʃ/   school /k/   character /k/   lunch /tʃ/
architecture /k/   chaos /k/   drench /tʃ/

5 a) cleaning done without water
b) catering done by yourself
c) to put something back
d) cleaning done in spring-time
e) you serve yourself
f) to pay back

SHORT STORY

1 Elaine, Toni and Jenny. The others are Toni's friends.

3 1 c   2 a   3 c   4 b   5 a

4 1 They share an interest in literature and writing. Toni
is a student while Elaine is a journalist. She lives alone
and rarely sees her parents. He lives with his parents.

Unit eight

LANGUAGE FOCUS

1 1 a   2 b   3 a   4 a   5 b   6 a   7 d   8 c   9 c   10 d

2

INFINITIVE	PAST TENSE	PAST PARTICLIPLE
blow	blew	blown
creep	crept	crept
hide	hid	hidden
shoot	shot	shot
sink	sank	sunk
spill	spilt	spilt
spring	sprang	sprung
steal	stole	stolen

3 Tapescript

JAMES: Paul . . . Cook?

PAUL: Yes, sorry . . . I don't . . .

JAMES: James Brady.

PAUL: Of course. How are you?

JAMES: I'm fine, thanks.

PAUL: Would you like to join me?

JAMES: Thank you very much.

PAUL: Are you still with MAP Advertising?

JAMES: No, I have my own company now. Well, I'm working with Julia Marsh.

PAUL: Oh, I remember Julia. How is she?

JAMES: Fine.

PAUL: How long have you been working together?

JAMES: For about three months . . . since May. What about you, are you still working for . . . um . . .

PAUL: Art and Design.

JAMES: Art and Design.

PAUL: Yes, I've been working there for ten years.

JAMES: What are you doing here in Manchester?

PAUL: I have an interview for a job.

JAMES: A job?

PAUL: Yes, I've been looking for a new job for ages. I've applied for a job with a newspaper company, here in Manchester.

JAMES: What kind of job?

PAUL: Well, they're starting a new weekly magazine for young people, and they're looking for a designer.

JAMES: Have you worked on a magazine before?

PAUL: No, but it's always been my ambition. Oh, I must go. I don't want to be late.

JAMES: Well, good luck.

PAUL: Thank you.

3 1 How long has James been working in the new company with Julia?

2 How long has Paul been working at Art and Design?

3 How long has Paul been looking for a new job?

4 Sample answer: What kind of job has Paul applied for?

5 What has Paul's ambition always been?

4 1 Sorry, I mean Bob.

2 Pardon?

3 I'm afraid I don't understand.

4 Could you give me an example?

5 Could you say that again?

EXPLORING VOCABULARY

2 1 literature   2 geography   3 biology   4 economics
5 architecture   6 physics

3 1 engineer   2 journalist   3 chef   4 solicitor/lawyer
5 veterinary surgeon (vet)   6 plumber   7 librarian

4 1 legal   2 patient   3 complex   4 tolerant
5 renewable

5 Tapescript and key
bi<u>o</u>logy   anthrop<u>o</u>logy   tech<u>no</u>logy   ec<u>o</u>logy
ge<u>o</u>logy   astr<u>o</u>logy   soci<u>o</u>logy   psych<u>o</u>logy
zo<u>o</u>logy   The ending -ology means 'the science/
study of something'.

SHORT STORY

All exercises have open answers.

2 Tapescript

Elaine sat on the balcony of their hotel room with a glass of fresh orange juice in her hand and gazed down at the peaceful scene below. Verino, a town that she had come to love, was beautiful in the clear early morning light. But she was thoughtful and sad. The holiday was almost at an end and, try as she might, she couldn't get her feelings for Toni out of her mind. As far as she could tell, though, Toni himself accepted without question that their friendship would soon be over.

'What shall I do, Jenny?' Elaine asked her friend, when she came out to join her for breakfast. 'I've never met anyone that I like so much. He's kind, he's interesting . . . but he lives so far away.'

'Oh, come on, Elaine – be realistic. You're on holiday here so you're happy and relaxed, and he's given you some attention. But that's all it is – a holiday relationship. You love your job – do you want to give it up? What would you do? And why on earth would he want to come to England? He's never talked about the possibility, has he?'

'No, no, he hasn't. And – well, I've got no idea how he really feels about me. I know I'm being silly.'

'You probably are – but it's your life. Why don't you just talk to him? Tell him how you feel and see what he says. Then at least you'll know if you've got any options to choose from.'

That evening was the last one that Elaine and Toni had together, and they ate together in a quiet restaurant just outside the town. At the end of the meal, Elaine took a deep breath.

'Toni,' she said slowly. 'I'm going to miss you, I really am. I don't know how to tell you, but . . .'

Toni reached across the table and put his hand over hers. 'You don't need to tell me, Elaine. I feel the same. But I haven't spoken about it because it's impossible. I can't come to England – I have my work and my studies . . . and when I finish my studies, I must help my parents in the business. I want to be here, and I would like very much for you to be here too, but what can we do?'

'Well, I've got to go tomorrow, you know that ... but if I *can* find a way to come back – after all, I'm a journalist, and they need reporters overseas – if I *can* find a way, will you truly be happy to see me?'

'You know I will, Elaine. Write to me for now and depend on it, I'll wait for you.'

Unit nine

LANGUAGE FOCUS

1 1 That looks delicious!
 2 He looks like a soldier.
 3 He looks like his father.
 4 They still don't look clean!
 5 He doesn't look ill!
 6 They don't look like sheep.
 7 That film doesn't look very funny.

2 1 C 2 B/D 3 F 4 E 5 A

3 Possible answers:
 1 I'm not sure. 2 Yes, maybe. 3 No, I'm sure they won't. 4 No, they definitely won't. 5 Yes, almost certainly.

4 Tapescript
JULIA: James, you know that model agency you went to see – when you were in Manchester?
JAMES: Yes?
JULIA: What did you tell them?
JAMES: I asked them to send us photographs of children – from 12 to 14 years old – that we could use to advertise an educational computer.
JULIA: Well, they sent photographs. But most of these aren't children, are they? I mean, look at this one.
JAMES: What's the matter with him?
JULIA: Well, he's too old. He must be at least 18. He could be 23.
JAMES: I don't think so.
JULIA: He must be! He looks like a professional footballer.
JAMES: It says here he's 16.
JULIA: He can't be! It must be a mistake. And look at this one.
JAMES: She looks great!
JULIA: Yes, she looks great, but she doesn't look like a schoolgirl, does she?
JAMES: I don't know ... schoolgirls look like that these days.
JULIA: She doesn't look like a schoolgirl who enjoys using a computer. She looks like a rock singer. And it says she's 14! She can't possibly be 14.
JAMES: What about this one? She looks about 14, she looks intelligent, and she looks like someone who enjoys doing homework.
JULIA: James ...
James: What?

JULIA: That's a photograph of me.
JAMES: Oh.
JULIA: When I was at university.

4 1 He must be at least 18. He could be 23.
 2 He looks like a professional footballer.
 3 He's 16.
 4 She doesn't look like a schoolgirl.
 5 She can't possibly be 14.
 6 She looks 14. She looks intelligent. She looks like someone who enjoys doing homework.
 7 About 18–21!
 8 Because the models from the agency look too old and don't look serious enough. The other one is of Julia!

EXPLORING VOCABULARY

2 A shave B tattoo C dye D pierce

3 1 unshaven 2 smart 3 slim 4 drab/dull
 5 unconventional
 a) clean-shaven b) slim c) conventional
 d) drab, smart

4 1 too crowded 2 too hot 3 too full 4 too busy

5 col<u>our</u>ful (1) aggr<u>e</u>ssive (1) inn<u>o</u>cent (2)
 conv<u>en</u>tional (3) reb<u>e</u>llious (1) forg<u>e</u>tful (2)
 sym<u>me</u>trical (1) unsh<u>a</u>ven (1)
 The /ə/ sound never occurs in a stressed syllable. These adjective endings commonly contain the /ə/ sound: -ent, al, -ous, -en. While the ending -ful is usually transcribed /fʊl/, it can also be interpreted as /fəl/ if it is said quickly.

HELP YOURSELF

1 1 stationary 2 stationery 3 I need to buy some stationery. 4 same

2 1 a) Boxing Day b) boxer c) box d) Boxing e) the box
 2 boxcar 3 the box (meaning TV), box someone's ears 4 four 5 in reply to newspaper advertisements
 6 buy tickets 7 never

3 1 appearance, foreigner, necessary, psychology
 2 foreigner, necessary

Unit ten

LANGUAGE FOCUS

1 1 managed 2 couldn't 3 managed/was able
 4 wasn't able 5 can 6 managed 7 will be able

2 1 Didn't they manage to book seats?
 2 Could he speak Spanish before he moved to Mexico?
 3 Will you be able to leave at the same time as me tomorrow?
 4 Is she able to learn her lines?
 5 Can you help me, please?

3 1 D   2 G   3 E   4 F   5 A   6 C   7 B

4 Tapescript

JAMES: Julia, I'm so sorry! I couldn't find a taxi.

JULIA: So how did you get here?

JAMES: By taxi.

JULIA: I thought you said you couldn't find one.

JAMES: I meant I wasn't able to find a taxi when I came out of my flat. What's the matter with you?

JULIA: Nothing. Here's your ticket.

JAMES: Thank you. How much did it cost?

JULIA: £27.

JAMES: £27? For a jazz concert?

JULIA: This is the Wilton Hall. It's expensive.

JAMES: But weren't there any cheaper tickets?

JULIA: Yes. But I wasn't able to get any.

JAMES: Why not?

JULIA: Because I forgot to get them last night . . . Come on, we'll miss the beginning.

4 1 Because he couldn't find a taxi.
2 He managed to find one after some time.
3 They cost £27 each.
4 It's called The Wilton Hall.
5 Julia wasn't able to get cheaper ones.

5 1 I did.   2 I wasn't.   3 she wasn't.   4 I won't.
5 we could.   6 I can't.

6 1 I am writing   2 In my opinion   3 as far as I'm concerned   4 Why don't   5 certainly   6 Let's

EXPLORING VOCABULARY

2 1 dolphin   2 bear   3 camel   4 tiger   5 monkey
6 seal   7 crocodile   8 elephant   9 lion

3 A feed   B operate   C raise   D attach

4 1 ringmaster   2 clowns   3 acrobat   4 cages
5 tricks   6 box office

5 greed   sophistication   sensitivity   laziness
honesty   tenderness

HELP YOURSELF

1 Tapescript
A Can I have some clean 'towels, please?
B Can I have some 'clean towels, please?

1 1 B clean   2 A towels

2 Tapescript
1 Have you got any 'fresh 'fish?
2 Have you got any 'fresh fish?
3 Have 'you got any fresh fish?

4 Do you like 'this coat?
5 Do you like this 'coat?
6 Do you 'like this coat?
7 Do 'you like this coat?

2 1 B fresh fish   2 A fresh   3 C you   4 E this
5 G coat   6 D like   7 F you

3 Tapescript
A: Why didn't you ring me?
B: But I 'did ring you.
A: I'm a complete failure.
B: 'No, you 'aren't.

1 Why weren't you there?
2 Why isn't it Friday?
3 My hair looks awful.
4 I've never met her.

PRESENTER: Now listen to the complete dialogues.
1 A: Why weren't you there?
   B: But I 'was there.
2 A: Why isn't it Friday?
   B: But it 'is Friday.
3 A: My hair looks awful.
   B: 'No, it 'doesn't.
4 A: I've never met her.
   B: 'Yes, you 'have.

3 But I did ring you.
No, you aren't.
1 But I was there.
2 But it is Friday.
3 No, it doesn't.
4 Yes, you have.

4 Tapescript
1 MAN: It's a lovely day, isn't it?
   WOMAN: Yes, beautiful.

2 Man: It's a lovely day, isn't it?
   Woman: Yes, beautiful.

PRESENTER: Now listen and repeat.
A: It was a great lesson, wasn't it?
B: Yes, very interesting.

A: It was a great lesson, wasn't it?
B: Yes, very interesting.

4 1 a) 1   b) 2

5 Tapescript
1 Oh yes? He will? (questioning)
2 Oh yes. He will. (reassuring)
3 Oh yes he will. (expressing anger)
4 Oh yes he will. (showing fear)
5 Oh yes! He will! (expressing excitement)

5 A 4   B 2   C 3   D 1   E 5

Unit eleven

LANGUAGE FOCUS

1 1 –   2 the   3 a   4 a   5 the   6 The   7 the
8 –   9 –   10 the   11 the   12 the   13 The   14 –
15 –   16 The   17 –   18 –   19 the   20 a

2 1 Is the system likely to be expensive?
2 Are you certain the system will save money?
3 Are you seriously going to consider installing it?

4 Do you intend to think about other options?
5 Will the system work in your offices?

3 1 We're not/We aren't going to have a long discussion.
2 They won't be able to express their opinions.
3 I may not have to leave early.
4 The directors probably won't join us.
5 I'm not likely/unlikely to lose my temper.

4 Possible answers:
1 They probably won't be very happy.
2 She might fall.
3 He'll definitely go to prison.
4 They're certain to get wet.
5 I'm sure the dog won't catch her.

5 Tapescript
KARL: Julia, this is Michael Preston.
JULIA: How do you do?
MICHAEL: How do you do?
KARL: Michael Preston, James Brady.
JAMES: How do you do?
MICHAEL: How do you do? Please sit down. Now, I'm thinking of investing in the new computer that Karl's company has produced. And I asked him if I could come to this meeting to talk about the advertising campaign. I'm very glad that you could come.
JAMES: Thank you.
MICHAEL: I've read your campaign plan. It looks very good. I only have a few questions, mainly about where you intend to place these advertisements.
JULIA: Well, as you can see from the plan, we intend to place them in family magazines and on early evening television. We want whole families – parents *and* children to see them.
MICHAEL: Hm. But are you sure they'll be the right families?
JULIA: The right families? Well …
MICHAEL: Are you certain that the parents who read those magazines and watch those television programmes are the people who will buy an educational computer for their children?
JULIA: Yes, we are quite certain. This research shows that …
MICHAEL: Good. I'm sure you're right. And I see that you're thinking of placing advertisements in teenage magazines.
JULIA: Yes, we intend to place them in *some* teenage magazines – the more serious ones.
JAMES: And we're thinking of putting them in Sunday newspapers – because it's likely that the whole family will be together on Sundays.
MICHAEL: I see. But do you really think that parents *and* children will like the same advertisements?
JAMES: We think they'll like our advertisements.
MICHAEL: Good.

5 1 might   2 are planning to   3 may   4 probably
5 likely to

6 1 Just a minute   2 What do you mean?
3 for instance   4 Could I ask a question?

EXPLORING VOCABULARY

2 1 coal   2 gas   3 petrol (AmE gas)   4 solar power

3 1 profit – commercial (BUSINESS)
2 household – domestic (HOME)
3 politician – election (GOVERNMENT)
4 ecosystem – rainforest (THE ENVIRONMENT)
5 planet – spaceship (SPACE TRAVEL)
6 ocean – wave (THE SEA)

4 pessimist – pessimistic   optimist – optimistic
benefit – beneficial   environment – environmental
theory – theoretical   commerce – commercial
gene – genetic   ridicule – ridiculous

5 1 a   2 an   3 –   4 –   5 an   6 a
crew [no code = countable]   petrol [U]   optimist [no code = countable]   emotion [C,U]   ridicule [U]
species [no code = countable]

SHORT STORY

1 Possible answer:
A boy is standing in a school yard with some older and taller boys standing around him. One of the bigger boys is smiling.

2 Possible answers:
1 T (They move because she changes jobs.)
2 T (She is probably older because she gives him advice.)   3 F   4 T   5 F (When they came up to him he thought they were being friendly at first.)   6 T

3 Because people look back at them as a time when they had few responsibilities and their worries were small.

Unit twelve

LANGUAGE FOCUS

1 Passive forms: was founded, was priced, was reduced was sold, was changed, is based, is owned, are taken, is aimed

2 1 When was *The Manchester Guardian* founded?
It was founded in 1821.
2 When was the price reduced?
The price was reduced in 1855.
3 Who became the editor in 1871?
The writer C P Scott became the editor.
4 When was the title changed?
The title was changed in 1959.
5 Where is the editor based now?
The editor is based in London.
6 How often does the international paper appear?
It appears every week.
7 Where is it sold?
It is sold outside Britain.

3 1 …in Belfast has been bombed.

2 …to cut awards for crime victims have been delayed.

3 …have been stolen from the Prince's apartment.

4 …have been discovered by a farmer in his fields.

5 …has been sold by a collector for one million pounds.

4 Tapescript

JULIA: Here it is. 'Listen and learn with the new talking computer'.

JAMES: Hey! That looks great!

JULIA: Are you surprised?

JAMES: No! I knew it would look good.

JULIA: Now … let's look through all these newspapers and magazines.

JAMES: Why?

JULIA: To see if there are any new advertisements for other computers.

JAMES: Oh. Right.

Part two.

JAMES: Hey! There's a story here you may wish to read.

JULIA: I'm too busy!

JAMES: It's about MAP.

JULIA: Really? MAP? Let me have a look. 'The prize for the best advertising campaign of the year has been presented to MAP Advertising.

JAMES: What for? Which campaign?

JULIA: Um … hold on … 'MAP were given the prize for' … where is it … ah … 'the Drake bicycles campaign'.

JAMES: What?

JULIA: Apparently Tom Hall was presented with the prize in London last night.

JAMES: Last night? Tom was in London last night?

JULIA: Yes. I'm surprised he didn't come and see us.

JAMES: Are you surprised? I'm not.

JULIA: Why?

JAMES: Because *he* has been given a prize for something that was done by *me.*

JULIA: What do you mean?

JAMES: Drake bicycles was my account. I managed that campaign.

JULIA: Oh, I see.

JAMES: I'd like to have a word with Tom Hall.

4 1 Because their advertisement looks great.

2 Because Tom Hall has been given a prize for some work that James did himself.

5 1 has been presented   2 were given
3 was presented   4 has been given, was done

EXPLORING VOCABULARY

2 1 huge   2 silent   3 filthy   4 feeble   5 evil
6 vicious

3 1 attacked   2 injured   3 sacked   4 arrested

4 powerless   defenceless
The ending -*less* means *without.*

5 1 She's <u>left</u>-<u>wing</u>   2 a <u>left</u>-wing <u>news</u>paper   3 He's <u>right</u>-<u>wing</u>   4 a <u>right</u>-wing <u>news</u>paper   5 He's <u>Chi</u>nese.   6 <u>Chi</u>nese food.   7 She's Japa<u>nese</u>.
8 Japa<u>nese</u> food.

6 edit – editor   report – reporter   publish – publisher
print – printer   own – owner

SHORT STORY

1 Possible answer:
Michael has been bullied at his new school. He has told his sister, but not his mother, about the problem.

3 Bullies are people who use their strength to hurt or frighten people who are not as strong as they are.

4 1 M   2 TB   3 M   4 G   5 TB   6 T

Unit thirteen

LANGUAGE FOCUS

1 Tapescript

JAMES: I think that's Ireland. Who's the photographer?

JULIA: … 126 .. er … John Patrick Brady.

JAMES: What! That's amazing!

JULIA: Do you know him?

JAMES: He's my cousin! Here's another one. Aren't they wonderful?

JULIA: They're very nice.

JAMES: No, what do you really think? Isn't he a great photographer?

JULIA: He's good. Yes, he's very good. Is he a professional photographer, or is this his hobby?

JAMES: I don't really know. He was still a student when I last saw him. He'd always been a keen photographer – like me. But he certainly hadn't had an exhibition when I left Ireland, I'm sure of that. He'd never even *sold* a photograph, as far as I can remember.

JULIA: Why didn't he tell you about this exhibition?

JAMES: Well, I haven't seen him for ages. I'm so pleased he's doing well.

1 1 Yes, he is.   2 Yes, she does.   3 No, he hasn't.
4 No, he didn't.   5 Yes, he had.   6 No, he hadn't.
7 No, he hadn't.

2 1/2 had just brought   3 had asked   4 As soon as
5 had had   6 had called   7 had identified   8 had disappeared   9 had been   10 had noticed
11 until then   12 By the time   13 had worked

3 1 – C   2 – G   3 – B   4 – A   5 – H   6 – D   7 – F
8 – E

4 1 Go up the escalator to the second floor. Turn left and left again and you'll see the hairdresser's in front of you near the restaurant.

2 Go up the stairs to the second floor. Then turn left. Go past the hairdresser's and the restaurant is in front of you.

EXPLORING VOCABULARY

2 1 sight   2 exhibit   3 curator   4 mouldy   5 wrinkles

3 1 embarrassed   2 cheerful   3 neglected   4 genuine
5 offensive

4 arrogant assistance
apple (A)   attractive (B)   alive (B)   attack (B)
addict (A)   arrest (B)

5 carefree
1 crime-free   2 meat-free   3 tax-free   4 disease-
free

SHORT STORY

1 1 a week   2 unhappy   3 sister   4 identify

2 Possible answers:
  1 He could tell his mother.
  2 He could identify the bullies to the teacher.
  3 He could hit the bullies back.

3 TAPESCRIPT
Option A:
Michael agreed to go with his teacher to see the head of
the school. He told them both what had happened and
named the three boys who were involved. A boy who
witnessed the second attack was able to confirm
Michael's story, and the head sent for the three boys.
Option B:
Michael was too frightened to tell the teacher about the
bullies. He knew what would happen if he did, because
he had tried it before in another school. Next time he saw
the boys he offered to give them his pocket money and
his bus money every week if they left him alone. They
agreed.
Option C:
Michael refused to talk about the attacks. He was so
frightened that he decided to stop going to school. He
didn't want his mother or sister to know, so he left home
every day at the usual time and spent his days wandering
around town. At least he felt safe.

3 Possible answers:
  1 B (or none of them)   2 B   3 A

5 Tapescript
Michael didn't feel able to talk about the bullying to
anyone. His mother would worry, he knew that. His
sister had her own life and had never mentioned their
conversation again. And he was afraid of what the
bullies might do to him if he told any of the teachers.
He should be able to deal with the situation on his
own, he thought – and if he couldn't, well, that was
his problem.
   He didn't even enjoy his lessons any more, because
it was a real struggle to concentrate. As he sat in class
each day, he thought about what might happen after
school and his mind went completely blank. And sure
enough, two or three times a week, the bullies were
out there waiting for him.

'Well, now, Jenkins, what've you got for us today?'
they shouted. He took the money from his pockets
and gave it to them without a word. Sometimes they
still hit him, for the fun of it, but usually they ran off
laughing.
   The day everything changed was the day before
half-term. Michael had stayed late at school because
he needed some advice about an English project. The
school grounds were empty by the time he left, but he
stayed tense and watchful on the short walk to the bus
stop.
   There was only one other boy from the school at
the bus stop, and Michael stared at him in disbelief. He
was in the lowest class, so he was probably eleven
years old, but he looked younger. His clothes were
dirty and torn, and he was crying quietly.
   'Hey, what happened to you? Are you OK?'
Michael asked, but he had a sick feeling in his
stomach.
   'These boys ... they said they'd hurt me if ... if I
didn't give them money,' the younger boy said. 'And I
haven't *got* any money – only my bus pass ... '
   'Were there three of them?' Michael asked quickly.
'They're from school, aren't they?'
   The child looked at him with suprise and nodded.
Tears dripped from his cheeks to the ground. Michael
took a deep breath.
   'It happens to me too,' he said, 'and there's only
one way to stop it. We've got to tell someone. Come
with me.'
   He led the way back to the school, and found his
English teacher. As Michael told his story, the boys
could see sympathy and anger in her face. When he
finished, there was a short silence.
   'Is this right, Ben?' she said to the younger boy. 'Are
you sure the bullies who hurt you are the same ones?'
   'Yes,' he whispered. 'The same ones.'
   She looked at each of them in turn. 'You can leave it
to me now,' she said quietly. 'I'll see the head first
thing in the morning. And don't worry, either of you.
This won't happen again, I promise you.'

5 1 talk   2 concentrate   3 went   4 continued
5 hit   6 stayed   7 was threatened   8 realised
9 tell

Unit fourteen

LANGUAGE FOCUS

1 Tapescript
JULIA: What did you say to Tom?
JAMES: I said I was very unhappy that he hadn't spoken to
   me about the prize.
JULIA: And what did he say?
JAMES: Well, he said he was sorry that I was unhappy, but
   he also said that the *agency* had won the prize, and
   not an individual employee.

JULIA: Well, he's right, of course.

JAMES: I suppose so ... Anyway, he said he wanted us to be friends. And he asked me if I would go and see him ... spend a weekend in the country.

JULIA: And what did you say?

JAMES: I said I would. And I asked if you could come with me.

JULIA: Oh, did you!

JAMES: Wouldn't you like a weekend in the country?

JULIA: Hmm. I'll think about it.

JAMES: Oh, come on – it'll be fun.

JULIA: I said I'd think about it.

1 1 Yes, they are.

2 JAMES: I'm very unhappy that you haven't spoken/didn't speak to me about the prize.

TOM: I'm sorry that you're unhappy. But the agency (has) won the prize, not an individual employee. I want us to be friends, James. Would you come and see me ... spend a weekend in the country?

JAMES: Yes, I'd like that. Can Julia come with me?

2 1 d   2 b   3 a   4 b   5 b   6 a   7 c   8 d   9 b
10 a

3 1 ... me (us) there.   2 ... is ours (mine)!
3 ... then ... in a week's time (the following week).
4 ... taken him ...

4 Possible answer:

SECRETARY: Bradford College. Can I help you?

SECRETARY: No, this is the forestry department. Who's speaking, please?

SECRETARY: Hold the line a moment. I'll try to put you through to him.

SECRETARY: I'm afraid he's engaged at the moment. Would you like to call again later?

EXPLORING VOCABULARY

2 1 database, program, software
2 hold on, put through
3 a) fortnight   b) tool   c) enthusiasm
4 a) casual   b) engaged/restricted   c) familiar
   d) valuable

3 1 survey   2 confirms/confirmed/has confirmed
3 average   4 cost   5 bargain   6 alarmed
7 revolution

4 unconscious   insecurity   unenthusiastic   unfamiliar
unreasonably   inconclusive   unrestricted
insignificant

5 access A   alarmed B   aware B   confirm B
consult B   danger A   delay B   dial A   drawback A
engaged B   excuse B   express B   imply B

HELP YOURSELF

This page contains only linguistic contrasts: open answers.

Unit fifteen

LANGUAGE FOCUS

1 Tapescript

JAMES: I don't know which platform we want, do you?

JULIA: It's platform 2 – I think ... but I'm not sure if it's the same at weekends.

JAMES: Excuse me?

EMPLOYEE: Yes?

JAMES: Do you know where the Banbury train leaves from?

EMPLOYEE: Yes, Platform 1.

JAMES: Is Platform 1 on this side?

EMPLOYEE: No, it's the last platform – over there.

JAMES: Oh ... Er ... Excuse me ... Could you help me, please?

EMPLOYEE: Of course. But I must deliver this parcel first. Would you mind waiting a moment?

JAMES: No, not at all ... Thank you.

JAMES: What are you reading?

JULIA: A book about India.

JAMES: Oh, I've always wanted to go there. I read a wonderful book about India when I was a boy. I don't know who wrote it. It was called *The Forgotten Land*. What's that one about?

JULIA: The writer describes a journey through India. He travelled by slow train, by boat ... he even went 200 kilometres by taxi.

JAMES: That sounds wonderful. I'd love to do something like that.

JULIA: I wonder if I would like it ...

JAMES: I think you would. Maybe we could go there together.

JULIA: Together? You and me on a slow train through India? I'm not a very good travelling companion.

JAMES: I'm sure you'd love it.

JULIA: Would I, James?

JAMES: Yes, you would.

JULIA: India ... with you ... I wonder.

1 1 ... which platform we want   2 ... if it's the same
3 ... where the Banbury train leaves   4 ... who wrote
5 ... if I would like

2 1 Which platform do we want?   2 Is it the same at weekends?   3 Where does the Banbury train leave from?   4 Who wrote it?   5 Would I like it?

3 Possible answers:
1 Can you tell me if you are open on Sundays?
2 Can you tell me what your fax number is?
3 Do you know how much a return ticket to Oxford is?
4 Do you know if the London train is on time?
5 Can you tell me if the train stops at Reading?

4 1 I'll call you as soon as her plane takes off (✓).
2 When he reaches Argentina (✓), we'll be on our way to Ecuador (✓).

3 Before they go to lunch we'll meet for a drink (✓).

4 You'll arrive there after he does (✓).

5 I'll give him your note when he hears the good news (✓).

6 As soon as I get it (✓), I'll spend it.

5 1 unless   2 If   3 if   4 unless   5 Unless

6 1 Do not enter unless you are wearing protective clothing.

2 If you (don't) take a number, an assistant will (won't) call you.

3 If you travel without a valid ticket, you will have to pay a penalty of £50.

4 You won't get a free gift unless you spend £25 or more.

5 You should give up this seat if an elderly or disabled person needs it.

6 Do not pull the handle unless there is an emergency.

7 If the train is at a station, don't use the toilets.

EXPLORING VOCABULARY

2 Possible answers:

1 resort   2 tour guide   3 delights   4 luxury
5 overlooks   6 spectacular/stunning   7 handicrafts
8 excursions   9 contact   10 convenient

3 1 dazzling, radiant   2 vast   3 vibrant
Adjectives to describe attractive scenery: glorious, spectacular, stunning

4 coast   culture   season   ritual/rite   agricultural
malarial   spiritual   trivial   vital

HELP YOURSELF

1 1 Possible answers:
card, licence, driving document, driving permit, official document, driving licence

2 plastic licence, photo-licence, plastic card

3 British motorists, drivers, licence holders

4 European Union, the Union, EU

2 Possible answers:

1 tin, box

2 baby, toddler

3 cruise, ride

3 1 vehicles/(means of) transport   2 criminals/thieves
3 break   4 old

4 Possible answers:
1 end   2 start   3 appear   4 job   5 place   6 view
7 fantastic   8 unhappy   9 hard

5 1 don't earn   2 caught   3 became   4 bought
5 won   6 receive

Wordlist

These lists include key vocabulary from the Students' Book. They also include the words from the Workbook Exploring Vocabulary sections.

Unit 1

aerial (n) / 'eəriəl/
alive (adj) / ə'laɪv/
area (n) / 'eəriə/
background (n) / 'bækgraʊnd/
bare (adj) / beər/
barge (n) / bɑːdʒ/
bathe (v) / beɪð/
block of flats (n) / ˌblɒk əv 'flæts/
brick (n) / brɪk/
caravan (n) / 'kærəvæn/
care for (v) / 'keə ˌfɔːr/
cave (n) / keɪv/
childhood (n) / 'tʃaɪldhʊd/
chimney (n) / 'tʃɪmni/
close-knit (adj) / ˌkləʊs 'nɪt/
community (n) / kə'mjuːniti/
concrete (n) / 'kɒnkriːt/
conjuror (n) / 'kʌndʒərər/
cool (adj) / kuːl/
cottage (n) / 'kɒtɪdʒ/
council (n) / 'kaʊnsəl/
cruise (n) / kruːz/
cycle (v) / 'saɪkəl/
depend on (v) / dɪ'pend ˌɒn/
deserted (adj) / dɪ'zɜːtɪd/
detached (adj) / dɪ'tætʃt/

dock (v) / dɒk/
docker (n) / 'dɒkər/
docks (n pl) / dɒks/
dramatically (adv) / drə'mætɪkli/
dress (v) / dres/
dwelling (n) / 'dwelɪŋ/
environment (n) / ɪn'vaɪərənmənt/
especially (adv) / ɪ'speʃəli/
estate (n) / ɪ'steɪt/
executive (n) / ɪg'zekjətɪv/
facade (n) / fə'sɑːd/
farmhouse (n) / 'fɑːmhaʊs/
foreground (n) / 'fɔːgraʊnd/
foreman (n) / 'fɔːmən/
hardly ever (adv) / ˌhɑːdli 'evər/
hill (n) / hɪl/
hook (n) / hʊk/
hostel (n) / 'hɒstəl/
houseboat (n) / 'haʊsbəʊt/
housing (n) / 'haʊzɪŋ/
identify (v) / aɪ'dentɪfaɪ/
identity (n) / aɪ'dentɪti/
imagination (n) / ɪˌmædʒɪ'neɪʃən/
industry (n) / 'ɪndəstri/
insurance (n) / ɪn'ʃʊərəns/
ladder (n) / 'lædər/

lampshade (n) / 'læmpʃeɪd/
launch (n) / lɔːntʃ/
lawyer (n) / 'lɔːjər/
left-over (adj) / 'leftəʊvər/
lifestyle (n) / 'laɪfstaɪl/
load (v) / ləʊd/
magical (adj) / 'mædʒɪkəl/
memory (n) / 'meməri/
mobile home (n) / ˌməʊbaɪl 'həʊm/
mortgage (n) / 'mɔːgɪdʒ/
passenger (n) / 'pæsɪndʒər/
pension (n) / 'penʃən/
plain (n) / pleɪn/
plateau (n) / 'plætəʊ/
playing card (n) / 'pleɪ-ɪŋ ˌkɑːd/
pleasure (n) / 'pleʒər/
porch (n) / pɔːtʃ/
professional (adj) / prə'feʃənəl/
purchase (v) / 'pɜːtʃəs/
rabbit (n) / 'ræbɪt/
range (n) / reɪndʒ/
relevant (adj) / 'reləvənt/
responsible (adj) / rɪ'spɒnsəbəl/
rock (n) / rɒk/
row (n) / rəʊ/
rubbish (n) / 'rʌbɪʃ/
search (n) / sɜːtʃ/
seaside (n) / 'siːsaɪd/

semi-detached (adj) / ˌsemɪdɪ'tætʃt/
setting (n) / 'setɪŋ/
shabby (adj) / 'ʃæbi/
sink (v) / sɪŋk/
skilled (adj) / skɪld/
skip (n) / skɪp/
slate (n) / sleɪt/
slope (n/v) / sləʊp/
spirit (n) / 'spɪrɪt/
stevedore (n) / 'stiːvədɔːr/
stone (n) / stəʊn/
surrounding (adj) / sə'raʊndɪŋ/
tent (n) / tent/
terraced (adj) / 'terəst/
thrive (v) / θraɪv/
tile (n) / taɪl/
tiny (adj) / 'taɪni/
toy (n) / tɔɪ/
tug (n) / tʌg/
unload (v) / ʌn'ləʊd/
used to (v) / 'juːstə/
vegetation (n) / ˌvedʒɪ'teɪʃən/
wash-house (n) / 'wɒʃhaʊs/
washing line (n) / 'wɒʃɪŋ ˌlaɪn/
waste (n) / weɪst/
watering can (n) / 'wɔːtərɪŋ ˌkæn/

Unit 2

accept (v) / əkˈsept/
addict (n) / ˈædɪkt/
affect (v) / əˈfekt/
ahead of (adv) / əˈhed əv/
amazing (adj) / əˈmeɪzɪŋ/
aquamarine (adj)
  / ˌækwəməˈriːn/
assortment (n) / əˈsɔːtmənt/
attraction (n) / əˈtrækʃən/
bend (n) / bend/
blood (n) / blʌd/
board game (n) / ˈbɔːd ˌɡeɪm/
breath (n) / breθ/
breathtakingly (adv)
  / ˈbreθteɪkɪŋli/
breeze (n) / briːz/
bright (adj) / braɪt/
brilliant (adj) / ˈbrɪljənt/
bury (v) / ˈberi/
candle (n) / ˈkændl/
chess (n) / tʃes/
close (adj) / kləʊs/
collapse (v) / kəˈlæps/
control (n) / kənˈtrəʊl/
cove (n) / kəʊv/
crush (v) / krʌʃ/
dawn (n) / dɔːn/

deep (adj) / diːp/
depressing (adj) / dɪˈpresɪŋ/
diamond (n) / ˈdaɪəmənd/
discover (v) / dɪsˈkʌvər/
dusk (n) / dʌsk/
earthquake (n) / ˈɜːθkweɪk/
effects (n pl) / ɪˈfekts/
escape (v) / ɪˈskeɪp/
experiment (n) / ɪkˈsperɪmənt/
face (v) / feɪs/
faint (adj) / feɪnt/
fantasy (n) / ˈfæntəsi/
favourite (adj) / ˈfeɪvərɪt/
flash (v) / flæʃ/
flicker (v) / ˈflɪkər/
gather (v) / ˈɡæðər/
ghost (n) / ɡəʊst/
giant (adj) / ˈdʒaɪənt/
gun (n) / ɡʌn/
high-tech (adj) / ˌhaɪ ˈtek/
hillside (n) / ˈhɪlsaɪd/
honeysuckle (n) / ˈhʌniˌsʌkəl/
hopelessly (adv) / ˈhəʊpləsli/
ideal (adj) / aɪˈdɪəl/
imaginary (adj) / ɪˈmædʒɪnəri/
imagine (v) / ɪˈmædʒɪn/
incredible (adj) / ɪnˈkredəbəl/
jagged (adj) / ˈdʒæɡɪd/
jet (n) / dʒet/

job-share (v) / ˈdʒɒbʃeər/
lightning (n) / ˈlaɪtnɪŋ/
limit (v) / ˈlɪmɪt/
look-out (n) / ˈlʊk-aʊt/
magic (n) / ˈmædʒɪk/
monster (n) / ˈmɒnstər/
mud (n) / mʌd/
nag (v) / næɡ/
nightmare (n) / ˈnaɪtmeər/
pale (adj) / peɪl/
patio (n) / ˈpætiəʊ/
peaceful (adj) / ˈpiːsfəl/
pine (n) / paɪn/
production (n) / prəˈdʌkʃən/
promotion (n) / prəˈməʊʃən/
reality (n) / riˈæləti/
refuse (v) / rɪˈfjuːz/
result (n) / rɪˈzʌlt/
ride (n) / raɪd/
roar (v) / rɔːr/
rose (n) / rəʊz/
rough (adj) / rʌf/
runaway (adj) / ˈrʌnəweɪ/
rush (v) / rʌʃ/
satellite (n) / ˈsætəlaɪt/
satisfied (adj) / ˈsætɪsfaɪd/
scent (n) / sent/
sea level (n) / ˈsiː ˌlevəl/
secret (n) / ˈsiːkrət/

seductive (adj) / sɪˈdʌktɪv/
set (n) / set/
sharp (adj) / ʃɑːp/
sheer (adj) / ʃɪər/
skyscraper (n) / ˈskaɪˌskreɪpər/
sliver (n) / ˈslɪvər/
smell (v) / smel/
sparkle (v) / ˈspɑːkəl/
spill (v) / spɪl/
studio (n) / ˈstjuːdiəʊ/
take part in (v) / ˌteɪk ˈpɑːt ɪn/
tanker (n) / ˈtæŋkər/
taste (v) / teɪst/
terrified (adj) / ˈterɪfaɪd/
terrifying (adj) / ˈterɪfaɪ-ɪŋ/
thirsty (adj) / ˈθɜːsti/
tram (n) / træm/
trap (v) / træp/
twinkling (adj) / ˈtwɪŋklɪŋ/
typical (adj) / ˈtɪpɪkəl/
ultimate (adj) / ˈʌltɪmət/
visual (adj) / ˈvɪʒuəl/
whisper (n/v) / ˈwɪspər/
wild (adj) / waɪld/
would rather (v adv) / ˌwʊd
  ˈrɑːðə/

Unit 3

appalling (adj) / əˈpɔːlɪŋ/
boarding (adj) / ˈbɔːdɪŋ/
border (n) / ˈbɔːdər/
border post (n) / ˈbɔːdə ˌpəʊst/
brain (n) / breɪn/
brand-new (adj) / ˌbrænd
  ˈnjuː/
campsite (n) / ˈkæmpsaɪt/
check-in clerk (n) / ˈtʃekɪn
  ˌklɑːk/
citizen (n) / ˈsɪtɪzən/
comment (n) / ˈkɒment/
confident (adj) / ˈkɒnfɪdənt/
cross (adj/v) / krɒs/
currency (n) / ˈkʌrənsi/
declaration (n) / ˌdekləˈreɪʃən/
deeply rooted (adj) / ˌdiːpli
  ˈruːtɪd/
deportation (n) / ˌdiːpɔːˈteɪʃən/
depressed (adj) / dɪˈprest/
detention (n) / dɪˈtenʃən/
disappointed (adj)
  / ˌdɪsəˈpɔɪntɪd/

disgusting (adj) / dɪsˈɡʌstɪŋ/
drawing book (n) / ˈdrɔːɪŋ
  ˌbʊk/
dreadful (adj) / ˈdredfəl/
duty-free (v) / ˌdjuːti ˈfriː/
echo (v) / ˈekəʊ/
enormous (adj) / ɪˈnɔːməs/
equal (adj) / ˈiːkwəl/
explore (v) / ɪkˈsplɔːr/
extradition (n) / ˌekstrəˈdɪʃən/
fasten (v) / ˈfɑːsən/
feature (n) / ˈfiːtʃə/
flat (adj) / flæt/
flight attendant (n) / ˈflaɪt
  əˌtendənt/
forbidden (adj) / fəˈbɪdn/
former (adj) / ˈfɔːmər/
frontier (n) / ˈfrʌntɪər/
gift (n) / ɡɪft/
guard (n) / ɡɑːd/
hang-gliding (n) / ˈhæŋ
  ˌɡlaɪdɪŋ/
hike (v) / haɪk/
hire (v) / haɪər/
hut (n) / hʌt/

illegally (adv) / ɪˈliːɡəli/
immense (adj) / ɪˈmens/
immigration official (n)
  / ˌɪmɪˈɡreɪʃən əˈfɪʃəl/
indeed (adv) / ɪnˈdiːd/
inn (n) / ɪn/
item (n) / ˈaɪtəm/
linger (v) / ˈlɪŋɡər/
lock (n) / lɒk/
lounge (n) / laʊndʒ/
marvellous (adj) / ˈmɑːvələs/
miserable (adj) / ˈmɪzərəbəl/
official (n) / əˈfɪʃəl/
painful (adj) / ˈpeɪnfəl/
patch (n) / pætʃ/
perfume (n) / ˈpɜːfjuːm/
porter (n) / ˈpɔːtər/
purchase (n) / ˈpɜːtʃəs/
receive (v) / rɪˈsiːv/
recommendation (n)
  / ˌrekəmenˈdeɪʃən/
relaxed (adj) / rɪˈlækst/
relief (n) / rɪˈliːf/
require (v) / rɪˈkwaɪər/
resident (n/adj) / ˈrezɪdənt/

rocky (adj) / ˈrɒki/
rotten (adj) / ˈrɒtən/
sandy (adj) / ˈsændi/
scared (adj) / skeəd/
seat (n) / siːt/
seat belt (n) / ˈsiːt ˌbelt/
sheltered (adj) / ˈʃeltəd/
showdown (n) / ˈʃəʊdaʊn/
sigh (n) / saɪ/
similar (adj) / ˈsɪmələr/
stony (adj) / ˈstəʊni/
stuff (n) / stʌf/
stupid (adj) / ˈstjuːpɪd/
superb (adj) / sjuːˈpɜːb/
surround (v) / səˈraʊnd/
sycophantic (adj)
  / ˌsɪkəˈfæntɪk/
tolerable (adj) / ˈtɒlərəbəl/
valley (n) / ˈvæli/
visa (n) / ˈviːzə/
vision (n) / ˈvɪʒən/
wave (v) / weɪv/
worry (v) / ˈwʌri/

Unit 4

academy (n) /əˈkædəmi/
act (v) /ækt/
apparently (adv) /əˈpærəntli/
arson (n) /ˈɑːsən/
arsonist (n) /ˈɑːsənɪst/
authoritarian (adj)
   /ɔːˌθɒrɪˈteəriən/
authority (n) /ɔːˈθɒrəti/
believable (adj) /bəˈliːvəbəl/
blow (v) /bləʊ/
burglar (n) /ˈbɜːɡləʳ/
burglary (n) /ˈbɜːɡləri/
burgle (v) /ˈbɜːɡəl/
burn (v) /bɜːn/
cadet (n) /kəˈdet/
camp (n) /kæmp/
career (n) /kəˈrɪəʳ/
circumstance (n)
   /ˈsɜːkəmstæns/
companion (n) /kəmˈpænjən/
confrontation (n)
   /ˌkɒnfrənˈteɪʃən/
courage (n) /ˈkʌrɪdʒ/
creep (v) /kriːp/
crime (n) /kraɪm/
criminal (n) /ˈkrɪmɪnəl/

currently (adv) /ˈkʌrəntli/
defend (v) /dɪˈfend/
delighted (adj) /dɪˈlaɪtɪd/
demand (v) /dɪˈmɑːnd/
detective (n) /dɪˈtektɪv/
distraught (adj) /dɪˈstrɔːt/
division (n) /dɪˈvɪʒən/
embarrassment (n)
   /ɪmˈbærəsmənt/
embezzlement (n)
   /ɪmˈbezəlmənt/
enemy (n) /ˈenəmi/
entail (v) /ɪnˈteɪl/
event (n) /ɪˈvent/
fact (n) /fækt/
female (adj) /ˈfiːmeɪl/
fiction (n) /ˈfɪkʃən/
fine (n) /faɪn/
foam (n) /fəʊm/
gang (n) /ɡæŋ/
half-eaten (adj) /ˈhɑːf ˌiːtən/
hero (n) /ˈhɪərəʊ/
hide (v) /haɪd/
impatience (n) /ɪmˈpeɪʃəns/
investigate (v) /ɪnˈvestɪɡeɪt/
justice (n) /ˈdʒʌstɪs/
knight (n) /naɪt/
landowner (n) /ˈlændəʊnəʳ/

lead (v) /liːd/
legend (n) /ˈledʒənd/
legendary (adj) /ˈledʒəndəri/
loan (n) /ləʊn/
local government (n) /ˌləʊkəl
   ˈɡʌvənmənt/
merry (adj) /ˈmeri/
mug (v) /mʌɡ/
mugger (n) /ˈmʌɡəʳ/
mugging (n) /ˈmʌɡɪŋ/
murder (n/v) /ˈmɜːdəʳ/
murderer (n) /ˈmɜːdərəʳ/
notice (v) /ˈnəʊtɪs/
outlaw (n) /ˈaʊtlɔː/
patrol (n) /pəˈtrəʊl/
pickpocket (n) /ˈpɪkˌpɒkɪt/
prison sentence (n) /ˈprɪzən
   ˌsentəns/
property (n) /ˈprɒpəti/
protect (v) /prəˈtekt/
punch (v) /pʌntʃ/
rebel (n/v) /ˈrebəl (n)
   rɪˈbel (v)/
representative (n)
   /ˌreprɪˈzentətɪv/
reputation (n) /ˌrepjʊˈteɪʃən/
riot (n) /ˈraɪət/
rob (v) /rɒb/

robber (n) /ˈrɒbəʳ/
robbery (n) /ˈrɒbəri/
series (n) /ˈsɪəriːz/
serve (n) /sɜːv/
several (det/pron) /ˈsevərəl/
shoot (v) /ʃuːt/
shoplifter (n) /ˈʃɒpˌlɪftəʳ/
shoplifting (n) /ˈʃɒpˌlɪftɪŋ/
snatch (v) /snætʃ/
spray (n) /spreɪ/
steal (v) /stiːl/
symbol (n) /ˈsɪmbəl/
theft (n) /θeft/
thief (n) /θiːf/
threaten (v) /ˈθretn/
till (n) /tɪl/
vandal (n) /ˈvændəl/
vandalise (v) /ˈvændəlaɪz/
vandalism (n) /ˈvændəlɪzəm/
violent (adj) /ˈvaɪələnt/
washing machine (n) /ˈwɒʃɪŋ
   məˌʃiːn/
while (conj) /waɪl/
white collar (adj) /ˌwaɪt ˈkɒləʳ/
witness (n/v) /ˈwɪtnɪs/

Unit 5

abbreviate (v) /əˈbriːvieɪt/
abbreviation (n)
   /əˌbriːviˈeɪʃən/
accountant (n) /əˈkaʊntənt/
advertise (v) /ˈædvətaɪz/
agent (n) /ˈeɪdʒənt/
aisle (n) /aɪl/
aluminium (n) /ˌæljʊˈmɪniəm/
apology (n) /əˈpɒlədʒi/
applaud (v) /əˈplɔːd/
basic (adj) /ˈbeɪsɪk/
best-selling (adj) /ˈbest ˌselɪŋ/
book-keeping (n) /ˈbʊk
   ˌkiːpɪŋ/
chassis (n) /ˈʃæsi/
clockwise (adv) /ˈklɒk-waɪz/
complain (v) /kəmˈpleɪn/
component (n)
   /kəmˈpəʊnənt/
correspondence (n)
   /ˌkɒrɪˈspɒndəns/
delivery (n) /dɪˈlɪvəri/
deserve (v) /dɪˈzɜːv/
design (n/v) /dɪˈzaɪn/

desktop (n) /ˈdesktɒp/
differ (v) /ˈdɪfəʳ/
display (n/v) /dɪˈspleɪ/
distinction (n) /dɪˈstɪŋkʃən/
distribute (v) /dɪˈstrɪbjuːt/
employ (v) /ɪmˈplɔɪ/
enclose (v) /ɪnˈkləʊz/
encourage (v) /ɪnˈkʌrɪdʒ/
export (v) /ɪkˈspɔːt/
eye-level (n) /ˈaɪˌlevəl/
fuel tank (n) /ˈfjʊəl ˌtæŋk/
grow (v) /ɡrəʊ/
hand-crafted (adj) /ˌhænd
   ˈkrɑːftɪd/
hand made (adj) /ˌhænd
   ˈmeɪd/
huntsman (n) /ˈhʌntsmən/
image (n) /ˈɪmɪdʒ/
import (v) /ɪmˈpɔːt/
inspect (v) /ɪnˈspekt/
invoice (n) /ˈɪnvɔɪs/
karate (n) /kəˈrɑːti/
layout (n) /ˈleɪaʊt/
luxurious (adj) /lʌɡˈzʊərɪəs/
manufacturer (n)
   /ˌmænjəˈfæktʃərə/

mass-produced (adj)
   /ˌmæsprə ˈdjuːst/
necklace (n) /ˈnekləs/
order (n/v) /ˈɔːdəʳ/
original (adj) /əˈrɪdʒənəl/
package (n) /ˈpækɪdʒ/
panel (n) /ˈpænəl/
payment (n) /ˈpeɪmənt/
peasant (n) /ˈpezənt/
peel (v) /piːl/
persuade (v) /pəˈsweɪd/
pick (v) /pɪk/
practical (adj) /ˈpræktɪkəl/
product (n) /ˈprɒdʌkt/
publishing (n) /ˈpʌblɪʃɪŋ/
radiator (n) /ˈreɪdieɪtəʳ/
reaction (n) /riˈækʃən/
recently (adv) /ˈriːsəntli/
refund (n) /ˈriːfʌnd/
reliable (adj) /rɪˈlaɪəbəl/
repay (v) /ˈriːpeɪ/
ruler (n) /ˈruːləʳ/
science (n) /ˈsaɪəns/
semolina (n) /ˌseməˈliːnə/
sender (n) /ˈsendəʳ/
sensible (adj) /ˈsensɪbəl/

shelves (n pl) /ʃelvz/
shopper (n) /ˈʃɒpəʳ/
solid (adj) /ˈsɒlɪd/
space (n) /speɪs/
sports car (n) /ˈspɔːts ˌkɑːʳ/
steel (n) /stiːl/
storage (n) /ˈstɔːrɪdʒ/
store (n) /stɔːʳ/
supplier (n) /səˈplaɪəʳ/
supply (n) /səˈplaɪ/
technique (n) /tekˈniːk/
traditional (adj) /trəˈdɪʃənəl/
transport (v) /trænˈspɔːt/
trolley (n) /ˈtrɒli/
unacceptable (adj)
   /ˌʌnəkˈseptəbəl/
undoubtedly (adj)
   /ʌnˈdaʊtɪdli/
unique (adj) /juːˈniːk/
urgently (adv) /ˈɜːdʒəntli/
wholesaler (n) /ˈhəʊlˌseɪləʳ/
word-processing (n) /ˈwɜːd
   ˌprəʊsesɪŋ/

Unit 6

ache (v) /eɪk/
acupuncturist (n)
/ˈækjʊˌpʌŋktərɪst/
adulthood (n) /ˈædʌlthʊd/
afraid (adj) /əˈfreɪd/
aloud (adv) /əˈlaʊd/
anaesthetic (n) /ˌænəsˈθetɪk/
anxious (adj) /ˈæŋkʃəs/
appointment (n)
/əˈpɔɪntmənt/
author (n) /ˈɔːθər/
bleed (v) /bliːd/
bristle (v) /ˈbrɪsəl/
bump (n/v) /bʌmp/
care (n) /keər/
casement (n) /ˈkeɪsmənt/
child-minder (n)
/ˈtʃaɪldmaɪndər/
cigarette (n) /ˈsɪɡəret/
condition (n) /kənˈdɪʃən/
consequence (n)
/ˈkɒnsɪkwəns/
crack (v) /kræk/
creak (v) /kriːk/
dental (adj) /ˈdentəl/
dentist (n) /ˈdentɪst/
dependable (adj)
/dɪˈpendəbəl/
depths (n pl) /depθs/

development (n)
/dɪˈveləpmənt/
disposable (adj)
/dɪsˈpəʊzebəl/
drip (v) /drɪp/
drug (n) /drʌɡ/
emergency (n) /ɪˈmɜːdʒənsi/
emit (v) /ɪˈmɪt/
enjoyable (adj) /ɪnˈdʒɔɪəbəl/
equipment (n) /ɪˈkwɪpmənt/
erect (adj) /ɪˈrekt/
exercise (n/v) /ˈeksəsaɪz/
expert (n) /ˈekspɜːt/
eyesight (n) /ˈaɪsaɪt/
fashion (n) /ˈfæʃən/
feed (v) /fiːd/
fit (adj) /fɪt/
floorboard (n) /ˈflɔːbɔːd/
footstep (n) /ˈfʊtstep/
growl (n/v) /ɡraʊl/
gunshot (n) /ˈɡʌnʃɒt/
habit (n) /ˈhæbɪt/
herbalist (n) /ˈhɜːbəlɪst/
household (adj) /ˈhaʊshəʊld/
inactive (adj) /ɪnˈæktɪv/
intermittent (adj)
/ˌɪntəˈmɪtənt/
irritable (adj) /ˈɪrɪtəbəl/
jog (v) /dʒɒɡ/
likely (adv) /ˈlaɪkli/
marble (n) /ˈmɑːbəl/

medicine (n) /ˈmedsən/
moan (v) /məʊn/
muffled (adj) /ˈmʌfəld/
needle (n) /ˈniːdl/
ominous (adj) /ˈɒmɪnəs/
operation (n) /ˌɒpəˈreɪʃən/
optician (n) /ɒpˈtɪʃən/
ought to (v) /ˈɔːt tə/
overloaded (adj)
/ˌəʊvəˈləʊdɪd/
overpopulated (adj)
/ˌəʊvəˈpɒpjʊleɪtɪd/
overweight (adj) /ˌəʊvəˈweɪt/
overworked (adj)
/ˌəʊvəˈwɜːkt/
pace (n) /peɪs/
pain (n) /peɪn/
paralyse (v) /ˈpærəlaɪz/
parental (adj) /pəˈrentəl/
patient (n) /ˈpeɪʃənt/
persuasive (adj) /pəˈsweɪsɪv/
petrified (adj) /ˈpetrɪfaɪd/
pharmacist (n) /ˈfɑːməsɪst/
physically (adv) /ˈfɪzɪkli/
prick (v) /prɪk/
prickling (n) /ˈprɪklɪŋ/
psychiatrist (n) /saɪˈkaɪətrɪst/
pushchair (n) /ˈpʊʃtʃeər/
routine (n) /ruːˈtiːn/
rumble (n/v) /ˈrʌmbəl/
rustle (v) /ˈrʌsəl/

scream (v) /skriːm/
smoker (n) /ˈsməʊkər/
snuffle (v) /ˈsnʌfəl/
sore (adj) /sɔːr/
splash (v) /splæʃ/
spring (v) /sprɪŋ/
still (adj) /stɪl/
sting (n/v) /stɪŋ/
strain (v) /streɪn/
strength (n) /streŋθ/
structured (adj) /ˈstrʌktʃəd/
surgeon (n) /ˈsɜːdʒən/
surgery (n) /ˈsɜːdʒəri/
survival kit (n) /səˈvaɪvəl ˌkɪt/
tail (n) /teɪl/
tap (n) /tæp/
tense (adj) /tens/
thread (n) /θred/
throat (n) /θrəʊt/
tie (v) /taɪ/
toddler (n) /tɒdlər/
tot (n) /tɒt/
tranquilliser (n)
/ˈtræŋkwɪlaɪzər/
treatment (n) /ˈtriːtmənt/
uneasy (adj) /ʌnˈiːzi/
unfit (adj) /ʌnˈfɪt/
washable (adj) /ˈwɒʃəbəl/
weightlifting (n) /ˈweɪtlɪftɪŋ/
youngster (n) /ˈjʌŋstər/

Unit 7

annual (*adj*) /ˈænjuːəl/
architectural (*adj*) /ˌɑːkɪˈtektʃərəl/
attempt (*n*) /əˈtempt/
attract (*v*) /əˈtrækt/
babysitting (*n*) /ˈbeɪbiˌsɪtɪŋ/
balcony (*n*) /ˈbælkəni/
bark (*v*) /bɑːk/
base (*n*) /beɪs/
bewildered (*adj*) /bɪˈwɪldəd/
certificate (*n*) /səˈtɪfɪkət/
chaos (*n*) /ˈkeɪ-ɒs/
complicated (*adj*) /ˈkɒmplɪkeɪtɪd/
conclusion (*n*) /kənˈkluːʒən/
confetti (*n*) /kənˈfeti/
contest (*n*) /ˈkɒntest/
desperately (*adv*) /ˈdespərətli/
drench (*v*) /drentʃ/
drop (*v*) /drɒp/
dry-cleaning (*n*) /ˌdraɪ ˈkliːnɪŋ/

enrage (*v*) /ɪnˈreɪdʒ/
experienced (*adj*) /ɪkˈspɪəriənst/
fail (*v*) /feɪl/
fit (*v*) /fɪt/
flick (*n/v*) /flɪk/
freeze (*v*) /friːz/
fright (*n*) /fraɪt/
gasp (*v*) /ɡɑːsp/
gear (*n*) /ɡɪəʳ/
generation (*n*) /ˌdʒenəˈreɪʃən/
hire (*v*) /haɪəʳ/
hurl (*v*) /hɜːl/
igloo (*n*) /ˈɪɡluː/
infestation (*n*) /ˌɪnfesˈteɪʃən/
key (*n*) /kiː/
laundry (*n*) /ˈlɔːndri/
leap (*v*) /liːp/
light (*v*) /laɪt/
major (*adj*) /ˈmeɪdʒəʳ/
matchbox (*n*) /ˈmætʃbɒks/
melt (*v*) /melt/
mend (*v*) /mend/
midway (*adv*) /ˌmɪdˈweɪ/
napkin (*n*) /ˈnæpkɪn/

naturalist (*n*) /ˈnætʃərəlɪst/
overturn (*v*) /ˌəʊvəˈtɜːn/
pandemonium (*n*) /ˌpændɪˈməʊniəm/
peace (*n*) /piːs/
peer (*v*) /pɪəʳ/
pile (*v*) /paɪl/
pitch (*v*) /pɪtʃ/
plague (*n*) /pleɪɡ/
playground (*n*) /ˈpleɪɡraʊnd/
promptly (*adv*) /ˈprɒmptli/
protest (*v*) /prəˈtest/
proud (*adj*) /praʊd/
quiver (*v*) /ˈkwɪvəʳ/
rapid (*adj*) /ˈræpɪd/
react (*v*) /riˈækt/
realistic (*adj*) /rɪəˈlɪstɪk/
recreation (*n*) /ˌrekriˈeɪʃən/
remove (*v*) /rɪˈmuːv/
replace (*v*) /rɪˈpleɪs/
rider (*n*) /ˈraɪdəʳ/
roll (*v*) /rəʊl/
safari (*n*) /səˈfɑːri/
sale (*n*) /seɪl/
sarcastic (*adj*) /sɑːˈkæstɪk/

scatter (*v*) /ˈskætəʳ/
scorpion (*n*) /ˈskɔːpiən/
secretarial (*adj*) /ˌsekrəˈteəriəl/
self-catering (*adj*) /ˌself ˈkeɪtərɪŋ/
slide show (*n*) /ˈslaɪd ˌʃəʊ/
speed (*v*) /spiːd/
stable (*n*) /ˈsteɪbəl/
stick (*v*) /stɪk/
surface (*n*) /ˈsɜːfɪs/
survival (*n*) /səˈvaɪvəl/
swarm (*v*) /swɔːm/
thump (*v*) /θʌmp/
unfortunate (*adj*) /ʌnˈfɔːtʃənət/
utter (*v*) /ˈʌtəʳ/
vain (*adj*) /veɪn/
view (*n*) /vjuː/
volunteer (*n*) /ˌvɒlənˈtɪəʳ/
wardrobe (*n*) /ˈwɔːdrəʊb/
wrangler (*n*) /ˈræŋɡləʳ/
youth hostel (*n*) /ˈjuːθ ˌhɒstəl/

Unit 8

ambition (*n*) /æmˈbɪʃən/
anthropology (*n*) /ˌænθrəˈpɒlədʒi/
applicant (*n*) /ˈæplɪkənt/
architecture (*n*) /ˈɑːkɪtektʃəʳ/
au pair (*n*) /ˌəʊ ˈpeəʳ/
biology (*n*) /baɪˈɒlədʒi/
carpenter (*n*) /ˈkɑːpəntəʳ/
carpentry (*n*) /ˈkɑːpəntri/
ceramics (*n*) /səˈræmɪks/
chef (*n*) /ʃef/
chemistry (*n*) /ˈkemɪstri/
clarification (*n*) /ˌklærɪfɪˈkeɪʃən/
cleaner (*n*) /ˈkliːnəʳ/
collage (*n*) /ˈkɒlɑːʒ/
complex (*adj*) /ˈkɒmpleks/

contact (*n*) /ˈkɒntækt/
contract (*n*) /ˈkɒntrækt/
courier (*n*) /ˈkʊriəʳ/
craft (*n*) /krɑːft/
curvaceous (*adj*) /kɜːˈveɪʃəs/
degree (*n*) /dɪˈɡriː/
economics (*n*) /ˌekəˈnɒmɪks/
engineer (*n*) /ˌendʒəˈnɪəʳ/
essential (*adj*) /ɪˈsenʃəl/
flexible (*adj*) /ˈfleksəbəl/
fortune (*n*) /ˈfɔːtʃən/
geography (*n*) /dʒiˈɒɡrəfi/
graduate (*v*) /ˈɡrædʒueɪt/
humour (*n*) /ˈhjuːməʳ/
interviewee (*n*) /ˌɪntəvjuˈiː/
invent (*v*) /ɪnˈvent/
irritating (*adj*) /ˈɪrɪteɪtɪŋ/
journalist (*n*) /ˈdʒɜːnəlɪst/
knowledge (*n*) /ˈnɒlɪdʒ/

lawyer (*n*) /ˈlɔːjəʳ/
legal (*adj*) /ˈliːɡəl/
librarian (*n*) /laɪˈbreəriən/
literature (*n*) /ˈlɪtərətʃəʳ/
mathematics/maths (*n*) /ˌmæθəˈmætɪks, mæθs/
patient (*adj*) /ˈpeɪʃənt/
physics (*n*) /ˈfɪzɪks/
plumber (*n*) /ˈplʌməʳ/
postgraduate (*adj*) /ˌpəʊstˈɡrædʒuət/
primary school (*n*) /ˈpraɪməri ˌskuːl/
project (*n*) /ˈprɒdʒekt/
provide (*v*) /prəˈvaɪd/
qualification (*n*) /ˌkwɒlɪfɪˈkeɪʃən/
religion (*n*) /rɪˈlɪdʒən/
renewable (*adj*) /rɪˈnjuːəbəl/

repetition (*n*) /ˌrepəˈtɪʃən/
research (*n*) /rɪˈsɜːtʃ/
sculpture (*n*) /ˈskʌlptʃəʳ/
secondary school (*n*) /ˈsekəndəri ˌskuːl/
sequence (*n*) /ˈsiːkwəns/
solicitor (*n*) /səˈlɪsɪtəʳ/
specifically (*adv*) /spəˈsɪfɪkli/
stripy (*adj*) /ˈstraɪpi/
technology (*n*) /tekˈnɒlədʒi/
theme (*n*) /θiːm/
thesis (*n*) /ˈθiːsɪs/
tolerant (*adj*) /ˈtɒlərənt/
trainee (*n*) /treɪˈniː/
veterinary surgeon/vet (*n*) /ˈvetərɪnəri ˌsɜːdʒən, vet/
window dresser (*n*) /ˈwɪndəʊ ˌdresəʳ/
youth (*n*) /juːθ/

Unit 9

accent (n) /ˈæksənt/
affected by (adj) /əˈfektɪd ˌbaɪ/
aggressive (adj) /əˈgresɪv/
artificial (adj) /ˌɑːtɪˈfɪʃəl/
attitude (n) /ˈætɪtjuːd/
beauty (n) /ˈbjuːti/
blonde (n) /blɒnd/
bona fide (adj) /ˌbəʊnə ˈfaɪdi/
booker (n) /ˈbʊkər/
bright-eyed (adj) /ˌbraɪtˈaɪd/
butterfly (n) /ˈbʌtəflaɪ/
certainty (n) /ˈsɜːtənti/
clean-shaven (adj) /ˌkliːn ˈʃeɪvən/
colourful (adj) /ˈkʌləfʊl/
competition (n) /ˌkɒmpəˈtɪʃən/
concert (n) /ˈkɒnsət/
conventional (adj) /kənˈvenʃənəl/
cosmetic surgery (n) /ˌkɒsmetɪk ˈsɜːdʒəri/
drab (adj) /dræb/
dye (v) /daɪ/
exotic (adj) /ɪgˈzɒtɪk/
forgetful (adj) /fəˈgetfəl/
fun-loving (adj) /ˈfʌnlʌvɪŋ/
good-looking (adj) /ˌgʊd ˈlʊkɪŋ/
guess (n) /ges/
hair style (n) /ˈheəstaɪl/
hairy (adj) /ˈheəri/
horn (n) /hɔːn/
immature (adj) /ˌɪməˈtʃʊər/
innocent (adj) /ˈɪnəsənt/
mature (adj) /məˈtʃʊər/
middle eastern (adj) /ˌmɪdl ˈiːstən/
middle-aged (adj) /ˌmɪdl ˈeɪdʒd/
modelling (n) /ˈmɒdlɪŋ/
nail (n) /neɪl/
occasion (n) /əˈkeɪʒən/
opera (n) /ˈɒpərə/
overweight (adj) /ˌəʊvəˈweɪt/
personality (n) /ˌpɜːsəˈnæləti/
pierce (v) /pɪəs/
policy (n) /ˈpɒləsi/
portfolio (n) /pɔːtˈfəʊliəʊ/
possibly (adv) /ˈpɒsəbli/
profile (n) /ˈprəʊfaɪl/
rebellious (adj) /rɪˈbeljəs/
reindeer (n) /ˈreɪndɪər/
risky (adj) /ˈrɪski/
scout (v) /skaʊt/
scruffy (adj) /ˈskrʌfi/
shave (v) /ʃeɪv/
shot (n) /ʃɒt/
sign up (v) /ˌsaɪn ˈʌp/
skin (n) /skɪn/
slim (adj) /slɪm/
smart (adj) /smɑːt/
straighten (v) /ˈstreɪtən/
sun-bleached (adj) /ˈsʌnbliːtʃt/
symmetrical (adj) /sɪˈmetrɪkəl/
tattoo (n/v) /təˈtuː/
tramp (n) /træmp/
unconventional (adj) /ˌʌnkənˈvenʃənəl/
unshaven (adj) /ʌnˈʃeɪvən/
well-built (adj) /ˌwel ˈbɪlt/
wig (n) /wɪg/
worthwhile (adj) /ˌwɜːθ ˈwaɪl/

Unit 10

acrobat (n) /ˈækrəbæt/
amusement arcade (n) /əˈmjuːzmənt ɑːkeɪd/
animation (n) /ˌænɪˈmeɪʃən/
argue (v) /ˈɑːgjuː/
attach (v) /əˈtætʃ/
ban (v) /bæn/
base on (v) /ˈbeɪs ˌɒn/
bear (n) /beər/
box (n) /bɒks/
box office (n) /ˈbɒks ˌɒfɪs/
cage (n) /keɪdʒ/
camel (n) /ˈkæməl/
chin (n) /tʃɪn/
circus (n) /ˈsɜːkəs/
clap (v) /klæp/
claw (n) /klɔː/
clown (n) /klaʊn/
comic (adj) /ˈkɒmɪk/
comparison (n) /kəmˈpærɪsən/
councillor (n) /ˈkaʊnsələr/
crocodile (n) /ˈkrɒkədaɪl/
cruelty (n) /ˈkruəlti/
disappear (v) /ˌdɪsəˈpɪər/
dolphin (n) /ˈdɒlfɪn/
dozen (n) /ˈdʌzən/
dramatist (n) /ˈdræmətɪst/
dress circle (n) /ˈdres ˌsɜːkəl/
elephant (n) /ˈeləfənt/
emphasis (n) /ˈemfəsɪs/
epic (n) /ˈepɪk/
exit (n) /ˈeksɪt/
exploitation (n) /ˌɪksplɔɪˈteɪʃən/
feed (v) /fiːd/
free (adj) /friː/
funfair (n) /ˈfʌnfeər/
greedy (adj) /ˈgriːdi/
hangman (n) /ˈhæŋmən/
harm (v) /hɑːm/
historical (adj) /hɪˈstɒrɪkəl/
hole (n) /həʊl/
honest (adj) /ˈɒnɪst/
humiliate (v) /hjuːˈmɪlieɪt/
illuminate (v) /ɪˈluːmɪneɪt/
impolite (adj) /ˌɪmpəˈlaɪt/
inexcusable (adj) /ˌɪnɪkˈskjuːzəbəl/
infant (n) /ˈɪnfənt/
influence (n) /ˈɪnfluəns/
invariably (adv) /ɪnˈveəriəbli/
lazy (adj) /ˈleɪzi/
leopard (n) /ˈlepəd/
lion (n) /ˈlaɪən/
lion tamer (n) /ˈlaɪən ˌteɪmər/
logical (adj) /ˈlɒdʒɪkəl/
manipulate (v) /məˈnɪpjʊleɪt/
marionette (n) /ˌmæriəˈnet/
maul (v) /mɔːl/
merely (adv) /ˈmɪəli/
mixture (n) /ˈmɪkstʃər/
monkey (n) /ˈmʌŋki/
moral (adj) /ˈmɒrəl/
musical (n) /ˈmjuːzɪkəl/
operate (v) /ˈɒpəreɪt/
orchestra (n) /ˈɔːkestrə/
originally (adv) /əˈrɪdʒɪnəli/
panther (n) /ˈpænθər/
patch (v) /pætʃ/
performer (n) /pəˈfɔːmər/
poet (n) /ˈpəʊɪt/
puma (n) /ˈpjuːmə/
puppet (n) /ˈpʌpɪt/
puppeteer (n) /ˌpʌpɪˈtɪər/
puppetry (n) /ˈpʌpɪtri/
quarrel (n) /ˈkwɒrəl/
quarrelsome (adj) /ˈkwɒrəlsəm/
raise (v) /reɪz/
rational (adj) /ˈræʃənəl/
reconstruct (v) /ˌriːkənˈstrʌkt/
ringmaster (n) /ˈrɪŋˌmɑːstər/
rod (n) /rɒd/
screen (n) /skriːn/
seal (n) /siːl/
sensitive (adj) /ˈsensətɪv/
shadow (n) /ˈʃædəʊ/
shark (n) /ʃɑːk/
skilful (adj) /ˈskɪlfəl/
small-scale (adj) /ˌsmɔːlˈskeɪl/
sophisticated (adj) /səˈfɪstɪkeɪtɪd/
spectacle (n) /ˈspektəkəl/
stage (n) /ˈsteɪdʒ/
stalls (n pl) /stɔːlz/
stick (n) /stɪk/
string (n) /strɪŋ/
survive (v) /səˈvaɪv/
sympathise (v) /ˈsɪmpəθaɪz/
tame (v/adj) /teɪm/
tender (adj) /ˈtendər/
tickle (v) /ˈtɪkəl/
tiger (n) /ˈtaɪgər/
tradition (n) /trəˈdɪʃən/
tragedy (n) /ˈtrædʒədi/
train (v) /treɪn/
trick (n) /trɪk/
trouble (n) /ˈtrʌbəl/
upper circle (n) /ˈʌpə ˌsɜːkəl/
variation (n) /ˌveəriˈeɪʃən/
vary (v) /ˈveəri/
warm-hearted (adj) /ˌwɔːm ˈhɑːtɪd/
wild (n/adj) /waɪld/
wound (n) /wuːnd/
zebra (n) /ˈzebrə/

Unit 11

accuse (v) /əˈkjuːz/
addition (n) /əˈdɪʃən/
algae (n) /ˈældʒiː/
assess (v) /əˈses/
benefit (n) /ˈbenəfɪt/
biologist (n) /baɪˈɒlədʒɪst/
biosphere (n) /ˈbaɪəsfɪər/
boldly (adv) /ˈbəʊldli/
choke (v) /tʃəʊk/
coal (n) /kəʊl/
commercial (adj) /kəˈmɜːʃəl/
conduct (v) /kənˈdʌkt/
convert (v) /kənˈvɜːt/
crew (n) /kruː/
criticism (n) /ˈkrɪtɪsɪzəm/
custodian (n) /kʌˈstəʊdiən/
defence (n) /dɪˈfens/
die (v) /daɪ/
domestic (adj) /dəˈmestɪk/
duty (n) /ˈdjuːti/
ecosystem (n) /ˈiːkəʊˌsɪstəm/
elderly (adj) /ˈeldəli/
election (n) /ɪˈlekʃən/
electrical (adj) /ɪˈlektrɪkəl/
emotion (n) /ɪˈməʊʃən/
enterprise (n) /ˈentəpraɪz/
environmental (adj)
    /ɪnˌvaɪərənˈmentəl/
explode (v) /ɪkˈspləʊd/
failure (n) /ˈfeɪljər/
far-fetched (adj) /ˌfɑːˈfetʃt/
fossil fuel (n) /ˈfɒsəl ˌfjʊəl/
gas (n) /gæs/
gene (n) /dʒiːn/
generalisation (n)
    /ˌdʒenərəlaɪˈzeɪʃən/
genetic (adj) /dʒəˈnetɪk/
geneticist (n) /dʒəˈnetɪsɪst/
greenhouse (n) /ˈgriːnhaʊs/
guarantee (n) /ˌgærənˈtiː/
harvest (n) /ˈhɑːvɪst/
hereditary (adj) /həˈredɪtəri/
household (n) /ˈhaʊshəʊld/
hydroelectric (adj) /ˌhaɪdrəʊ-
    ɪˈlektrɪk/
inhabitant (n) /ɪnˈhæbɪtənt/
intelligence (n) /ɪnˈtelɪdʒəns/
interfere (v) /ˌɪntəˈfɪər/
interrupt (v) /ˌɪntəˈrʌpt/
interruption (n) /ˌɪntəˈrʌpʃən/
justify (v) /ˈdʒʌstɪfaɪ/
lease (n) /liːs/
lighting (n) /ˈlaɪtɪŋ/
location (n) /ləʊˈkeɪʃən/
mainstream (adj)
    /ˈmeɪnstriːm/
marine biologist (n) /məˌriːn
    baɪˈɒlədʒɪst/
marsh (n) /mɑːʃ/
micro-organism (n) /ˌmaɪkrəʊ
    ˈɔːgənɪzəm/
nuclear (adj) /ˈnjuːkliər/
ocean (n) /ˈəʊʃən/
optimist (n) /ˈɒptəmɪst/
optimistic (adj) /ˌɒptəˈmɪstɪk/
pathetic (adj) /pəˈθetɪk/
pessimist (n) /ˈpesəmɪst/
pessimistic (adj) /ˌpesəˈmɪstɪk/
petrol (n) /ˈpetrəl/
photovoltaics (n)
    /ˌfəʊtəʊvɒlˈteɪ-ɪks/
planet (n) /ˈplænɪt/
plant (n) /plɑːnt/
politician (n) /ˌpɒləˈtɪʃən/
power (n) /ˈpaʊər/
process (v) /ˈprəʊses/
profit (n) /ˈprɒfɪt/
profitable (adj) /ˈprɒfɪtəbəl/
progress (n) /ˈprəʊgres/
rainforest (n) /ˈreɪnˌfɒrɪst/
reliance (n) /rɪˈlaɪəns/
rescue (v) /ˈreskjuː/
resource (n) /rɪˈzɔːs/
ridicule (v) /ˈrɪdɪkjuːl/
sacrifice (v) /ˈsækrɪfaɪs/
savanna (n) /səˈvænə/
sceptical (adj) /ˈskeptɪkəl/
science fiction (n) /ˌsaɪəns
    ˈfɪkʃən/
scientific (adj) /ˌsaɪənˈtɪfɪk/
scientist (n) /ˈsaɪəntɪst/
seek (v) /siːk/
self-defence (n) /ˌselfdɪˈfens/
self-sustaining (adj)
    /ˌselfsəˈsteɪnɪŋ/
self-taught (adj) /ˌself ˈtɔːt/
shrimp (n) /ʃrɪmp/
site (n) /saɪt/
solar (adj) /ˈsəʊlə/
source (n) /sɔːs/
souvenir (n) /ˌsuːvəˈnɪər/
spaceship (n) /ˈspeɪsˌʃɪp/
space-suit (n) /ˈspeɪs-suːt/
species (n) /ˈspiːʃiːz/
sponsor (n) /ˈspɒnsər/
storey (n) /ˈstɔːri/
structure (n) /ˈstrʌktʃər/
theme park (n) /ˈθiːm ˌpɑːk/
theory (n) /ˈθɪəri/
wave (n) /weɪv/
wealthy (adj) /ˈwelθi/

Unit 12

acclaim (n) /əˈkleɪm/
account (n) /əˈkaʊnt/
amend (v) /əˈmend/
arrest (v) /əˈrest/
attack (n) /əˈtæk/
attacker (n) /əˈtækər/
biased (adj) /ˈbaɪəst/
bid (n) /bɪd/
binoculars (n) /bəˈnɒkjuləz/
break down (v) /ˌbreɪk ˈdaʊn/
broadsheet (n) /ˈbrɔːdʃiːt/
burst (v) /bɜːst/
cancel (v) /ˈkænsəl/
candidate (n) /ˈkændɪdeɪt/
cane (adj) /keɪn/
caption (n) /ˈkæpʃən/
cartoonist (n) /kɑːˈtuːnɪst/
casualty (n) /ˈkæʒuəlti/
cheque book (n) /ˈtʃek ˌbʊk/
comic (n) /ˈkɒmɪk/
comment (n) /ˈkɒment/
content (n) /ˈkɒntent/
convoy (n) /ˈkɒnvɔɪ/
correspondent (n)
    /ˌkɒrɪˈspɒndənt/
couple (n) /ˈkʌpəl/
critic (n) /ˈkrɪtɪk/
daily (adj) /ˈdeɪli/

damage (n) /ˈdæmɪdʒ/
defenceless (adj) /dɪˈfensləs/
deny (v) /dɪˈnaɪ/
deputy (n) /ˈdepjuti/
disaster (n) /dɪˈzɑːstər/
discreet (adj) /dɪsˈkriːt/
disk (n) /dɪsk/
edit (v) /ˈedɪt/
edition (n) /ɪˈdɪʃən/
editor (n) /ˈedɪtər/
emergence (n) /ɪˈmɜːdʒəns/
evacuee (n) /ɪˌvækjuˈiː/
evil (adj) /ˈiːvəl/
exceptional (adj) /ɪkˈsepʃənəl/
exclusive (adj) /ɪkˈskluːsɪv/
factory (n) /ˈfæktəri/
fair (adj) /feər/
feeble (adj) /ˈfiːbəl/
filthy (adj) /ˈfɪlθi/
frail (adj) /freɪl/
gentle (adj) /ˈdʒentl/
greasy (adj) /ˈgriːsi/
harmless (adj) /ˈhɑːmləs/
helpless (adj) /ˈhelpləs/
huge (adj) /huːdʒ/
illegitimate (adj)
    /ˌɪləˈdʒɪtəmət/
independent (adj)
    /ˌɪndɪˈpendənt/
injure (v) /ˈɪndʒər/

isolated (adj) /ˈaɪsəleɪtɪd/
issue (v) /ˈɪʃuː/
journalism (n) /ˈdʒɜːnəlɪzəm/
leader (n) /ˈliːdər/
left-wing (adj) /ˌleft ˈwɪŋ/
mansion (n) /ˈmænʃən/
misery (n) /ˈmɪsəri/
muscular (adj) /ˈmʌskjʊlər/
naive (n) /naɪˈiːv/
nervously (adv) /ˈnɜːvəsli/
neutral (adj) /ˈnjuːtrəl/
objective (adj) /əbˈdʒektɪv/
own (v) /əʊn/
pamper (v) /ˈpæmpər/
powerful (adj) /ˈpaʊəfəl/
powerless (adj) /ˈpaʊələs/
province (n) /ˈprɒvɪns/
publish (v) /ˈpʌblɪʃ/
quote (n) /ˈkwəʊt/
recruit (v) /rɪˈkruːt/
refer to (v) /rɪˈfɜː tuː/
refinery (n) /rɪˈfaɪnəri/
region (n) /ˈriːdʒən/
report (n) /rɪˈpɔːt/
reporter (n) /rɪˈpɔːtər/
review (n) /rɪˈvjuː/
right-wing (adj) /ˌraɪt ˈwɪŋ/
sack (v) /sæk/
scenario (n) /səˈnɑːriəʊ/
section (n) /ˈsekʃən/

sensational (adj)
    /senˈseɪʃənəl/
sentient (adj) /ˈsenʃənt/
severe (adj) /səˈvɪər/
sharp (adj) /ʃɑːp/
silent (adj) /ˈsaɪlənt/
sinister (adj) /ˈsɪnɪstər/
sub-editor (n) /ˌsʌbˈedɪtər/
suppress (v) /səˈpres/
suspense (n) /səˈspens/
tabloid (n) /ˈtæblɔɪd/
tailor (n) /ˈteɪlər/
tax (n) /tæks/
tear (v) /teər/
territorial (adj) /ˌterɪˈtɔːriəl/
threatening (adj) /ˈθretnɪŋ/
torn (adj) /tɔːn/
trusting (adj) /ˈtrʌstɪŋ/
underclass (n) /ˌʌndəˈklɑːs/
unsteady (adj) /ʌnˈstedi/
vicious (adj) /ˈvɪʃəs/
victim (n) /ˈvɪktɪm/
villa (n) /ˈvɪlə/
vulnerable (adj) /ˈvʌlnərəbəl/
weak (adj) /ˈwiːk/
weekly (adj) /ˈwiːkli/
writ (n) /rɪt/

Unit 13

adopt (v) /əˈdɒpt/
apart from (adv) /əˈpɑːt ˌfrɒm/
arc (n) /ɑːk/
arrogant (adj) /ˈærəgənt/
art (n) /ɑːt/
assistance (n) /əˈsɪstəns/
banister (n) /ˈbænɪstər/
bead (n) /biːd/
beat (v) /biːt/
blind (adj) /blaɪnd/
care (n) /keər/
carefree (adj) /ˈkeəfriː/
cheerful (adj) /ˈtʃɪəfəl/
conflict (n) /ˈkɒnflɪkt/
creation (n) /kriˈeɪʃən/
crescent (n) /ˈkresənt/
cross (n) /krɒs/
curator (n) /kjʊˈreɪtər/
deaf (adj) /def/
decay (n) /dɪˈkeɪ/
dedicated (adj) /ˈdedɪkeɪtɪd/

dump (v) /dʌmp/
dustbin (n) /ˈdʌstˌbɪn/
elegant (adj) /ˈelɪgənt/
embarrassed (adj) /ɪmˈbærəst/
establish (v) /ɪˈstæblɪʃ/
exhibit (n) /ɪgˈzɪbɪt/
faceless (adj) /ˈfeɪsləs/
fascinating (adj) /ˈfæsɪneɪtɪŋ/
founder (n) /ˈfaʊndər/
gallery (n) /ˈgæləri/
gather (v) /ˈgæðər/
genuine (adj) /ˈdʒenjuɪn/
grand (adj) /grænd/
grope (v) /grəʊp/
grown-up (adj) /ˌgrəʊnˈʌp/
hesitate (v) /ˈhezɪteɪt/
index (n) /ˈɪndeks/
interactive (adj) /ˌɪntərˈæktɪv/
invade (v) /ɪnˈveɪd/
jelly (n) /ˈdʒeli/
jewel (n) /ˈdʒuːəl/
lack (n) /læk/
launch pad (n) /ˈlɔːntʃ ˌpæd/

leftovers (n) /ˈleftˌəʊvəz/
lively (adj) /ˈlaɪvli/
lonely (adj) /ˈləʊnli/
medical kit (n) /ˈmedɪkəl ˌkɪt/
metaphor (n) /ˈmetəfɔːr/
mistake (v) /mɪˈsteɪk/
mould (n) /məʊld/
mouldy (adj) /ˈməʊldi/
nappy (n) /ˈnæpi/
neglected (adj) /nɪˈglektɪd/
obviously (adv) /ˈɒbviəsli/
offensive (adj) /əˈfensɪv/
onyx (n) /ˈɒnɪks/
oppressive (adj) /əˈpresɪv/
playschool (n) /ˈpleɪskuːl/
prisoner (n) /ˈprɪzənər/
rail (n) /reɪl/
record (n) /ˈrekɔːd/
regardless (adv) /rɪˈgɑːdləs/
resemble (v) /rɪˈzembəl/
right (n) /raɪt/
scale (n) /skeɪl/
schedule (n) /ˈʃedjuːl/

scrape (v) /skreɪp/
secure (adj) /sɪˈkjʊər/
shiny (adj) /ˈʃaɪni/
shrivel (v) /ˈʃrɪvəl/
sight (n) /saɪt/
significance (n) /sɪgˈnɪfɪkəns/
snake (n) /sneɪk/
specialist (n) /ˈspeʃəlɪst/
spoilt (adj) /spɔɪlt/
stiff (adj) /stɪf/
stimulating (adj) /ˈstɪmjəˌleɪtɪŋ/
suffering (n) /ˈsʌfərɪŋ/
treat (v) /triːt/
tribute (n) /ˈtrɪbjuːt/
tube (n) /tjuːb/
vein (n) /veɪn/
volcanic eruption (n) /vɒlˈkænɪk ɪˈrʌpʃən/
war (n) /wɔːr/
well-fed (adj) /ˌwelˈfed/
wrinkle (n) /ˈrɪnkəl/

Unit 14

access (n) /ˈækses/
adolescent (n) /ˌædəˈlesənt/
alarmed (adj) /əˈlɑːmd/
ambulance (n) /ˈæmbjʊləns/
anti-social (adj) /ˌæntiˈsəʊʃəl/
aspect (n) /ˈæspekt/
average (adj/v) /ˈævərɪdʒ/
aware (adj) /əˈweər/
bargain (adj) /ˈbɑːgən/
bombing (n) /ˈbɒmɪŋ/
bruise (n) /bruːz/
capability (n) /ˌkeɪpəˈbɪləti/
casual (adj) /ˈkæʒuəl/
conclusive (adj) /kənˈkluːsɪv/
confirm (v) /kənˈfɜːm/
conscious (adj) /ˈkɒnʃəs/
consult (v) /kənˈsʌlt/
convince (v) /kənˈvɪns/
cost (n) /kɒst/
danger (n) /ˈdeɪndʒər/
database (n) /ˈdeɪtəbeɪs/
delay (n) /dɪˈleɪ/
demonstrate (v) /ˈdemənstreɪt/

destination (n) /ˌdestɪˈneɪʃən/
dial (n) /ˈdaɪəl/
drawback (n) /ˈdrɔːbæk/
encouragement (n) /ɪnˈkʌrɪdʒmənt/
engaged (adj) /ɪnˈgeɪdʒd/
enthusiasm (n) /ɪnˈθjuːziæzəm/
enthusiastic (adj) /ɪnˈθjuːziæstɪk/
evidence (n) /ˈevɪdəns/
excuse (n) /ɪkˈskjuːs/
express (adj) /ɪkˈspres/
familiar (adj) /fəˈmɪljər/
fancy (v) /ˈfænsi/
fare-paying (adj) /ˈfeə ˌpeɪ-ɪŋ/
fortnight (n) /ˈfɔːtnaɪt/
full-fare (adj) /ˈfʊl ˌfeər/
game boy (n) /ˈgeɪm ˌbɔɪ/
heart attack (n) /ˈhɑːt əˌtæk/
hold on (v) /ˌhəʊld ˈɒn/
imbalance (n) /ˈɪmbæləns/
immediate (adj) /ɪˈmiːdɪət/
imply (v) /ɪmˈplaɪ/
indicate (v) /ˈɪndɪkeɪt/
keen (adj) /kiːn/

last-minute (adj) /ˌlɑːstˈmɪnɪt/
lie (v) /laɪ/
line (n) /laɪn/
load (n) /ləʊd/
mail (n) /meɪl/
mark (v) /mɑːk/
nerve (n) /nɜːv/
observation (n) /ˌɒbsəˈveɪʃən/
obsess (v) /əbˈses/
outward (adj) /ˈaʊtwəd/
overall (adj/adv) /ˈəʊvərɔːl/
overnight (adj) /ˌəʊvəˈnaɪt/
parcel (n) /ˈpɑːsəl/
particularly (adv) /pəˈtɪkjʊləli/
point (v) /pɔɪnt/
procedure (n) /prəˈsiːdʒər/
program (n) /ˈprəʊgræm/
prove (v) /pruːv/
put through (v) /ˌpʊt ˈθruː/
question (v) /ˈkwestʃən/
reasonably (adv) /ˈriːzənəbli/
redress (v) /rɪˈdres/
respondent (n) /rɪˈspɒndənt/
restricted (adj) /rɪˈstrɪktɪd/
revolution (n) /ˌrevəˈluːʃən/
sample (n) /ˈsɑːmpəl/

security (n) /sɪˈkjʊərɪti/
service (n) /ˈsɜːvɪs/
sex (n) /seks/
sexual (adj) /ˈsekʃʊəl/
shock (n) /ʃɒk/
significant (adj) /sɪgˈnɪfɪkənt/
software (n) /ˈsɒftweər/
speed (n) /spiːd/
split up (v) /ˌsplɪt ˈʌp/
steady (adj) /ˈstedi/
stereotype (v) /ˈsteriətaɪp/
successive (adj) /səkˈsesɪv/
support (v) /səˈpɔːt/
survey (n) /ˈsɜːveɪ/
teenage (adj) /ˈtiːneɪdʒ/
toiletries (n pl) /ˈtɔɪlətriz/
tool (n) /tuːl/
training shoes (n pl) /ˈtreɪnɪŋ ʃuːz/
truth (n) /truːθ/
urgent (adj) /ˈɜːdʒənt/
user (n) /ˈjuːzər/
valuable (adj) /ˈvæljuəbəl/

Unit 15

accompany (v) /əˈkʌmpəni/
adviser (n) /ədˈvaɪzəʳ/
agriculture (n) /ˈægrɪˌkʌltʃəʳ/
airline (n) /ˈeəlaɪn/
allowance (n) /əˈlaʊəns/
as soon as (conj) /ˌəz ˈsuːn ˌəz/
balance (n) /ˈbæləns/
bless (v) /bles/
boiling (adj) /ˈbɔɪlɪŋ/
carnival (n) /ˈkɑːnɪvəl/
coastal (adj) /ˈkəʊstəl/
combine (v) /kəmˈbaɪn/
compass (n) /ˈkʌmpəs/
complete (adj) /kəmˈpliːt/
contact (v) /ˈkɒntækt/
convenient (adj)
    /kənˈviːniənt/
cultural (adj) /ˈkʌltʃərəl/
dazzling (adj) /ˈdæzlɪŋ/
delight (n) /dɪˈlaɪt/

deposit (n) /dɪˈpɒzɪt/
discount (n) /ˈdɪskaʊnt/
embassy (n) /ˈembəsi/
employment (n)
    /ɪmˈplɔɪmənt/
escalator (n) /ˈeskəleɪtəʳ/
evocative (adj) /ɪˈvɒkətɪv/
exchange rate (n) /ɪksˈtʃeɪndʒ
    ˌreɪt/
excursion (n) /ɪkˈskɜːʃən/
expect (v) /ɪkˈspekt/
get rid of (v) /ˌget ˈrɪd əv/
glorious (adj) /ˈglɔːriəs/
guidebook (n) /ˈgaɪdbʊk/
handicraft (n) /ˈhændɪkrɑːft/
immerse (v) /ɪˈmɜːs/
insider (n) /ɪnˈsaɪdəʳ/
insurance (n) /ɪnˈʃʊərəns/
kid (n) /kɪd/
landscape (n) /ˈlændskeɪp/
luxury (n) /ˈlʌkʃəri/
malaria (n) /məˈleəriə/

nanny (n) /ˈnæni/
non-smoking (adj) /ˌnɒn
    ˈsməʊkɪŋ/
opening (n) /ˈəʊpənɪŋ/
opportunity (n) /ˌɒpəˈtjuːnəti/
overlook (v) /ˌəʊvəˈlʊk/
paradise (n) /ˈpærədaɪs/
pick (v) /pɪk/
prose (n) /prəʊz/
radiant (adj) /ˈreɪdiənt/
resort (n) /rɪˈzɔːt/
responsible (adj)
    /rɪˈspɒnsəbəl/
ritual (adj) /ˈrɪtʃuəl/
sack (n) /sæk/
samba (n) /ˈsæmbə/
scenery (n) /ˈsiːnəri/
season (n) /ˈsiːzən/
seasonal (adj) /ˈsiːzənəl/
sell out (v) /ˌsel ˈaʊt/
share (v) /ʃeəʳ/

spectacular (adj)
    /spekˈtækjʊləʳ/
spirituality (n) /ˌspɪrɪtʃuˈæləti/
stunning (adj) /ˈstʌnɪŋ/
sunburn (n) /ˈsʌnbɜːn/
tablet (n) /ˈtæblɪt/
taxi rank (n) /ˈtæksi ˌræŋk/
temple (n) /ˈtempəl/
thrill (n) /θrɪl/
tour guide (n) /ˌtʊə ˈgaɪd/
tourism (n) /ˈtʊərɪzəm/
travel agency (n) /ˈtrævəl
    ˌeɪdʒənsi/
trivia (n pl) /ˈtrɪviə/
unless (conj) /ənˈles/
vacation (n) /vəˈkeɪʃən/
vast (adj) /vɑːst/
verdant (adj) /ˈvɜːdənt/
vibrant (adj) /ˈvaɪbrənt/
vitality (n) /vaɪˈtæləti/
worth (adj) /wɜːθ/